THE ILLUSION
OF A
CONSERVATIVE
REAGAN
REVOLUTION

THE ILLUSION OF A CONSERVATIVE REAGAN REVOLUTION

Larry M. Schwab

Transaction Publishers
New Brunswick (U.S.A.) and London (U.K.)

Library of Congress Catalog Number: 90-21812
ISBN: 0-88738-413-7
Printed in the United States of America

Library of Congress Cataloging-in-Publication Data

Schwab, Larry M.
    The illusion of a conservative Reagan revolution / Larry M.
Schwab.
        p.   cm.
    Includes index.
    ISBN 0-88738-413-7
    1. Party affiliation—United States.   2. Government spending
policy—United States.   3. Conservatism—United States.
    4. United States—Politics and government—1981–
1989.   I. Title.
JK2661.S36   1991
320.5′2′0973—dc20   90-21812
                                                              CIP

Contents

List of Tables

Preface

Several political commentators argue that the 1980s were a period of fundamental Republican and conservative change. Some of them believe the changes are so important that the 1980s should be seen as a watershed period in U.S. political history as significant as the 1930s. I oppose this thesis and point out why politics and policy have not fundamentally changed in a Republican and conservative direction. I demonstrate how policy developments and the political system during the 1980s often moved in the opposite direction from what should have happened in a fundamental conservative change or a Reagan revolution.

The early 1990s are an excellent time to study the political and policy developments of the 1980s because all the years of the decade can be examined. The analyses that were completed several years earlier missed important events, such as the Iran-Contra scandal, which occurred in the late 1980s. In addition, an analysis in the early 1990s provides the opportunity to examine what happened in policy and the political system after Ronald Reagan left office. Previous studies could only predict what would occur after 1988.

I wish to thank my family for the encouragement and help they gave me in writing this book. I also welcome the opportunity to acknowledge the assistance of Irving Louis Horowitz, Mary E. Curtis, and the other members of the Transaction staff. In addition, I want to thank Jean Belin and Carolyn Van Voorhis for typing the manuscript.

Acknowledgments

The author gratefully acknowledges the following publisher and publication for permission to use previously published material:

Larry M. Schwab, "The Myth of the Conservative Shift in American Politics: A Research Note," *Western Political Quarterly* 41 (December 1988): 817–823. Reprinted by permission of the University of Utah, Copyright Holder.

1

Introduction

An important debate has evolved during the past few years over the historical significance of the political and policy developments during the 1980s. After events such as the election victories of Ronald Reagan and George Bush, the Republican takeover of the Senate (1981–1986), and changes in the spending patterns of the federal budget, some political analysts began arguing that the political and policy developments in the 1980s represented a fundamental change in the U.S. system. They believe the 1980s have been a watershed period, similar to the 1930s, that will be seen as a turning point in the American political system.

The political analysts who support this viewpoint do not completely agree on the significance of the events of the 1980s. Their interpretations vary somewhat. But they do agree on the central point that the 1980s represented a fundamental historic change in U.S. politics and public policies.

Rowland Evans and Robert Novak were among the first political commentators to use the concept of the "Reagan revolution." They stated in 1981:

> While Nixon spoke in the contentious rhetoric of hyperbole, his policies as president were moderate if not downright liberal, careful not to disturb the national political consensus dating back to Franklin Roosevelt. In contrast, Reagan spoke in moderate language while pursuing policies whose only intent was to destroy that consensus. . . .
>
> If measured in overall governmental change rather than the journalistic standard of legislative accomplishment, Reagan's Hundred Days could be compared to Roosevelt's. What was so quickly started then in

1

regulatory relaxation, spending cuts and tax cut proposals was just the beginning. Removing the regulatory wedge was a continuing process; Stockman was making plans for further and deeper budget cuts in years ahead; Reagan saw tax rate reduction as a process that would not cease so long as he was president. Even the Moral Majority's social issues would be pursued in due time.

This was the Reagan Revolution.[1]

In the mid-1980s, John Chubb and Paul Peterson presented the fundamental change thesis in *The New Direction in American Politics*. They stated:

The American political system, during the presidency of Ronald Reagan, has been transformed to an extent unknown since the days of Franklin Delano Roosevelt. The terms of political debate, the course of domestic and foreign policy, and the dominant line of partisan cleavage have all been fundamentally changed. Only rarely in American history has the political system broken as sharply with governing customs to address festering national problems or to confront social and economic issues head-on.[2]

Similarly, in an article entitled "Why Reaganism Will Be With Us Into the 21st Century," Martin Shefter and Benjamin Ginsberg concluded:

The half-dozen party systems that have governed the United States since Jefferson have been distinguished by more than their electoral bases. At least five characteristics distinguish a durable and stable regime in American national politics. . . .

The regime constructed by Ronald Reagan seems to meet all of these criteria and thus could last long after Reagan leaves office.[3]

In the late 1980s, Martin Anderson, who had been on Reagan's White House staff, also concluded that the Reagan administration produced a fundamental change in the U.S. political system.

But there is mounting evidence that suggests that the main element of what became known as the Reagan revolution will continue. . . . But whether the new administration in January 1989 is Democrat or Republican, it will be largely irrelevant to the major policy changes that will likely dominate this republic for the next decade or so.

What Reagan and his comrades have done is to shape America's policy agenda well into the twenty-first century.[4]

In this analysis, I take issue with this point of view and argue that the Reagan revolution is an illusion.[5] The U.S. political system did not experience a fundamental conservative change in the 1980s. In fact, the results of many of the major political, policy, and institutional developments of the 1980s (e.g., an enormous increase in the federal budget deficits, defense cuts in the late 1980s, and Democratic victories in 1980–88 House elections) were just the opposite of what should have occurred in a Reagan revolution.

The central thesis of the book is that in the 1980s the United States did not enter a new conservative and Republican era in politics and public policies, but remained in the New Deal–Great Society era. Major social, economic, and political developments of the 1930s and 1940s produced the New Deal–Great Society era. These developments changed U.S. government and politics significantly from the previous conservative and Republican era (1896–1932). This earlier period featured more laissez-faire capitalism, a relatively small federal government, and Republican dominance in a two-party system. Beginning with the New Deal, the nation developed a more mixed economy, the federal government became much larger and more influential than the state and local governments, and the Democrats replaced the Republicans as number one in the overall system. For the United States to have changed to a conservative and Republican era in the 1980s, these key features of the New Deal–Great Society era would need to have reverted to the conditions of the early 1900s. However, the New Deal–Great Society conditions remained in the 1980s as the country continued with a mixed economy, a dominant federal government, and a two-party system with the Democrats as the top party overall.

This chapter summarizes the fundamental change (i.e., Reagan revolution) thesis and then analyzes each part of it. The other chapters will expand on the points outlined in this introduction.

Reagan Revolution Thesis

Since 1932, according to this thesis, the United States experienced nearly fifty liberal years of public policy in a political system largely dominated by Democrats. However, by 1980 a massive conservative shift in public opinion had taken place in the country. This conservative shift in opinion produced Ronald Reagan's landslide victories and the first Republican Senate majority in over twenty-five years. President Reagan became one of the most popular presidents in modern times and successfully used his popularity and the conservative shift in public opinion to dramatically change the political system. Supposedly, the conservative mood and Reagan's leadership produced massive changes in public policies, party politics, and the political process. The policy changes led to a significant decline in the role of the federal government, which rivals the historic significance of the increase in the role of the federal government produced by the New Deal. The Republicans became the number one political party. And, fundamental changes occurred in the federal government and in the relationship between the federal government and state and local governments.

With the explanation of the thesis completed, the next step is to divide it into its basic components and indicate the weaknesses and problems with each of these components.

Fifty Liberal Years?

In order to create as much contrast as possible between the 1980s and the previous period, those supporting the fundamental change thesis usually portray the years between 1932 and 1980 as a period of enormous liberal gains. Supposedly, liberals dominated the federal government and won victory after victory in civil rights, social programs, environmental programs, and in many other policy areas. The size of the federal government, according to the thesis, continually increased during this period.

Although there is some truth to this historical analysis, it contains a number of questionable inferences. Liberals certainly did not dominate the federal government for fifty years. The coalition of conservative southern Democrats and conservative Republicans was a powerful force in Congress during most of this period. Before the mid-1960s, conservative and moderate southern Democrats controlled most of the powerful positions in Congress.

In the executive branch as well, it is ridiculous to talk of fifty liberal years. From 1948 to 1980, each party controlled the presidency for sixteen years. Eisenhower, Nixon, and Ford were certainly not liberals. Even the Democratic presidents during this period came from the moderate or moderate-liberal sections of the Democratic party. Moreover, people in the bureaucracy could not be characterized as primarily liberal. The federal bureaucracy consisted of individuals with political points of view which covered the mainstream ideological spectrum from left to right. In addition, the Defense Department, which has been by far the largest part of the executive branch, was more often an ally of conservative rather than liberal groups.

Both liberal and conservative trends were present in the federal courts. These years saw Supreme Court eras as diverse as the Warren Court, the Burger Court, and the conservative Court of the early 1930s. The number of liberal and conservative judges in the lower federal courts increased or decreased as the parties exchanged the presidency.

Besides the three branches, liberal dominance never occurred among interest groups. The power of liberal groups was effectively countered by conservative groups, especially the numerous and powerful business lobbies.

Furthermore, the assumption of continual policy victories by liberals represents a faulty historical interpretation. Conservatives won in many important areas of public policy. For example, they won many battles on gun control. The Equal Rights Amendment never received the required amount of support from state legislatures. Liberals failed to enact a national health insurance program. The defense budget increased by billions and billions of dollars during this period.

Even most of the liberal victories came after many years of defeat. Black civil rights legislation and federal aid to education are good examples. Most of the major consumer and environmental legislation did not pass until the mid-1960s and the 1970s.

Consequently, the view of fifty liberal years presents an inaccurate interpretation of history. Rather than a period of liberal dominance, the period should be seen as one which produced a complex mix of conservative-to-liberal political leaders and conservative-to-liberal public policies.

Public Opinion

The media continually presented the message that American public opinion shifted to the right. Supposedly, the late 1970s and the 1980s were conservative periods which created conservative social, political, and economic attitudes.

An examination of the national polls and the public opinion literature, however, provides overwhelming evidence that this thesis is incorrect. The major conclusion which can be drawn from the data and analyses is that U.S. public opinion has remained stable over the last two decades. Substantial changes in public opinion have been rare in recent years. The majority of Americans continually support the liberal position on some issues and the conservative position on others. The general direction of the public on major issues has shown only limited change during the past fifteen years.

And within this overall stability, a long-term liberal trend can be observed in several social issues such as black civil rights, women's rights, and birth control information. Moreover, an analysis of the data during the 1980s suggests a slight movement to the left rather than the right.

The shift in attitudes on defense spending was the major reason why public opinion moved more toward the liberal side in the 1980s. While public opinion remained stable on most issues, an enormous decline occurred in support for defense programs.

Survey research data in other policy areas offers no support for the conservative shift thesis. For example, national polls during the 1980s revealed strong support by Americans for most of the federal social programs.

Little appears to have changed on controversial social policy issues through the 1970s and 1980s. The image of the United States as a country in the midst of a Moral Majority social revolution was certainly false. Other than crime, the other social policy issues, such as school prayer and abortion, did not appear to be major concerns of most Americans. Other issues, especially economic issues, were usually rated as much more important by most Americans.

The majority of Americans continued to be on the liberal side on several of these social issues and on the conservative side on others. The majority of the public still opposed a constitutional amendment banning abortions and supported the ERA and stronger gun control laws. On the other hand, they favored prayers in public schools and the death penalty, while they opposed racial quota systems.

The overall attitude toward the role of the federal government in the economy remained stable. Americans continued to support government influence and regulation in some aspects of the economy, but opposed it in others. No strong conservative swing toward laissez-faire capitalism and away from the mixed economy position can be found in the public opinion data.

Most citizens remained supportive of the capitalistic system and opposed major changes in the economic structure. However, they wanted the federal government to still play a big role in improving the economy and providing a mechanism to ease some of the harsh results which might be produced by a completely unregulated economic system.

Public support for environmental programs remained high and even increased in the 1980s. Only a small percentage of the public supported the Reagan administration's attempt to cut back on the environmental laws.

Reagan's Popularity

Besides the myth of a conservative opinion change on policies, many political commentators created the myth that Reagan was a highly popular president. However, an examination of poll data shows that Reagan's popularity ratings were not higher than other recent presidents. His ratings were considerably lower than Eisenhower's and Kennedy's and about the same overall as the other presidents in the 1953–88 period. President Bush's standing in the polls has been much higher than Reagan's for comparable periods in their administrations.

Conservative Voting in the Elections

Supposedly, a conservative surge in public opinion led to Reagan's and Bush's victories and conservative gains in congressional elections. But again, the evidence does not support this hypothesis.

Most survey research data and election studies indicate that Reagan did not win because of support for his conservative ideology. Instead of a conservative ideological vote for Reagan, the 1980 presidential election was primarily an anti-Carter vote. While Carter's poll ratings were moderate-to-good early in his term, his public support dropped into the poor range in the months before the election. Most of the voters casting their ballots for Reagan voted for someone to replace an unpopular president. The election was not an overwhelming endorsement of Reagan's conservative programs.

Economic factors influenced voters in the 1984 presidential election more than any other variable. The difference in support between Reagan and Mondale developed largely from people who were satisfied with the economy.

Not only were there no indications that conservative ideological trends caused the landslide victories, but perceptions of Reagan's conservative ideology actually hurt his electoral chances. Since the vote for Reagan in 1980 was largely an anti-Carter vote and no conservative shift occurred in public opinion, more moderate Republican candidates (e.g., Gerald Ford, George Bush, or Howard Baker) probably would have been able to beat Carter by an even higher percentage.

Similarly in 1984, Reagan won despite his position on many issues. Polls showed strong opposition to several of Reagan's major policies. The economic recovery, however, hit at the right time for the administration and canceled many of the adverse effects produced by the conservative policies.

Survey research findings indicated a similar pattern in the 1988 presidential election. Bush was elected primarily because of favorable economic conditions and not because of voter support for conservative policies.

Besides presidential elections, results from congressional elections refuted the conservative shift thesis. An analysis of the vote in the 1980 congressional election indicated that no relationship existed between the votes candidates received and their ideological position.[6] The election failed to produce a proconservative voting pattern. Liberals gained more electoral support than conservatives in the congressional elections from 1982 to 1988. Democrats won a big victory in the House in 1982. In 1984 Democrats won big again in the House and gained seats in the Senate despite Reagan's big victory. In the 1986 and 1988 elections, Democrats won landslide victories in the House and regained control of the Senate.

Reagan's Legislative Record

According to the next step in the Reagan–conservative revolution thesis, President Reagan won victory after victory in Congress with his brilliant skills in legislative leadership. Reagan supposedly dominated Congress almost completely. While other recent presidents failed in their role as chief legislator, the thesis suggests that Reagan was a great success. He was called the greatest legislative leader since either LBJ or FDR, or even the greatest of all time.

This is another illusion created by many political commentators and members of the media. The available evidence disputes this assertion. Measures of how often members of Congress support the president's position show that President Reagan had only poor-to-moderate success in relation to other recent presidents.[7] In the 1953–88 period, Reagan's yearly average in congressional support was the second lowest among the seven presidents. In 1987 and 1988, Reagan received the lowest scores recorded during the past thirty-five years.

So much of the political discussion concerning the 1980s concentrates on the events of 1981. Admittedly, the Reagan administration and conservatives achieved a number of legislative victories in 1981. But, during the following years, the administration had only modest success and many significant failures. For example, Congress failed to support most of the New Right agenda. Congressional majorities cut away several hundred billion dollars from Reagan's defense proposals and refused either to weaken environmental laws or to eliminate domestic programs on the administration's hit list. This inclination to emphasize the early legislative victories and to largely forget the failures after 1981 produced a distorted view of the national political events during the 1980s.

Generally, the budget proposals are the most important aspect of a president's legislative role. Instead of being one of the most successful presidents on budgetary policies, the record shows that Reagan was a dismal failure in budget politics. The Reagan administration promised that the budget would have a $100 billion surplus by the third year. However, the federal government ended up with budget deficits around $200 billion for most of the Reagan years. This budget failure is far beyond any other administration in history.

Also, the Reagan administration reached a level of incompetence in its budgetary relations with Congress unmatched by any other administration. No other president sent Congress so many budgets which were considered dead-on-arrival. Some years the Reagan budget was so out of step with political reality that the Senate Republican leadership was forced to write much of the budget for the administration.

Public Policies

While conservatives won some policy victories, no historic conservative change in policy occurred in the 1980s. Many policy outcomes were just the opposite of what should have happened in a conservative era.

The desire for a huge decline in the federal government and a balanced federal budget (or even a budget with a surplus) are two major components of modern conservative ideology. During this alleged conservative revolution, however, records were set in the opposite direction in these two areas. The federal budgets in the early and mid-1980s not only set records in total dollars spent, but also in percentage of Gross National Product (GNP) for the post–World War II period. Contrary to the assumption of an ever-expanding federal government before 1980, federal spending hit a plateau in the 20-to-22 percent range of GNP from the late 1960s through the 1970s. Then suddenly in the early 1980s, federal spending left this plateau and jumped to over 24 percent. Consequently, federal spending followed the opposite pattern from the conservative revolution thesis. Instead of the 1980s being a period of cutbacks in the government, most of the decade was a period of expansion of the federal government.

While the deficit generally declined as a percentage of GNP from 1976 to 1980, it expanded substantially in relation to GNP in the early 1980s. The total debt of the federal government doubled within a few years in the 1980s.

An examination of the trends in the major components of the federal budget also creates doubts about a conservative revolution.

Most of the major sections of the budget remained at about the same level as a percentage of the total federal budget and GNP. Very little changed in the overall composition of the budget from 1979 to the late 1980s.

Of the few important budget changes that did occur, the huge increase in the cost of debt financing was the most significant. This is another example of how the political system moved in the opposite direction from that envisioned by conservatives. Financing the federal debt shifted within a few years in the early 1980s from a relatively small spending category to one of the largest parts of the budget.

Besides overall government spending and the deficit, fundamental conservative changes failed to develop in a variety of other policy areas. In environmental and natural resources programs, the Reagan administration put a number of dedicated conservatives into key positions and tried to cut back on the regulations and the enforcement of several programs. While the administration had some initial success, the overall effort to restructure these programs ended in failure.

After scandals involving several administrative officials in high environmental and natural resources positions, President Reagan was forced to assure the American people that his administration would faithfully carry out the law in these areas. These scandals hurt Reagan's efforts to curtail these programs.

The situation in Congress was even worse for Reagan on environmental policy. Not only did the majority in Congress refuse to dismantle antipollution and natural resources programs, but they even strengthened some of the programs.

Defense was one of the most successful policy areas for Reagan and the conservatives in the early 1980s. But even here, the claim of a fundamental conservative change is an illusion. After military spending increased significantly in the early 1980s, Congress began cutting Reagan's military budget proposals in the mid-1980s. This changed the direction of the defense budget from a high-growth to a low-growth pattern. By the end of the Reagan administration, the rate of increase in the defense budget was at one of the lowest points in the post–World War II period.

In addition, the increase in the rate of growth of military spending began in the late 1970s, not in the early 1980s. If the late-1970s' growth rate had continued through the 1980s, the defense budget would have ended up much higher than it actually was in 1989.

Similar to defense spending, Reagan and the conservatives won some early battles in spending on social programs, but they eventually lost the war. They eliminated some relatively minor programs and created more stringent eligibility requirements in several welfare programs. However, all the major social programs survived, and compared to 1979, their budgets were many billions of dollars larger in 1988. The entitlement programs, which include most of the major social programs, *increased* rather than decreased as a percentage of the federal budget and GNP in the early 1980s.

Admittedly, the growth rate of several social programs slowed in the 1980s, but this development certainly fails to qualify as a fundamental change in the political system. The elimination of programs such as Social Security, Medicaid, and food stamps would be needed to qualify as a fundamental change.

Furthermore, the slowdown in the growth rate of federal social programs began in the mid-1970s, not in 1981. So the slower growth rate of the 1980s was just part of a broader trend toward smaller increases in these programs. A cut in the growth rate of these programs was inevitable because their budgets had increased faster than anticipated, and national economic problems had decreased the flow of revenue needed to finance them.

The legacy of the 1981–88 period was one of strengthening federal social programs rather than weakening them. These programs survived a conservative Republican president, who won two landslide victories, and a Senate with a Republican majority. And not only did these programs survive, but their total budgets increased enormously during this period. The public outcry after the 1981 cuts in social programs and the results of national polls showed the depth of public support for these programs. The majority in Congress followed these public attitudes and thwarted any further attempts to cut the programs. This ultimate victory for the federal social programs left them in a stronger position to face the budget battles of the future.

One of the major illusions of the Reagan revolution thesis is that a significant conservative shift occurred in economic policy. Political commentators often proclaimed the 1980s as a conservative period in economic policy without adequately examining policies and outcomes. They failed to discern the wide gap between Reagan's conservative economic rhetoric and what actually happened in economic policy. Three areas are particularly important here: the overall impact of the federal government, fiscal policy, and deregulation.

In many ways the federal government's impact on the economy increased during the 1980s, especially in agriculture and finances. These are two of the largest sectors in the economy, and federal policies affect them more than most other economic sectors.

An examination of Reagan's budget proposals shows that no conservative shift occurred in fiscal policy. The Reagan economic program was based on a hodgepodge of various conservative economic theories. It contained elements such as the traditional conservative Republican support for balanced budgets and the supply-side emphasis on tax cuts. What actually happened in fiscal policy, however, could not be characterized as either traditional conservative, or supply-side, or any other conservative economic theory. The only way to describe Reagan's fiscal policy would be as a policy of incredible incompetence.

Never before has so much difference existed between an administration's stated fiscal policy and the actual policy pursued. Reagan said before the 1980 election that the continual deficits of the federal government were a major economic problem, so his program would follow a fiscal policy of balanced budgets and even budgets with large surpluses. Yet what Reagan actually proposed to Congress year after year were budgets with enormous deficits. This was a completely new approach which was not supported by any ideological group from left to right in the political mainstream.

Finally on economic issues, the 1980s failed to produce a significant conservative shift in deregulation policy. In fact, much more economic deregulation (e.g., airlines and trucking) took place in the 1970s than the 1980s.

Conservatives failed in their attempts to alter social and civil rights policies. For example, all the major parts of the New Right social agenda were defeated in Congress. Conservatives were also defeated on important black civil rights measures. Congress, for instance, extended the 1965 Voting Rights Act and passed a law designating a national holiday in honor of Martin Luther King, Jr. In addition, the vote to oppose the confirmation of Robert Bork as a Supreme Court justice was an enormous setback for conservative civil rights and social policies.

Party Politics

Party realignment (Republicans replacing Democrats as the number one party) obviously never occurred in the 1980s. In the party realignment of the 1930s, Democrats won control of the presidency, Congress, and the majority of state and local offices. They also became the majority party in party identification. During the 1980s, the Republicans only won the presidency and the majority of the Senate in three elections. Democrats continued to dominate the political system under the presidency. After the 1988 elections, the Democrats still had the majority of House seats, Senate seats, governorships, and state legislatures. Also, they continued their lead in party identification and party registration.

Governance

The Reagan Administration did not produce long-lasting changes in the governmental process. The assertion that Ronald Reagan would have a significant impact on the presidency was disproved in the 1988 presidential election and the first year of the Bush administration. All the Democratic and Republican presidential candidates claimed that they would not use Reagan's "hands-off" administrative style. They all supported a more "hands-on" presidency where the president stays better informed about the major developments and becomes more actively involved than Reagan. Although George Bush did not stress his opposition to Reagan's administrative style during the campaign, his statements and actions during the first months of his administration demonstrated that he would not follow his predecessor's decision-making approach.

The basic structure and decision-making patterns in the federal bureaucracy continued through the 1980s. Furthermore, the number of federal employees did not decline sharply, but expanded during the decade.

The major changes in the Supreme Court occurred at the end of the 1960s and in the 1970s with the transition from the liberal

Warren Court to the more conservative Burger Court. The continuation of the Burger Court during the first half of the 1980s and the
earlier years of the Rehnquist Court in the second half did not
produce a new era of the Court.

Congressional politics changed in the late 1960s and the 1970s as
some power shifted away from southern Democrats, committee
chairs, and the full committees. The "postreform" period of the
late 1970s continued through the 1980s. In addition, moderate and
liberal Democrats, not conservative Republicans, dominated Congress at the end of the 1980s.

Finally, no historic shift of power from the federal government to
state and local governments happened in the 1980s. The major part
of Reagan's New Federalism program never even received serious
consideration in Congress. The federal share of total government
spending actually increased during the 1980s.

Conclusion

A significant shift in policy, public opinion, and politics never
happened in the 1980s. In fact, in several important measures, the
political system moved in the opposite direction from what should
have occurred in a fundamental conservative change. The Reagan
revolution was an illusion.

This is not to argue, however, that conservative Republicans are
similar to liberal Democrats, and thus no major policy changes can
take place in the U.S. political system. There are significant differences between these ideological groups, and their differences surfaced in clashes between Reagan's proposals and liberal Democrats' counter proposals. Significant changes could have occurred
in the system if Reagan and the conservatives had successfully
carried out their program, but they failed in their effort to fundamentally change the system. Several factors, such as the recession,
lack of public support, and their flawed budget plan, contributed to
the failure of the conservative program. Consequently, the 1980s
should be seen as a phase of the political era which has been in
existence for the last several decades rather than as a watershed
period marking the beginning of a new era. The basic framework of
public opinion, policies, and politics which existed during the
previous forty years continued through the 1980s.

The major points of this chapter are examined in more detail in the following chapters.

Notes

1. Rowland Evans and Robert Novak, *The Reagan Revolution* (New York: E. P. Dutton, 1981), 245–46.
2. John E. Chubb and Paul E. Peterson, "Realignment and Institutionalism," in *The New Direction in American Politics,* ed. John E. Chubb and Paul E. Peterson (Washington, D.C.: Brookings Institution, 1985), 1.
3. Martin Shefter and Benjamin Ginsburg, "Why Reaganism Will Be With Us Into the 21st Century," *Washington Post National Weekly Edition,* 30 September 1985, p. 21.
4. Martin Anderson, *Revolution* (San Diego: Harcourt Brace Jovanovich, 1988), 438.
5. Most analysts in the debate on the alleged Reagan revolution use the term *revolution* to mean a significant change similar to the New Deal. They do not mean changes of the magnitude associated with events such as the French Revolution or the Russian Revolution.
6. Demetrios Caraley, "Do Congressional Liberals Really Need to Tremble? A Quick Look at Some Hard Data," *Political Science Quarterly* 6 (Spring 1981): 27–30.
7. The measure is Congressional Quarterly's presidential support scores. It will be discussed more in later chapters.

2

No Conservative Shift in Public Opinion

Many reporters and political analysts proclaimed that a significant conservative shift in public opinion occurred in the late 1970s and the 1980s. News stories often presented this assumption of a conservative opinion change as an accepted fact.

However, an examination of public opinion studies shows that this assumption is yet another illusion presented to the American people during the 1980s. Analysis of polls indicates that no large-scale conservative shift in opinion on issues occurred through the period from the late 1970s to the late 1980s. In fact, U.S. public opinion shifted a little to the left during the 1980s.

The chances are small of any major shift in public opinion occurring either to the left or right in a short period of time. Overall, U.S. public opinion on issues remains fairly stable from decade to decade. One study, for example, examined over 600 questions from national polls and discovered considerable stability in the results during the 1935–79 period.[1] The majority opinion on broad issue areas may change somewhat, but these changes usually develop gradually over many years. Most of the long-term changes have been in the liberal direction (e.g., women's rights, minority rights, and sexual attitudes).

The majority of Americans are conservative on certain policies, moderate on some, and liberal on others. These patterns generally remained stable in the 1980s. A few shifts occurred, but the liberal side gained more than the conservative side. So instead of a massive conservative shift in public opinion in the 1980s, attitudes on issues shifted overall a little to the left.

Ferguson and Rogers provide a good summary of the stable ideological balance and gradual liberal trend of U.S. public opinion.

> American public opinion has long been best described as both ideologically conservative and programmatically liberal. That is, Americans are opposed to big government, and respond favorably to the myths and symbols of competitive capitalism in the abstract. When it comes to assessing specific government programs or the behavior of actual business enterprises, however, they support government spending in a variety of domestic areas and are profoundly suspicious of big business. . . .

> Within this structure, moreover, the trend in public opinion over the past generation has been toward greater liberalism.[2]

Self-Identified Conservatives

A conservative Reagan revolution should have produced an enormous increase in conservatives within the population. However, there is no evidence of a significant increase in Americans identifying themselves as conservatives. The proportion of the public listing their ideological preference as conservative remained stable in the polls.

From 1976 to 1986, Gallup found the percentage of conservatives remained almost the same (29 to 28). During most of this period, the percentage of self-identified conservatives varied only between the high twenties and low thirties. The proportion of conservatives actually dropped a little from the early 1980s to 1986.[3]

Ideological Orientation of Young Americans

Moreover, the assertion that young people became much more conservative in the 1980s is inaccurate. The majority of young Americans in the 1980s, particularly college students, held liberal positions on some issues and conservative positions on others. The 1980s also saw no consistent movement toward conservative stands on issues.

These findings were confirmed by the annual survey of college freshmen conducted by the University of California, Los Angeles's Higher Education Research Institute. Comparing the results of the surveys from the mid-1960s to the mid-1980s shows that the majority of freshmen continued to support the liberal position on many issues into the 1980s. For instance, a majority supported higher taxes for the rich and programs for national health care, consumer protection, and pollution control. In several issues, such as certain aspects of women's rights, college students have become more liberal in the past twenty years. In contrast, the survey indicated a more conservative direction on only a few issues. The percentage supporting the legalization of marijuana, for instance, declined. Alexander Austin, one of the directors of the survey, concluded: "Materialism in the job market may have been mistaken for conservatism in the political arena. But conservatism in politics is not a characteristic of most American college students today any more than it has been in the past. In some areas, they are even more liberal today."[4]

In addition, survey research studies show young adults in the 1980s were among the most liberal, not the most conservative, of the various age groups in their attitudes toward certain policies. For instance, young adults as a group were among the most supportive of many social-welfare policies.[5]

Contrary to what many political commentators stated, young people did not strongly support Reagan's policies. A 1987 poll, for instance, found that nearly six in ten of the people in the 18–29 age group wanted the next president to change direction from Reagan's policies. Their level of support for a policy change was higher than the national average.[6]

Federal Government Programs

Besides the ideological preferences of the public in general and of youth, it is useful to examine public opinion trends on government programs such as defense and environmental protection. If a conservative change occurred in public opinion, support for conservatives' programs (e.g., defense) should have soared while support for liberals' programs (e.g., social and environmental) should have plummeted. Here again, the assertion of a conservative change in opinion is not borne out by poll results.

Of all the important policy areas, public opinion changed the most on defense spending. The public moved in a liberal, not a conservative, direction. Support for increases in defense spending dropped dramatically. According to the Harris poll, only 9 percent of Americans supported an increase in military spending during the mid-1980s. This was one of the lowest levels of support for defense spending ever recorded in a Harris poll. In addition, Lou Harris said that the enormous shift against military spending during the 1980s was one of the most dramatic changes in public opinion he had ever observed.[7]

The Gallup poll found strong support for cutting defense spending to reduce the budget deficit. Sixty-six percent of the respondents approved cutting defense spending in April 1985 compared to only 28 percent who disapproved the cuts.[8] From 1981 to 1986 the proportion of Americans who believed that too much was being spent on the military increased from 15 to 47 percent.[9]

Findings from the National Election Studies (NES) also demonstrate that Americans swung sharply away from supporting defense spending during the 1980s. On one defense question, respondents placed their opinions on a seven-point scale with "greatly decrease defense spending" at one end and "greatly increase defense spending" at the other. From 1980 to 1986, the percentage of the public choosing the three increase spending positions dropped from 61 to 33. Support for the strongest prodefense spending position on the scale declined from 20 to 5 percent.[10]

While many political commentators talked of the conservative 1980s and the public's strong support of the military buildup, opinion had actually shifted against military spending. Not only did these commentators misinterpret the public's mood, but they failed to see that the military buildup was dead by the mid-1980s because Congress began following public opinion by greatly cutting back on the growth of the military budget.

Several national polls did record an increase in support for military spending during the late 1970s and early 1980s. However, this period of support lasted only a short time from late 1979 into 1981.[11] So these few months of higher support for military spending should not have been construed as a mandate for a huge increase in military spending. Also, it is ridiculous to characterize the period of the late 1970s through the 1980s as a pro-military spending period in public opinion because of a shift in the polls that lasted such a short time. Obviously, a much better case could be made that this was a period of low support for a military buildup. During most of the years from the late 1970s to the late 1980s, national polls showed more support for cutting the military budget rather than greatly increasing it.

Another myth of the 1980s was that the public supported large cuts in social programs. Most Americans wanted to expand these programs rather than reduce them. In the late 1970s, national polls showed over 80 percent of the respondents supported programs to help poor people buy food at cheap prices, to provide aid to poor one-parent families, and to pay health costs for poor people. When asked about specific cuts in federal spending, about three-fourths of the sample in a 1979 Harris poll opposed cuts in health and education programs and programs for the elderly, handicapped, and the poor.[12]

This strong support for federal social programs continued into the 1980s. When asked about various options to reduce the budget deficit, the public overwhelmingly rejected the option of cutting social programs. In a 1985 Gallup poll, 87 percent of the respondents opposed reducing the entitlement programs such as Social Security and Medicare. When asked about cuts in social programs, 55 percent disapproved, while only 39 percent approved.[13] By 1987, 88 percent still opposed cuts in entitlement programs, and 76 percent opposed cuts in social programs such as health and education.[14]

When given the option to cut either defense programs or social programs, the public chose cuts in defense by enormous margins. When forced to make a choice between defense and social spending cuts, respondents chose defense cuts by a two-to-one margin in national polls.

Not only did most Americans want to continue federal social programs, they also favored the expansion of social programs into new areas. Child care is an excellent example of this development. Polls showed strong support for significant increases in governmental programs in child care. For example, a 1989 Gallup poll found that 41 percent of the sample wanted to increase federal spending on child-care services, compared to only 13 percent who favored cuts in these services.[15]

So the public mood was just the opposite of that suggested by a conservative 1980s' thesis. The majority of Americans were not superconservatives demanding cuts in federal social programs and huge increases in military spending. Most Americans wanted to cut back on the military and either to maintain or even to expand social programs.

Support for environmental programs also remained strong in the 1970s and 1980s. For instance, a *Los Angeles Times* poll in 1982 asked a sample of Americans whether they supported keeping or easing regulations which President Reagan thought were holding back free enterprise.[16] In environmental concerns, those who favored keeping the regulations outnumbered those who favored easing the regulations by a large amount (49 to 28 percent). In 1981, the CBS/*New York Times* poll gave the options of either relaxing environmental laws to achieve economic growth or maintaining present environmental laws to preserve the environment. By the margin of 67 to 21 percent, the respondents chose the option of protecting the environment. According to a 1981 Roper poll, only one fifth of the public believed that environmental regulations had gone too far.[17] The environment became one of the major issues in the 1988 presidential campaign largely because the polls showed that Americans' high support for environmental programs continued through the decade.

Not only did the public's approval of environmental laws remain strong in the 1980s, some evidence suggests increased support for the liberal environmental position. For example, in 1986 the Gallup poll asked: "Do you feel that nuclear power plants operating today are safe enough with present safety regulations, or do you feel that their operations should be cut back until more strict regulations can be put into practice?" The majority (66 to 25 percent) favored cutting back on the nuclear power plants. Only 40 percent had favored nuclear power cuts in 1976.[18]

Finally, support for government services in general remained high in the 1980s. No conservative backlash developed against the general idea of the government providing services. The responses to a question from the NES analyses illustrate this point. The question provided seven responses on a continuum with the response of the government providing fewer services at one end and the option of the government providing more services at the other. In 1980 the proportion of the population choosing the three pro-government services' choices was 38 percent compared to 28 percent selecting the three antigovernment services' positions. By 1986 those supporting more government services expanded to 41 percent, while those favoring fewer government services declined to 24 percent.[19]

Economics

The attitude of the public on the role of the government in the economy remained stable during the 1980s. No significant shift toward laissez-faire economics was evident in the national polls. The majority of respondents continued to support the overall framework of a free enterprise system. However, they remained suspicious of uncontrolled business actions and thus favored many regulatory activities. Strong support continued, for example, for a consumer protection agency and product safety programs.[20]

Americans' attitudes about the debates on the minimum wage and plant-closing notification during the 1980s provide a good illustration of public opinion on the government's role in the economy. In both of these cases, government policies would violate laissez-faire capitalism because the government would be regulating important decisions of private businesses. According to survey studies, even though most Americans continued to support capitalism in the abstract, a high percentage of the public approved the bills to increase the minimum wage and to set guidelines on notifying workers on plant closings. If a conservative shift in public opinion toward laissez-faire capitalism had developed, the overwhelming proportion of the public would have not only rejected the increase in the minimum wage, but also the whole concept of a minimum wage. Similarly, if this public opinion change had happened, the public would have strongly opposed the basic idea of a law concerning plant closings.

Social and Moral Issues

No evidence can be found that a massive conservative shift occurred in attitudes on social and moral issues such as women's rights and abortion. The basic public opinion patterns on most of these issues remained the same in the 1980s. The majority continued to support either the conservative or liberal position on some of these issues and remained deeply divided on others. The changes that occurred on these issues over the last several decades were generally in a liberal direction. The majority continued to support the conservative side on issues such as the death penalty, sentencing of criminals, and busing. On the other hand, liberal majorities could still be found, for instance, on gun registration, integrated schools, and many women's rights issues.[21]

Findings from public opinion studies on women's rights, minority rights, sexual practices, religion, poverty, abortion, crime, and gambling provide evidence that most Americans did not embrace the New Right philosophy in the 1980s. In these areas, the New Right position either lost ground during the 1980s or failed to gain significantly greater acceptance.

Contrary to what would be expected in a conservative period, support for the liberal position on women's rights continued to grow in the 1980s. Survey research indicated a continual shift toward the acceptance of women taking a greater role in the workplace and other aspects of society. The NES questionnaire has a question with a seven-point continuum in which women should have an "equal role with men in running business, industry, and government" and "women's place is in the home" are at the ends. From 1972 to 1984, support for the three responses favoring equal rights expanded from 47 to 54 percent, while support for the strongest position of women staying home declined from 19 to 5 percent.[22]

Attitudes about women as candidates for public office also provide a good example of this trend. In 1987, 82 percent of the respondents in a national poll answered yes when asked whether they would vote for a qualified woman for president if she were nominated by their party. In 1969 only 54 percent accepted women as presidential candidates for their party.[23]

No backlash developed against the black civil rights movement. Public opinion generally continued either to move in the liberal direction during the 1980s or to remain fairly stable on various aspects of minority rights. On the question of the pace of civil rights leaders' actions, the majority of the public between the 1960s and the 1980s changed from believing the pace was too fast to feeling the pace was about right, according to NES findings. Those believing the pace was too fast dropped from 63 to 14 percent between 1964 and 1986.[24]

Acceptance of blacks as political candidates increased substantially during the past thirty years. According to a national poll, the proportion of Americans willing to vote for a well-qualified black candidate who had been nominated by their party increased from 38 to 77 percent between 1958 and 1978. This proportion remained about the same in the 1980s, as it moved up to 79 percent in 1987.[25]

According to a national study, nearly 80 percent of Americans in the late 1980s believed private clubs should not have the right to exclude blacks. This again raises questions about the alleged conservative shift in public opinion.[26]

Busing for school desegregation is one aspect of the black civil rights movement for which the conservative position receives overwhelming public support. Polls generally indicate that well over a majority of Americans oppose this type of integration program. While this pattern continued in the 1980s, the proportion of the public opposing busing programs declined a little in the 1980s.[27]

Also, NES data show that a somewhat higher percentage of the public believe the "government should not make a special effort to help minorities because they should help themselves" as compared to those who feel the "government in Washington should make every possible effort to improve the social and economic position of blacks and other minority groups." But again, no significant conservative shift occurred in the 1980s. The proportion supporting each position remained about the same between the early 1970s and the 1980s. The support for the conservative position of no special government aid dropped slightly from 1970 to 1986.[28]

While many in the New Right movement oppose granting certain rights and privileges to homosexuals, national public opinion has generally moved in the opposite direction. Support for the rights of homosexuals appears to have increased in the 1980s. While Gallup found some drop in the acceptance for the legality of homosexual relations in 1986 and 1987, by 1989 the public's support for allowing these relationships to be legal increased to a higher percentage than in 1977 (47 to 43 percent).[29] From 1977 to 1989 an increasing proportion of the public accepted the hiring of homosexuals in several important occupations (doctors, 44 to 56 percent; salespersons, 68 to 79 percent; armed forces, 51 to 60 percent; clergy, 36 to 44 percent; and elementary school teachers, 27 to 42 percent).[30]

Trends in Americans' attitudes about several other sexual matters would also not please the New Right. The results of a national poll, for example, indicated a substantial shift away from the belief that premarital sex is wrong. In 1987 only 46 percent of the respondents considered premarital sex to be wrong, compared to 68 percent in 1969.[31]

Since the New Right and Religious Right strongly oppose sex education in schools, the supposed Reagan revolution should have produced an enormous shift in opinion against this practice. But just the opposite happened in the 1980s. Support for sex education in elementary schools, according to a national study, soared from 45 percent in 1981 to 71 percent in 1987. Only 21 percent of the respondents in 1987 opposed sex education in elementary schools.[32]

Most conservatives strongly oppose TV commercials for birth control devices, yet a national poll found that over two thirds of the public favored condom commercials on TV.[33] How could the 1980s be considered a conservative period in public opinion when most Americans accepted sex education in elementary schools and TV condom advertisements?

A significant increase in the support for the Religious Right's views would have been part of any conservative change in public opinion. But the findings from public opinion studies do not show this type of shift in views. The NES has an excellent question to measure an aspect of the support for the fundamentalist position. Respondents are given four options to choose from on the accuracy of the Bible: "(1) The Bible is God's word and all it says is true; (2) The Bible was written by men inspired by God but it contains some human errors; (3) The Bible is a good book because it was written by wise men, but God has nothing to do with it; (4) The Bible was written by men who lived so long ago that it is worth very little today." The first option is the closest to the views of the Religious Right. This option should have received a surge of support in the 1980s if opinion changed toward their position, but the responses remained fairly stable from the 1960s through the 1980s. About 50 percent of the people consistently chose the first option, and about 40 percent opted for the second answer. The percentage of respondents choosing the first answer dropped slightly from 53 in 1964 to 51 in 1986 rather than increasing to 70 or 80 percent as would be expected in a conservative era.[34]

The scandals involving TV evangelists damaged the reputation of the Religious Right considerably. Many people associated these ministers with the conservative religious movement, and the reputation of TV preachers was at an extremely low point in the late 1980s. A 1989 Gallup poll found that most Americans believed these ministers were not trustworthy with money (79 percent), dishonest (70 percent), insincere (67 percent), had no special relationship with God (67 percent), and didn't care about people (62 percent).[35]

One of the key reasons people support or oppose social programs, especially welfare programs, is their attitude about why people end up in poverty. An important difference develops between liberals and conservatives on this issue. Liberals generally stress uncontrollable factors as the cause of poverty, while many conservatives believe that people often create many of their own problems. This leads liberals to be more willing than conservatives to accept government programs to help the disadvantaged. In a conservative period, a high portion of the population would accept the "blame-the-poor" attitude.

Contrary to the Reagan revolution thesis, a 1989 poll did not show a significant shift toward the attitude that poverty developed from individual lack of effort and away from the position that it developed from circumstances in people's lives. While the percentage accepting the choice that lack of effort causes poverty increased a little (33 to 38 percent) between 1964 and 1989, the proportion of respondents believing circumstances caused poverty increased much more (29 to 42 percent). Those feeling that both factors equally caused poverty dropped (32 to 17 percent) during the period.[36]

Abortion probably has been the most controversial social issue during the past twenty years. It also ranks high in media attention.

The majority of Americans continued to oppose the New Right position on abortion in the 1980s. None of the national polls recorded a surge of support for the antiabortion position during the decade. U.S. public opinion appears to have remained fairly stable on abortion. Only a small portion of Americans agree with the view held by many conservatives that abortion should be illegal in all situations. About 25 to 40 percent of the public continued to support the right of a woman to choose to have an abortion in all cases. About half the population accept abortion under several circumstances.

This pattern holds in most national studies, but the findings vary depending on the options given and the wording of the options. The NES abortion question presents four options: (1) abortion never allowed; (2) abortion permitted in cases of rape, incest, and when a woman's life is in danger; (3) abortion permitted only when the need is clearly established; (4) abortion is a woman's personal choice. In 1986 the results were as follows: (1) 13 percent; (2) 28 percent; (3) 18 percent; (4) 39 percent.[37] Gallup found the following in 1988 from three possible responses: 24 percent, abortion always legal; 57 percent, abortion legal under certain circumstances; 17 percent, abortion always illegal.[38]

The major policy goals of the New Right are to get the major abortion decision, *Roe v. Wade,* overturned and to pass a constitutional amendment to ban abortions. According to public opinion data, the majority of Americans oppose both of these goals.

Crime is another important social issue for conservatives and all Americans. The majority of U.S. citizens hold conservative views on some crime issues and liberal views on others. In the sentencing of criminals, for instance, the majority of the public usually supports the conservative hard-line approach. The death penalty is a good example. Well over a majority support the death penalty in murder cases. Approval of the death penalty increased during the 1980s in national polls, but the support for it was already high at the end of the 1970s.[39]

On the other hand, support for the liberal position on gun control, another of the major crime prevention issues, remained strong during the 1980s. According to national studies, the majority of Americans continued to oppose most aspects of the conservative position on gun control. In a 1988 poll, 67 percent of the public supported registration of all firearms, 84 percent favored licensing for all guns carried outside the home, and a whopping 91 percent supported a seven-day waiting period and background check for handgun purchases.[40]

The majority, however, still oppose a ban on handgun possession. Many liberals propose registration, licensing, and waiting periods instead of bans. Moreover, support for banning handguns increased during the 1980s. One poll recorded an increase from 31 to 42 percent between 1979 and 1987 in the public's approval of a handgun ban.[41]

Finally, gambling is another social issue of concern to the New Right. Many conservatives are worried about what they see as the moral decay represented by the increasing amount of gambling in general and legalized gambling. While many Americans may share some of their concerns about gambling, no significant shift in opinion against legalized gambling occurred in the 1980s. Polls indicate that the majority of U.S. citizens hold views on this topic far different from those of the New Right conservatives. Gallup, for instance, found the majority of Americans supported the legalization of cash prizes in bingo games (75 percent), casino gambling in resort areas (55 percent), state lotteries for cash prizes (78 percent), and offtrack betting on horse races (54 percent).[42]

Foreign Policy

Similar to domestic policy, American public opinion did not become more conservative on foreign policy matters. In fact, the majority of Americans opposed several of the major conservative foreign policy initiatives of the Reagan administration. For example, poll after poll showed strong opposition by the majority of Americans to the administration's policy in Nicaragua.

Moreover, the easing of the cold war produced a shift in the public's attitudes about communism, which was unimaginable just a few years ago. Now, most Americans reject the past hard-line, anticommunist views of conservatives.

The conciliatory policy of Mikhail Gorbachev was a major factor in this change. Gorbachev received an amazingly favorable rating of 54 percent in a 1987 poll. This compares to a favorable rating of only 5 to 10 percent for Nikita Krushchev in the late 1950s and early 1960s.[43] Incredibly, Gorbachev ranked second in America's list of the most admired men in a 1988 poll. Gorbachev ranked higher than men such as Pope Paul, Billy Graham, and Lee Iacocca.[44]

An almost unbelievable change also occurred in America's attitudes toward the Soviet Union and China. According to Gallup polls, the percentage of Americans with favorable opinions of the Soviet Union and China increased from 21 to 62 percent and 20 to 72 percent respectively between 1976 and 1989.[45]

Conclusion

The assumption of a conservative shift in public opinion is yet another illusion of the 1980s. The evidence from the national polls shows that the majority of Americans did not change to the conservative position on a large number of issues. American public opinion remained stable on most issues. The liberal position continued to be supported on some issues, while the conservative position was still favored on others. And in the changes which did occur, opinion usually shifted more toward the liberal direction.

If a massive conservative shift in public opinion had taken place in the 1980s, Americans would have strongly supported the continuation of Reagan's policies into the 1990s. In a 1987 Gallup poll about the policies of the next administration, however, 58 percent of the respondents wanted the next president to shift policies in a direction different from President Reagan.[46]

Even many delegates at the 1988 Republican National Convention rejected many of Reagan's conservative policies. Overall, those delegates held amazingly liberal views. The following is a summary of several key findings from a survey of a representative sample of these delegates:

> Although two-thirds want to keep military spending at present levels, only 18% want to increase it, compared with 37% who would expand government programs to create jobs. . . . Although the Reagan administration has called for more study of acid rain, three-fourths of the delegates favor government action now to cut by 50% the pollution that causes acid rain. . . . 61% of this year's delegates believe "abortion is a private matter between a woman, her family and her doctor and oppose the government getting involved" . . . and 76% believe the public schools should offer sex education.[47]

Where was the conservative Reagan revolution? Neither the Republican convention delegates nor the public in general developed predominately conservative views in the 1980s.

Notes

1. Benjamin I. Page and Robert Y. Shapiro, "Changes in America's Policy Preferences 1935–1979," *Public Opinion Quarterly* 46 (September 1982): 24–42.

2. Thomas Ferguson and Joel Rogers, "The Myth of America's Turn to the Right," *The Atlantic,* May 1986, 43–53.
3. *The Gallup Report,* June 1986, 19–21.
4. "80s College Students Still Liberals," *The Plain Dealer,* 1 November 1986, p. 8-A. The story was originally published in the *Los Angeles Times.*
5. Robert Y. Shapiro and Kelly D. Patterson, "The Dynamics of Public Opinion Toward Social Welfare Policy." Paper presented at the 1986 Meeting of the American Political Science Association, Washington, D.C.
6. *The Gallup Report,* September 1987, 26–27.
7. Pamela Fessler, "From Home: Slash Those Deficits, But . . ." *Congressional Quarterly Weekly Report* 43 (20 April 1985): 718.
8. *The Gallup Report,* March 1985, 4.
9. *The Gallup Report,* April 1986, 15.
10. Warren E. Miller and Santa A. Traugott, *American National Election Studies Data Sourcebook, 1952–1986* (Cambridge, Mass.: Harvard University Press, 1989), 170.
11. Alvin Richman, "Public Attitudes on Military Power," *Public Opinion* 41 (December 1981/January 1982): 44–46.
12. Kathleen Maurer Smith and William Spinrod, "The Popular Political Mood," *Social Policy* 11 (March/April 1981): 37–45.
13. *The Gallup Report,* June 1985, 5 and 7.
14. *The Gallup Report,* August 1987, 23–27.
15. *The Gallup Report,* October 1989, 10.
16. Ferguson and Rogers, "The Myth of America's Turn to the Right," 38.
17. Everett Carll Ladd, "Public Opinion on Environmental Policy," *Public Opinion* 15 (February/March 1982): 16–20.
18. *The Gallup Report,* July 1986, 17.
19. Miller and Traugott, *American National Election Studies Data Sourcebook, 1952–1986,* 159.
20. Robert Y. Shapiro and John M. Gilroy, "The Polls: Regulation—Parts 1 and 2," *Public Opinion Quarterly* 48 (Summer 1984): 531–542 and 666–667.
21. Richard F. Hamilton and James D. Wright, *The State of the Masses* (New York: Aldine Publishing, 1986).
22. Miller and Traugott, *American National Election Studies Data Sourcebook, 1952–1986,* 164.
23. *The Gallup Report,* July 1987, 17.
24. Miller and Traugott, *American National Election Studies Data Sourcebook, 1952–1986,* 161.
25. *The Gallup Report,* July 1987, 19.
26. *The Gallup Report,* August 1988, 5.
27. Miller and Traugott, *American National Election Studies Data Sourcebook, 1952–1986,* 163.

28. Ibid., 162.
29. *The Gallup Report,* October 1989, 13.
30. *The Gallup Report,* October 1989, 15.
31. *The Gallup Report,* August 1987, 20–21.
32. *The Gallup Report,* March 1987, 19.
33. Ibid.
34. Miller and Traugott, *American National Election Studies Data Source-book, 1952–1986,* 167.
35. *The Gallup Report,* September 1989, 17.
36. *The Gallup Report,* August 1989, 7.
37. Miller and Traugott, *American National Election Studies Data Source-book, 1952–1986,* 166.
38. *The Gallup Report,* February 1989, 17.
39. *The Gallup Report,* January 1989, 27.
40. *The Gallup Report,* January 1989, 26.
41. *The Gallup Report,* August 1988, 4.
42. *The Gallup Report,* June 1989, 38–39.
43. *The Gallup Report,* August 1987, 30.
44. *The Gallup Report,* January 1989, 16.
45. *The Gallup Report,* May 1989, 6.
46. *The Gallup Report,* September 1987, 27.
47. Thomas J. Brazaitis, "Delegates Divided Over GOP Platform," *The Plain Dealer,* 10 August 1988, p. 2–A.

3

The Illusion of President Reagan's High Popularity

During the 1980s the media and political commentators often portrayed President Reagan as one of the most popular presidents of the twentieth century. This thesis was presented over and over as if it were a given fact.

Political analysts debated why Reagan was so incredibly popular among the American people. Reagan's personality, ideology, and television performances were some of the reasons suggested to explain why he received such high public opinion ratings.

President Reagan's high popularity is part of the Reagan revolution thesis. Proponents of the thesis argue that Reagan's popularity was a major asset he used to significantly change the country's politics and policies.

But an analysis of public opinion polls indicates that Reagan was only a moderately popular president, at best, compared to other recent presidents. In comparison with presidents since FDR, Reagan's public opinion ratings were way below the most popular presidents and close to the overall ratings of the least popular.[1]

Because of the landslide victory in the 1980 presidential election, Reagan was portrayed as a very popular president on entering office, as well as during the early part of his first term. This high public support was often mentioned as a major factor contributing to Reagan's legislative successes in 1981 and 1982.

An examination of poll data, however, shows that Reagan was the most unpopular president of the 1953–88 period during the early part of his first term. Of the seven presidents, Reagan received by far the lowest popularity rating (see table 3.1) in the first Gallup poll taken in each administration. Other presidents were much more popular than Reagan when they began their first term. Reagan received an extremely low rating of 51 percent in January 1981. The next lowest first-poll rating was Nixon's rating of 59 percent. The other presidents began their terms with ratings in the 66–78 percent range.

Reagan's very low popularity at the start of his presidency, after a landslide victory, corroborates the findings of several election studies that the vote in 1980 was primarily a strong anti-Carter vote and not an overwhelming pro-Reagan vote. Reagan's low popularity at the beginning of his first term indicates that he was a fairly weak candidate in 1980 who was fortunate to have the chance to run against an unpopular incumbent president.

Of the seven presidents during the 1953–88 period, Reagan not only had the lowest popularity at the start of his presidency, but his ratings were also among the lowest overall in the second and third years. In fact, Reagan had the lowest popularity rating at the beginning of the third year. The huge recession in the early 1980s was probably the main reason for Reagan's low popularity in 1982 and 1983.

With the end of the recession, Reagan's poll ratings gradually increased from the thirties to the fifties and sixties in 1985 and 1986. Then the Iran-Contra scandal hit and brought Reagan's popularity down to the forties for most of 1987. His approval ratings gradually increased again in 1988 and ended up in the sixties by the end of his presidency.

TABLE 3.1
Results of the First Gallup Poll Rating in Each Administration from Eisenhower to Reagan

Eisenhower	78%
Kennedy	72%
Johnson	78%
Nixon	59%
Ford	71%
Carter	66%
Reagan	51%

Source: Gallup poll.

As table 3.2 indicates, Reagan's approval ratings followed a different trend from the other presidents in the 1953–1988 period. Generally, the popularity of the other presidents gradually declined from the earlier years of their administrations until the end. Reagan's popularity, on the other hand, was higher during several periods of his second term than it had been in the first term.

This divergent pattern was presented by some political commentators as evidence of Reagan's high popularity. They argued that Reagan had higher approval ratings in the later years than the other recent presidents, and his popularity increased while theirs decreased. Much was also made of the fact that Reagan left office with the highest final approval rating in the polls of any president since FDR.[2]

The argument that Reagan was a very popular president because he had relatively high ratings during the later years of his administration has several weaknesses. First, Reagan had relatively high ratings in his second term for only a short period of time. His ratings for most of the last two years of his presidency were not high. The yearly average for 1987 and 1988 was only about 50 percent.

Second, the difference in the timing of major events, not greater popularity, caused Reagan's divergent pattern. For several of the other presidents, the major events that hurt their reputation and gradually brought their popularity down (e.g., Watergate for Nixon) occurred in the later years of their presidencies. For Reagan, on

TABLE 3.2
Yearly Average of Presidential Popularity Ratings, 1953–88

President	1st Year	2d Year	3d Year	4th Year	5th Year	6th Year	7th Year	8th Year
Eisenhower	70	65	71	73	65	55	63	61
Kennedy	76	72	63					
Johnson	74	66	51	44	42			
Nixon	61	57	50	56	42	26		
Ford	54	43	48					
Carter	62	45	37	41				
Reagan	57	44	44	56	61	62	48	51

Source: Based on data from the Gallup poll and Gary King and Lyn Ragsdale, *The Elusive Executive* (Washington, D.C.: CQ Press, 1988).

the other hand, the major event to adversely affect his popularity—the recession—happened early in his administration. Consequently, his popularity declined relatively early and simply returned to normal after the recession. If the recession had occurred in 1987 and 1988 instead of the early 1980s, Reagan's popularity would have declined in the later years, following the pattern of the other recent presidents.

Third, receiving a relatively high rating in the final poll is not, by itself, adequate proof that a president was highly popular. It is ridiculous to ignore all the many months in which Reagan received popularity ratings in the moderate or poor range and then to proclaim him a popular president because his last rating was high.

Based on Gallup poll results, the presidents since 1932 fall into two categories in popularity. Three presidents had high overall averages: Kennedy, 70; Roosevelt, 68; and Eisenhower, 66. The other six presidents had much lower averages: Johnson, 54; Reagan, 52; Nixon, 48; Carter, 47; Truman, 46; and Ford, 46.[3] So Reagan definitely was not a popular president in comparison to the presidents in office during the 1932–88 period. Kennedy, Roosevelt, and Eisenhower were relatively popular presidents. In comparison to these three presidents, Reagan's overall popularity was in the moderate range, along with the five other presidents.

For Reagan to be considered one of the most popular presidents of the last several decades, he should have a relatively large number of very high ratings. As the data in table 3.3 indicates, however, Reagan and Nixon were the only presidents in the 1953–88 period who never received approval ratings in either the seventies or the eighties.

The difference between Eisenhower and Kennedy, two presidents with high popularity ratings, and Reagan is enormous (see table 3.3). The huge gap between Reagan and these two popular presidents unquestionably shows that Reagan should not be considered a popular president. The distribution patterns between the two popular presidents and Reagan are nearly opposite. Whereas most of Eisenhower's and Kennedy's ratings were in the moderately high or high range, most of Reagan's were in the moderate or low range. Over 70 percent of Eisenhower's ratings and over 90 percent of Kennedy's were 60 or above. In contrast, almost 80 percent of Reagan's ratings were below 60.

TABLE 3.3
Distribution of Presidential Popularity Ratings from Eisenhower to Reagan

Eisenhower	N	%	Nixon	N	%	Reagan	N	%
80–89	0	0	80–89	0	0	80–89	0	0
70–79	31	29	70–79	0	0	70–79	0	0
60–69	48	45	60–69	19	20	60–69	26	22
50–59	26	25	50–59	38	40	50–59	42	35
40–49	1	1	40–49	13	14	40–49	49	41
	106	100	30–39	7	7	30–39	3	3
			20–29	17	18		120	101
				94	99			

Kennedy	N	%	Ford	N	%
80–89	1	3	80–89	0	0
70–79	23	58	70–79	1	3
60–69	13	33	60–69	1	3
50–59	3	8	50–59	7	20
	40	102	40–49	20	57
			30–39	6	17
				35	100

Johnson	N	%	Carter	N	%
80–89	1	1	80–89	0	0
70–79	17	20	70–79	3	4
60–69	18	22	60–69	11	13
50–59	9	11	50–59	21	26
40–49	33	40	40–49	24	29
30–39	5	6	30–39	23	28
	83	100	20–29	0	0
				82	100

Note: Some percentage totals do not equal one hundred because of rounding.
Source: Same as table 3.2.

Even Johnson had a much larger proportion of higher ratings than Reagan. Forty-three percent of LBJ's ratings were in the 60-or-above range, compared to only 22 percent of Reagan's.

If the distribution pattern of Reagan's ratings had been similar to Ike's and JFK's, political commentators would have been justified in proclaiming Reagan a highly popular president. However, since Reagan's ratings were so much lower than these two presidents, it is very difficult to understand why Reagan was considered a highly popular president when one of the most accepted measures of presidential popularity showed otherwise. Instead of creating the illusion that Reagan was a very popular president, reporters and political analysts should have concentrated on why Reagan generally received low-to-moderate popularity ratings similar to Nixon, Ford, and Carter.

Finally, some political commentators created the perception that George Bush would never be as popular a president as Ronald Reagan. Bush was often compared unfavorably with Reagan in his ability to gain public support. But in the early part of his administration, Bush received much higher popularity ratings than Reagan did in a comparable period. At the end of the first seven months, Bush had an approval rating of 70 percent compared to Reagan's 60 percent.[4] After his first year, Reagan had a rating of only 49 percent. In contrast, Bush received an incredible rating of 80 percent at the end of his first year.[5]

Conclusion

President Reagan's popularity was greatly exaggerated. According to public opinion polls, Reagan's popularity ratings were much lower than the ratings of FDR, Eisenhower, and Kennedy. And his overall average was only a little higher than the recent presidents with the lowest ratings.

During his first term, Reagan had some of the lowest approval ratings of any president in office during the past several decades. While his ratings increased at the end of his first term and in the early part of the second term, his popularity again dropped considerably in 1987 with the Iran-Contra scandal. Overall, most of Reagan's approval ratings were in the moderate or poor range compared to the popular presidents who received ratings largely in the moderately high or high range.

Notes

1. The analysis in this chapter is based on data from the Gallup poll compiled by Gary King and Lyn Ragsdale, *The Elusive Executive* (Washington, D.C.: CQ Press, 1988).

2. *The Gallup Report,* January 1989, 12–13.
3. Ibid., 13.
4. *The Gallup Report,* September 1989, 3.
5. *The Gallup Poll Monthly,* January 1990, 16.

4

No Conservative Shift in the 1980s' Election

President Reagan's two landslide victories suggested to many people that the elections of the 1980s reflected a move to the right in American politics. According to political analysts from a wide range of ideological perspectives, the election outcomes were the result of a significant conservative shift. For example, the liberal columnist Anthony Lewis stated: "What happened in the 1980 election reflected a profound and general turn to conservatism in this country."[1] And the conservative *National Review* concluded that recent presidential elections illustrated "the plain fact that the voters are rejecting liberal extremism."[2]

This chapter examines the thesis that the national elections from 1980 to 1988 reflected a profound conservative shift in public opinion. The first section analyzes the presidential elections, while the second section explores the congressional elections. The last section focuses on the elections in the California Assembly.

Ideological Voting and the Presidential Elections

If the conservative shift thesis is accurate, ideology should have been the key factor in the 1980, 1984, and 1988 presidential elections. Election data should indicate that conservative ideological voting was the main reason why Ronald Reagan and George Bush won these elections. However, most studies of these elections concluded that other factors besides support for conservative policies produced the victories. In fact, Reagan's conservative positions lessened his support among many American voters.

41

The overwhelming conclusion from the studies of the 1980 presidential election was that Reagan did not win the election because of ideological support, but won because of the public's low evaluation of Carter's performance in office. The election was not a mandate for conservative policies, but a rejection of the Carter administration. As Abramson, Aldrich, and Rohde concluded in their book on the 1980 election:

> In short, the positional issues, while clearly related to voter choice, do not support the argument that Reagan received a mandate in favor of his particular policies. Instead, many people had quite mixed views. . . . Moreover, positional issues provide only one determinant of voter choice. Why, then, did Reagan win so handily. . . . Regardless of what the incumbent promised to do if returned to office, voters felt he had not done a very good job of managing policy during his incumbency.[3]

In another major book on the 1980 election, Frankovic came to similar conclusions.[4] Using data from CBS News/*New York Times* polls, she found no support for the ideological-mandate thesis.

> There is no clear ideological mandate for the Reagan administration. Dissatisfaction with the Carter administration's performance on the economy, concern over Carter's handling of Iran, and the consistent general dislike of the incumbent all contributed to the Reagan victory. . . . The new President does not have a mandate for conservative policies; instead, he has a mandate to be different from Jimmy Carter.[5]

Unfortunately for Carter, the 1980 election occurred at a time when his popularity had reached a low level. While his poll ratings were moderate-to-high during the early period of his administration, these evaluations had dropped drastically by November 1980.

A comparison of the presidential elections from 1952 to 1980 also provides evidence that the 1980 election represented a referendum on Carter's performance rather than on ideology. According to an analysis of the Survey Research Center (SRC) presidential election data (1952–1980), "policy considerations exerted more influence over the collective voting decision than performance assessments" only in the 1964 and 1972 elections.[6]

The enormous impact of the public's negative assessment of Carter's performance can readily be seen by comparing the retrospective performance ratings (percent positive minus percent negative) in the SRC data. The five incumbent presidents running for reelection during the 1952–1980 period had the following retrospective performance ratings at the time of the election: Eisenhower (1956), 15.0; Johnson (1964), 10.6; Nixon (1972), 12.7; Ford (1976), −3.1; and Carter (1980), −25.0.[7] Carter's incredibly low performance rating was far more important to voters than Reagan's policy positions.

The state of the economy was a major reason why many people gave President Carter such low ratings.[8] Polls indicated that most Americans considered economic problems, not social problems, as the most important issue in 1980. Only a small portion of the voters were greatly worried about the social issues which concern the New Right. The Gallup poll found that over three-fourths of their sample mentioned economic issues as the most important issues, while less than 15 percent mentioned social and political issues.[9] Most respondents in the CBS News/*New York Times* Election Day poll also mentioned economic issues (e.g., inflation and jobs) as the most important issues affecting their vote.[10] So the poll data indicated that most voters did not cast their ballots in support of the New Right's position on social issues, but against the perceived mismanagement of the economy by President Carter.

A comparison between voter support in 1976 and 1980 also demonstrates the importance of the perception of economic conditions. Carter won in 1976 largely because of the support from voters who felt their economic situation had declined. In 1980 Reagan was able to make the same case against the economic performance of the incumbent administration. Again, these voting patterns show little ideological voting, but rather voting based on the judgment of the performance of an incumbent administration. These judgments were unrelated to an ideological assessment of the incumbent president's economic policy.

Another way to examine whether Reagan won in 1980 because of a conservative ideological shift is to study the ideological composition of the voters supporting the candidates. If an ideological change occurred, polls should have shown a shift in voting patterns among voters who considered themselves conservatives, moderates, and liberals. However, this was not the case because the proportion of liberals, moderates, and conservatives supporting Carter in 1980 was almost the same as in 1976.[11] Reagan also received similar support in 1980 from these three ideological groups as Ford received in 1976. Also, Carter suffered about the same percentage decline in support among liberal, moderate, and conservative Democrats. If Reagan's victory occurred because of a conservative shift in voting, a much larger proportion of conservative Democrats should have abandoned Carter compared to liberal and moderate Democrats.

Some supporters of the conservative shift thesis suggest that Reagan won primarily by acquiring the votes of newly-recruited voters from the lower-to-middle social classes who were more religious, alienated from the federal government, and supporters of the New Right social agenda. Himmelstein and McRae, however, found no support for this thesis in the data from the 1980 National Election Study.[12] The newly-recruited Republican voters "were not social conservatives who shifted to Reagan primarily on social issues."[13]

Just as in 1980, Reagan's 1984 victory was not a mandate for conservative policies. In fact, polls indicated that many voters opposed several of the President's major conservative policies. For example, a plurality of Americans opposed Reagan's position on abortion, the Equal Rights Amendment, defense spending, social programs, and Nicaragua.

The Survey Research Center data for the 1984 presidential election showed that Reagan's victory was not based on support for conservative policies. The respondents were asked to place Mondale's, Reagan's, and their position on an issue scale for seven major issues. On defense spending and Central American policy, the average citizen's position was much closer to Mondale's position. The average response was about halfway between the two candidates on government services, aid to women, relations with Russia, jobs, and standard of living guarantee. Only on aid to minorities was the average response significantly closer to Reagan's position.[14]

Amazingly, the recession in the early 1980s was a major factor in Reagan's victory. It would seem that a recession should hurt the reelection prospects of an incumbent president. However, the overall economic conditions during an incumbent president's term often are not as important in the election as the timing of the economic developments.[15] The economic conditions the year before the election are usually much more important than economic developments early in the term.

The recession hit early in Reagan's first term and his popularity dropped dramatically. At the time of the recession, Reagan's reelection changes looked rather bleak. The polls suggested that he was one of the least popular of the recent presidents during his second year. But the recession turned out to be the best thing that could have happened to Ronald Reagan. A recovery period set in after the recession and the economic conditions were generally favorable during the year before the election. The timing of the economic events was nearly perfect for Reagan's reelection campaign. By November 1984 many voters were thinking much more about the improving economy than the recession. Lipset summarized the changes in public opinion:

> The growth in negative evaluations of the President, closely related to the worsening economy and an increase in unemployment from seven to 11 percent, had direct effects on political choices. In early and mid-1981, Reagan invariably led Mondale by a decisive margin in all the surveys. . . . By late 1982, the former vice-president had taken the lead. . . . From the spring of 1983 on, as the various economic indicators steadily improved . . . Americans expressed a sharp increase in optimism both for themselves and for the nation. . . . Not surprisingly, the national surveys reported that Ronald Reagan and his economic policies were given credit for these improvements. . . . His approval rating in the ABC News/*Washington Post* survey climbed from 41 percent in January to 49 in mid-April, to 53 in mid-June, and remained in the mid-fifties to low sixties from then on in most polls taken up to the 1984 election.[16]

If the recession had occurred in 1984 rather than in 1982, Reagan probably would have lost the 1984 election. And then political commentators would have discussed why Reagan was so unpopular rather than why he was so popular. They would have analyzed why the election was such a repudiation of conservative policies rather than a mandate for these policies.

Finally, George Bush's election in 1988 was not based on ideological voting. As the public opinion chapter indicated, no conservative shift in public opinion occurred in the 1980s. Therefore, George Bush was not voted into office because of a large increase in support for conservative policies.

Furthermore, Bush's campaign was not solely based on a hard-line conservative policy agenda. While he did stress some conservative themes, he also emphasized several liberal policies. For example, he campaigned on patriotism and no new taxes, but he also promised child-care legislation and strong environmental laws.

Once again, the timing of the economic events was an important factor in the Republican victory. An economic downturn in late 1987 or in 1988 would have greatly helped Michael Dukakis. Whereas some Americans were upset with the economic conditions in 1988, the majority seemed to be fairly satisfied. A few weeks before the election a CBS/*New York Times* poll found that 68 percent of the respondents described the economy as good compared with only 31 percent who indicated it was bad.[17] A slowdown in the economy would have significantly improved Dukakis's chances of convincing voters that his administration would have been better for the economy.

Ideological Voting and the Congressional Elections

Caraley compared the electoral support of members of Congress to their roll-call votes on federal social programs.[18] Voting for a program was considered liberal, and voting against it was considered conservative. The results indicated that the more liberal candidates in the 1980 congressional elections fared as well as the more conservative candidates.

This section attempts to expand upon Caraley's analysis. The research consists of an examination of ideological ratings and election results (1976–88) for members of the U.S. Senate and the U.S. House of Representatives.[19] The ideological ratings used in the study come from the liberal Americans for Democratic Action (ADA) and the conservative Americans for Constitutional Action (ACA) and American Conservative Union (ACU).

For the conservative shift thesis to be supported, a high relationship should exist between conservative voting in Congress and the votes in the elections. Conservative members of Congress should have received much higher support in the 1980–88 elections than liberals. Also, conservative electoral support should have been much higher in the 1980–88 elections than the 1976–78 elections. If the more liberal candidates received about as many votes as the more conservative candidates, this indicates support for the position that no significant conservative swing took place in the 1980s.[20]

Results from congressional elections show that voting did not shift toward conservatives in the 1980–88 elections. Little, if any, support can be found for the conservative shift thesis.

If a major conservative shift had taken place, House conservatives should have enjoyed a much higher election percentage than liberals and a big increase in electoral support compared to the last elections in the 1970s. However, table 4.1 shows similar results in the House for liberals and conservatives, with a small liberal advantage. The mean election percentage for liberal representatives was 71 compared to 69 for conservative representatives in the 1980–88 elections. Since the mean for the 1976–78 elections indicates a small conservative advantage, the 1980s produced a slight shift in favor of the liberals.

If an electoral trend has taken place that favors one group over another, the group gaining electoral support should win more elections and hold more safe seats. On the other hand, the group losing ground should lose more elections and become involved in a higher proportion of competitive races as their opponents gain voter support. Therefore, most defeated incumbents should have been

TABLE 4.1
Comparison of the Electoral Support of Liberal, Moderate, and Conservative Members of Congress, 1976–88 Elections

Election	House of Representatives			Senate		
	Lib.	Mod.	Con.	Lib.	Mod.	Con.
1976	68	69	67	61	58	61
1978	69	68	72	52	64	57
1980	67	68	70	56	55	59
1982	70	67	65	60	58	55
1984	70	68	72	62	64	63
1986	75	75	70	58	59	57
1988	74	73	71	61	64	55
1976–78	68	68	70	58	60	58
1980–88	71	70	69	60	60	58

The entries are the mean percentages of the vote for liberals, moderates, and conservatives (incumbents or winners in open seats) in the elections.

liberals, and many more liberals than conservatives should have faced competitive races if an enormous conservative swing occurred in the 1980s.

Again, however, the data on incumbent defeats (table 4.2) and electoral competition (table 4.3) do not support the conservative shift thesis. In fact, liberals compiled a better record than conservatives. Only twenty-one liberal incumbents lost in the five House elections from 1980 to 1988, and only 12 percent of the House liberals had competitive races (winner with 55 percent or less) during these elections. This is compared to thirty-two conservative defeats and 18 percent of the conservatives in competitive elections. Also, a higher proportion of liberals as compared with conservatives won with over 65 percent of the vote. Of the eighty-eight elections (1980–88) in which incumbents lost, twenty-eight involved liberals against conservaties. Liberals won over a majority (sixteen) of these races.

A comparison of data for the 1970s and 1980s in tables 4.2 and 4.3 shows a small improvement for House liberals and a slight decline for House conservatives. The conservatives' share of the incumbent losses and competitive elections increased, while the liberals' portion of losses and competitive seats declined from the late 1970s to the five elections of the 1980s.

In addition, data in table 4.4 (correlation coefficients for ADA or ACA/ACU ratings and election percentages) indicate no support for the conservative shift thesis. Most of the coefficients are close to

TABLE 4.2
Ideology of Incumbents Defeated in 1976–88 Congressional Elections

	House of Representatives Defeated Incumbents				Senate Defeated Incumbents			
	1976–78		1980–88		1976–78		1980–88	
	N	%	N	%	N	%	N	%
Liberal	10	31	21	24	6	38	6	24
Moderate	13	41	35	40	7	44	10	40
Conservative	9	28	32	36	3	19	9	36
	32	100	88	100	16	101	25	100

TABLE 4.3
Comparison of the Competitiveness of Liberals, Moderates, and Conservatives in the 1976–88 Congressional Elections

Election Percentage of Incumbents and Open Seat Winners	Liberal		Moderate		Conservative	
	1976–78	1980–88	1976–78	1980–88	1976–78	1980–88
	House of Representatives					
55 or below	21%	12%	19%	17%	16%	18%
56–60	9%	12%	15%	12%	14%	11%
61–65	13%	14%	14%	16%	18%	14%
66 or more	57%	63%	52%	55%	52%	57%
	100%	101%	100%	100%	100%	100%
	N = 236	N = 748	N = 340	N = 722	N = 292	N = 704
	Senate					
55 or below	31%	37%	43%	38%	47%	48%
56–60	39%	13%	16%	21%	24%	12%
61–65	15%	28%	14%	18%	6%	15%
66 or more	15%	22%	27%	24%	24%	25%
	100%	100%	100%	101%	101%	100%
	N = 14	N = 46	N = 37	N = 68	N = 17	N = 52

TABLE 4.4
Correlation Between House Members' Ideological Ratings and Election Percentages, 1976–88 Elections

Elections	ADA	ACA/ACU
1976	− .004	− .02
1978	.09*	.05
1980	− .14*	.05
1982	.24*	− .24*
1984	− .08*	.08*
1986	.15*	− .15*
1988	.10*	− .14*

Note: The entries are the Pearson correlation coefficients for the House members' ratings by the Americans for Democratic Action (ADA) or the Americans for Constitutional Action (ACA) and their percentage of the vote in the 1976–88 elections. Ratings by the American Conservative Union (ACU) are substituted for ACA ratings in the 1986 and 1988 analysis.
*p < .05.

zero. If a strong conservative voting surge had occurred, the correlations between the votes and the ACA/ACU ratings would be high and positive and the correlations with the ADA ratings would be high and negative.

Although the Republicans won control of the Senate in the 1980–84 elections, the election data do not demonstrate a conservative shift in voting. Most data either show about equal voting strength for Senate liberals and conservatives or a small liberal advantage. Liberal senators had a higher mean percent of the vote (table 4.1) than conservative senators for the 1980–88 period. The correlation coefficients (data not shown) indicate no relationship between the ideological ratings and the election percentages. In addition, a higher percentage (48 to 37) of the conservative senators were in competitive races than liberal incumbents. Only six liberal incumbent senators lost in the 1980–88 elections.

Liberals even made some gains from the 1976–78 elections to the 1980–88 elections. Liberal senators' share of the total number of defeated incumbents dropped from the 1976–78 period to the 1980–88 period.

Ideological Voting and the California Assembly Elections

The California Assembly is included in the analysis because California is Ronald Reagan's home state, and it has such a significant social, economic, and political impact on the country. If a conservative shift occurred in the United States, it certainly should have hit California.

Just as in Congress, no conservative shift in voting developed in the elections. Voters did not support conservative candidates at a substantially higher rate than liberal candidates in the 1980–86 elections for the California Assembly.[21] Liberals and conservatives received a similar proportion of the vote. The mean vote percentage (table 4.5) for liberal and conservative legislators was the same. In addition, the correlation coefficients indicate no relationship existed between the amount of voter support for the legislators and their ideology. The coefficients for ADA scores and percentages of the vote were as follows for the 1976–86 elections: .12, .06, .08, − .08, .06, − .09. If a strong conservative voting pattern had devel-

TABLE 4.5

Comparison of the Voter Support Received by Liberal, Moderate, and Conservative Legislators in the 1976–86 California Assembly Elections

Elections	Liberals	Moderates	Conservatives
1976	69	64	65
1978	66	67	64
1980	67	61	65
1982	67	73	67
1984	72	72	72
1986	70	64	72
1980–86	69	68	69

Note: The entries are the mean election percentages of liberals, moderates, and conservatives for each election.

oped, the coefficients would have been high and negative rather than being close to zero.

Conclusion

Most analyses of the 1980 and 1984 presidential elections indicate that Ronald Reagan won primarily because of the unpopularity of the Carter administration and the timing of economic events. Therefore, Reagan's victories were not the result of a conservative shift in voting. In addition, George Bush's victory in 1988 was not based primarily on the voters' support for conservative policies. Similarly, the election results from the late 1970s and the 1980s for Congress and the California Assembly show that no liberal-to-conservative shift occurred during the 1980s. Candidates with conservative voting records in these legislative bodies did not receive significantly more electoral support than candidates with liberal records. In fact, some measures of voting strength during the period show that liberal legislators received higher support than conservative candidates. In addition, the election data on the legislators indicate no liberal-to-conservative voting trend developed from the mid-to-late 1970s to the 1980s.

Notes

1. Anthony Lewis, "The Tidal Wave," *New York Times,* 6 November, 1980, p. A5.

2. "The Week," *National Review,* 30 November, 1984, p. 14.
3. Paul R. Abramson, John H. Aldrich, and David W. Rohde, *Change and Continuity in the 1980 Elections,* rev. ed. (Washington, D.C.: Congressional Quarterly, 1983), 138.
4. Kathleen A. Frankovic, "Public Opinion Trends" in *The Election of 1980,* ed. Gerald M. Pomper (Chatham, N.J.: Chatham House Publishers, 1981), 97–118.
5. Ibid., 116–117.
6. Arthur H. Miller and Martin P. Wattenberg, "Throwing the Rascals Out: Policy and Performance Evaluations of Presidential Candidates, 1952–1980," *American Political Science Review* 79 (June 1985): 369.
7. Ibid., 368.
8. For example, see Douglas H. Hibbs, Jr., "President Reagan's Mandate from the 1980 Elections: a Shift to the Right?" *American Politics Quarterly* 10 (October 1982): 387–420.
9. Ibid., 398.
10. Ibid., 400–01.
11. Gerald M. Pomper, "The Presidential Election," *The Election of 1980,* 85–87.
12. Jerome L. Himmelstein and James A. McRae, Jr., "Social Conservatism, New Republicans, and the 1980 Election," *Public Opinion Quarterly* 48 (Fall 1984): 592–605.
13. Ibid., 602.
14. Paul R. Abramson, John H. Aldrich, and David W. Rohde, *Change and Continuity in the 1984 Elections,* rev. ed. (Washington, D.C.: CQ Press, 1987), 168–172.
15. D. Roderick Kiewiet and Douglas Rivers, "The Economic Basis of Reagan's Appeal," in *The New Direction in American Politics,* ed. John E. Chubb and Paul E. Peterson (Washington, D.C.: Brookings Institution, 1985), 69–90.
16. Seymour Martin Lipset, "The Elections, the Economy, and Public Opinion: 1984," *PS* 18 (Winter 1985): 32–33.
17. See Everett Carll Ladd, "The 1988 Elections: Continuation of the Post–New Deal System," *Political Science Quarterly* 104 (Spring 1989): 3.
18. Demetrios Caraley, "Do Congressional Liberals Really Need to Tremble? A Quick Look at Some Hard Data," *Political Science Quarterly* 96 (Spring 1981): 27–30.
19. The last two sections of the chapter are a revision of Larry M. Schwab, "The Myth of the Conservative Shift in American Politics: A Research Note," *Western Political Quarterly* 41 (December 1988): 817–823. I gratefully acknowledge the permission granted by *Western Political Quarterly* to reprint some of the material from the article.
20. The operational definitions for the ideological categories are as follows: liberal ADA − ACA = 50 to 100; moderate ADA − ACA = −49 to 49; conservative ADA − ACA = −50 to −100. Ratings by the

American Conservative Union (ACU) are substituted for the Americans for Constitutional Action (ACA) for the analyses of the 1986 and 1988 elections.

21. The operational definitions for the ideological categories are as follows: liberal = 68 to 100 ADA; moderates = 34 to 67 ADA; conservative = 0 to 33 ADA.

5

No Party Realignment

Many political scientists divide U.S. party politics during the twentieth century into two eras. The Republicans dominated the two-party system during the first three decades, while the Democrats dominated after 1932. Part of the Reagan revolution thesis is the assertion that the 1980s produced a party realignment which made the Republicans the number one party again.

An examination of the election results during the 1980s indicates that this assertion is incorrect. The Democratic party remained the top party in the political system overall.

This chapter analyzes three aspects of the debate on party realignment. The first section deals with the basic question of whether a party realignment occurred during the 1980s. The second section focuses on the debate about whether the party system moved into a new phase. And the third section examines the thesis that a party realignment occurred, but the results cannot be seen in legislatures because of Democratic gerrymandering.

Party Realignment Debate

The Democrats continued to dominate the political system during the 1980s. By the end of the decade, they held the majority of seats and positions in all major parts of the system except the presidency. Not only did the Democrats remain the number one party during the 1980s, but they set a record for party dominance. By remaining the top party through the 1980s, the Democrats extended the present political era to nearly fifty years. Never has one party maintained its lead in the overall system for such a long period of time. The Republicans' success in presidential elections is the only evidence that can be produced to support the realignment thesis. Republican candidates won all three presidential elections in the 1980s and five of the last six elections. These facts, however, do not prove that a party realignment took place in the 1980s. A party realignment means that one party gains the majority of offices in most of the components of the political system. The presidency is just one part of the political system. It is absurd to argue that the Republicans were the number one party at the end of the 1980s when the majority of representatives, senators, governors, state legislators, and big city mayors were Democrats. In the party realignment of the 1930s, the Democrats won control of all the major parts of the political system, not just the presidency.

Moreover, presidential elections are the worst measure of party strength among all the partisan elections. Since voters know more about candidates and issues in presidential elections, party identification has less impact on their voting decision than in most other races. Party identification remains important in presidential voting, but relatively less important than in other offices. Voters in elections for the U.S. House and state legislatures, for example, must rely more on their party identification because they have less knowledge about candidates and issues in comparison to their presidential voting. During the past several decades, a strong relationship existed between the percent of people who identify with each party at election time and the percent of the national vote each party received in House elections. The Democrats generally had a majority in party identification and received a majority of the vote. In contrast, wide differences often existed between the proportion of the electorate supporting a political party and that party's percent of the presidential vote. This difference was the greatest when Republican presidential candidates won by landslides.

In addition, the Republican success in presidential elections during the 1980s does not denote a new political era because the GOP had success in winning the presidency in earlier periods of the present era. In the 1952–72 period, for example, Republicans won four of the six presidential elections. After FDR died, Republicans were usually highly competitive in presidential races, but Democrats dominated in elections below the presidency. This pattern continued through the 1980s.

If a party realignment happened in the 1980s, the seats in Congress should have shifted from the Democrats to the Republicans between the 1970s and 1980s in a pattern similar to the Republican-to-Democrat change between the 1920s and 1930s. But as the data in table 5.1 demonstrates, the partisan shift toward Republicans failed to match the incredible shift toward the Democrats in the 1930s.

In the House of Representatives, of course, no partisan shift occurred at all because the Democrats won every House election in the 1980s, most of them by landslide proportions. In the 1920s, the Republicans won all the House elections and then lost every one

TABLE 5.1
Party Control of House and Senate Seats, 1920–38 and 1970–88

Year	House Elections		Senate Elections	
	Democrat	Republican	Democrat	Republican
1920	132	300	37	59
1922	207	225	43	51
1924	183	247	40	54
1926	195	237	47	48
1928	163	267	39	56
1930	216	218	47	48
1932	313	117	59	36
1934	322	103	69	25
1936	383	89	75	17
1938	262	169	69	23
1970	255	180	54	44
1972	242	192	56	42
1974	291	144	61	37
1976	292	143	61	38
1978	277	158	58	41
1980	243	192	46	53
1982	268	167	46	54
1984	253	182	47	53
1986	258	177	55	45
1988	260	175	55	45

Source: Norman J. Ornstein, Thomas E. Mann, and Michael J. Malbin, *Vital Statistics on Congress: 1989–1990* (Washington, D.C.: Congressional Quarterly, 1990).

(except 1930) in the 1930s. They won, on average, 255 seats in the House elections during the 1920s compared with only 139 seats in the 1930s. In the 1980s, on the other hand, the Democrats continued the pattern from the 1960s and 1970s by winning well over a majority of seats in each election. The Democrats' average number of seats for each election in the 1980s was even slightly higher (256 seats) than the Republicans' average in the 1920s.

Democrats not only maintained their majority of House seats, but they also continued to win the majority of the national vote in the 1980s House elections. And, as table 5.2 indicates, the Democratic percentage of the national House vote remained at about the same level in the 1980s as it had been in the 1970s and 1960s. The average for the 1960s, 1970s, and 1980s was 53, 54, and 53 respectively. So no shift toward the Republicans developed in the 1980s' House elections. Where was the Reagan revolution?

The Democrats have an amazing hold on the House of Representatives. They have won every House election since 1952. From 1932

TABLE 5.2
Democratic and Republican Percentage of the Popular Vote in House
Elections, 1960–88

Year	Democrat	Republican
1960	54.4	44.8
1962	52.1	47.1
1964	56.9	42.4
1966	50.5	48.0
1968	50.0	48.2
1970	53.0	44.5
1972	51.7	46.4
1974	57.1	40.5
1976	56.2	42.1
1978	53.4	44.7
1980	50.4	48.0
1982	55.2	43.3
1984	52.1	47.0
1986	54.5	44.6
1988	53.3	45.5

Source: Norman J. Ornstein, Thomas E. Mann, and Michael J. Malbin, *Vital Statistics on Congress: 1989–1990* (Washington, D.C.: Congressional Quarterly, 1990).

to 1988, the Democrats held the majority of House seats for all but four years. Never before in U.S. history has one party had such dominance of a house of Congress. The continuation of this record into the 1980s is yet another example of a record going in the wrong direction compared to what should have happened with a conservative Reagan revolution.

The Republicans had more success in the Senate. They held the majority of Senate seats for six years during the 1980s. These victories, however, did not mean that a party realignment happened in Senate elections.

First, the Republican Senate victories were based on special circumstances and not on a shift in national voting patterns. The Democrats won well over a majority of the combined national vote for the three elections (1980, 1982, and 1984) in which the Republicans won a majority of the seats. In fact, the Democrats won a near-landslide proportion of the popular vote in 1982, so no party realignment took place in Senate elections, since the Democrats remained the top party in voter support.

Republicans won the majority of Senate seats with a minority of the national vote through malapportionment and uncanny success in close elections. The large difference in the population of the states produces the high degree of malapportionment among the Senate seats. This unequal representation in the Senate allows a party with well below a majority of the national vote to win a majority of the seats. For example, a party would gain the same number of Senate seats with many fewer votes by winning three-fourths of the sixteen smallest states compared to winning the same proportion of the sixteen biggest seats.

This pattern developed in the first half of the 1980s. After the 1980, 1982, and 1984 elections, Senate Republicans held fifteen of the twenty seats in the ten states smallest in population. In contrast, Senate Republicans gained victories in only eight of the twenty seats in the ten largest states. This variation in Republican success between the large and small states helped produce their takeover of the Senate with a minority of the national vote.

Besides malapportionment, the Republicans' Senate success was based on an incredible winning percentage in close elections, especially in 1980. Instead of the winners in close elections dividing equally between the two parties in 1980, the Republicans won nine of the eleven races in which the winning candidate won with 51 percent or less of the vote. A shift of only about forty thousand votes in four of the close Republican victories would have given the Democrats a majority of the Senate seats in 1980, so the Republican majority in 1980 developed from a little over forty thousand votes out of a total of fifty-five million. This small number of votes needed to switch the majority party in the Senate, coupled with the fact that the Democrats won the majority of the national vote, shows that the 1980 Republican victory was a fluke and not the result of a surge in popular support.

Fortunately for the Democrats, they won most of the close elections in the 1986 election. In the Democrats' case in 1986, however, their success in close races allowed the party with the majority of the votes to receive a majority of the seats. In contrast to this, the Republicans' success in close races aided them in acquiring a majority of seats with a minority of the vote in 1980.

The Democratic victories in the 1986 and 1988 Senate elections also raise serious questions about the realignment thesis. Many supporters of the realignment thesis predicted that by the late 1980s Republicans would control the majority of House and Senate seats. Obviously, their predictions missed the mark by a wide margin. If a party realignment had happened in the 1980s, the Republicans should have been able to win the majority of House and Senate seats in the 1986 and 1988 elections with well over a majority of the national vote.

Just as in Congress, no party realignment happened in state government. Democrats remained the dominant party in state elections through the 1980s (see table 5.3). The Republicans' situation in state legislatures is just the opposite of what would be expected from a Reagan revolution. The Republican party is in deep trouble in the state legislative bodies. They controlled both houses in only eight state legislatures at the end of the decade. How could any political analyst even consider the possibility of a party realignment when the alleged top party won only 16 percent of the state legislatures?

Furthermore, Republicans have lost ground during the past twenty years in elections for state legislatures. In the late 1960s, Republicans controlled twenty state legislatures, whereas they only held eleven, on average, during the 1970s and 1980s.

TABLE 5.3
Party Control of State Legislatures and
the Office of Governor, 1960–89

Year	State Legislatures			Governors	
	Democratic Control	Split Party or Tie	Republican Control	Democratic	Republican
1961	27	6	15	34	16
1963	25	7	16	34	16
1965	32	10	6	33	17
1967	24	8	16	25	25
1969	20	9	20	20	30
1971	23	9	16	29	21
1973	27	6	16	31	19
1975	37	7	5	36	13
1977	36	8	6	37	12
1979	30	7	12	32	18
1981	28	6	15	27	23
1983	34	4	11	34	16
1985	27	11	11	34	16
1987	28	12	9	26	24
1989	28	13	8	29	21

Source: U.S. Bureau of the Census, *Statistical Abstract of the United States: 1990* (Washington, D.C.: U.S. Government Printing Office, 1990).

Voting in state legislative races provides an excellent measure of party strength among the electorate because of the voters' limited knowledge of candidates and issues in these contacts. If a surge in Republican support occurred in the 1980s, the number of state legislatures held by Republicans should have soared to twenty-five or thirty rather than remaining around ten.

It is amazing that almost fifty years after the Great Depression and the New Deal, the Republican party is able to win control of only about ten state legislatures. After all these years since the Democratic realignment, the Republican party should have gained enough strength to provide more competition for the Democrats in state legislative races. From a nationwide view, the elections for state legislatures could be better classified as a one-and-a-half-party system rather than a two-party system.

Democrats also maintained their lead in winning the office of governor during the 1980s. The Democrats' advantage has remained stable over the last three decades. The average number of Democratic governors for the 1960s, 1970s, and 1980s was twenty-nine, thirty-one, and thirty respectively. If a party realignment had taken place in the 1980s, the number of Republican governors should have increased to thirty or thirty-five rather than remaining around twenty. The Republicans could claim only sixteen governors in the mid-1980s. Furthermore, the trend since the late 1960s has been toward fewer Republican governors. After holding thirty governorships in 1969, the Republicans have failed to even win twenty-five positions since then.

Besides election results, data on party identification and voter registration provide useful measures of party strength. These measures also indicate that there was no party realignment in the 1980s.

In party identification studies, pollsters and political scientists ask Americans in sample surveys whether they consider themselves Democrats, Republicans, or independents. Over forty years of survey research questions are available on party identification.

During this period, the Democrats usually maintained a lead over the Republicans (see table 5.4). Their lead has not remained stable but has varied from as low as a few percentage points difference to a high of over twenty-five. A party realignment in the 1980s should have produced a similar pattern, with the Republicans overtaking the Democrats and holding a lead of five to twenty points throughout most of the decade.

Unfortunately for the Republicans, this pattern never developed. While they pulled close to the Democrats a few times during the decade, the Republicans never managed to move decisively ahead and keep a ten or fifteen point lead for several years. Certainly a consistent and decisive lead in party identification by the new number one party is a condition that must be met to declare a party realignment. The Republicans failed to meet this condition.

Republicans nearly closed the party identification gap with the Democrats before the 1984 elections, but the Republican strength faded after the election as the Democrats' lead increased to over ten in several national polls. The effect of the landslide Republican victory in the presidential race seemed to have a short-term impact on the poll results, but the Democratic advantage in party identification continued after the short-term factors abated.

By 1988 the Democrats had improved their lead to fourteen points

TABLE 5.4
Political Party Identification, 1937–88

Year	% Republican	% Democrat	% Independent
1988	29	43	28
1987	30	41	29
1986	32	39	29
1985	33	38	29
1984	31	40	29
1983	25	44	31
1982	26	45	29
1981	28	42	30
1980	24	46	30
1979	22	45	33
1976	23	47	30
1975	22	45	33
1972	28	43	29
1968	27	46	27
1964	25	53	22
1960	30	47	23
1954	34	46	20
1950	33	45	22
1946	40	39	21
1937	34	50	16

Source: Gallup poll.

(table 5.4) on the Gallup poll's question on party identification. This advantage nearly matched the average lead of fifteen that the Democrats held in the fifty-one year period during which Gallup measured party identification.[1] So by the end of the Reagan administration, the Democrats had basically regained their normal lead in party identification which they had maintained during the post–New Deal era.

The Republicans also failed to take a decisive lead in voter registration. In fact, the Democrats continued to hold their lead over the Republicans in many states. Although it is difficult to obtain accurate voter registration data for all the states, some reliable records are available. Table 5.5 presents the voter registration data from the *Statistical Abstract*.[2] As the data show, the Democrats had more registered voters than the Republicans in most of the twenty-two states listed, and they also held a large lead over the GOP in many of these states. The Democrats continued to

TABLE 5.5
Percentage of Democratic and
Republican Registered Voters
in Several States, 1988

State	Party Registration	
	% Democratic	% Republican
Arkansas	20.5	20.7
Arizona	42.7	45.7
California	50.4	38.6
Colorado	30.5	32.9
Connecticut	39.1	27.1
Delaware	43.6	36.1
Florida	54.0	39.0
Iowa	36.1	31.1
Kansas	28.5	41.3
Kentucky	67.2	29.4
Louisiana	75.2	16.4
Maryland	64.2	27.6
Nebraska	42.1	50.7
Nevada	47.0	42.4
New Hampshire	30.4	38.9
New Mexico	58.4	35.4
Oklahoma	65.3	32.1
Oregon	48.3	38.7
Pennsylvania	52.2	42.9
South Dakota	42.8	49.2
West Virginia	66.1	31.3
Wyoming	35.8	34.9

Source: Bureau of the Census, *Statistical Abstract of the United States: 1989*.

maintain big leads over the Republicans in several of the largest states such as California, Florida, and Pennsylvania. The Democratic advantage in California and Florida is especially noteworthy because these two states are the superstars of the growing sunbelt. A Republican realignment would have produced a large Republican lead in voter registration in these two key states.

Finally, another aspect of the Republican realignment thesis is the assertion that the major population shifts within the country are producing a Republican majority. Supposedly, the patterns of population growth and decline are enhancing Republican strength and hurting Democratic strength. Kevin Phillips made this argument in *The Emerging Republican Majority:*

Unluckily for Democrats, their major impetus is centered in stagnant Northern industrial states—and within those states, in old decaying cities. . . . From space-center Florida across the booming Texas plains to the Los Angeles–San Diego suburban corridor, the nation's fastest-growing areas are strongly Republican and conservative. Even in the Northeast, the few rapidly growing suburbs are conservative-trending areas. . . .[3]

This assertion is another myth. The two major population shifts of the past several decades have been first the increase in the suburban population and the decrease or slower growth in the nonmetropolitan and the central city population, and second the much higher rate of growth in the sunbelt compared to the snow-belt.[4] Contrary to the conventional view, these two population trends did not greatly increase Republican strength and decrease Democratic strength in the overall system. One of the major reasons why the Republicans still cannot successfully compete with the Democrats below the presidency is the fact that they did not gain significantly from these population trends.

Admittedly, Ronald Reagan won by wide margins in the suburbs and the sunbelt in 1980 and 1984, but he still would have won easily without the shifts in population. As mentioned in the chapter on elections, Reagan won primarily because of the timing of major economic events. The population shifts had very little impact on the outcome of those elections. If, for example, the recession had hit in 1984 rather than in 1982, Reagan's popularity would have been low at the time of the election. He would have received many fewer votes in the suburbs and the sunbelt as well as in the rest of the country.

Below the presidency, Democrats have adjusted amazingly well to the major population shifts. The Republicans failed to obtain the predicted electoral bonanza.

The population growth of suburbia and the sunbelt did not help the Republicans very much at the state level. In the mid-1980s, the Republicans controlled both houses of the state legislature in just one sunbelt state, and only two sunbelt states had Republican governors.

Much of the suburban population in the United States is in the twenty largest states. Indiana was the only one of these large states with a Republican-controlled state legislature in the mid-1980s.

Republicans controlled the legislature mostly in rural states, such as Idaho and North Dakota, which had little or no suburban population.

Republicans do not dominate the suburban districts in most state legislatures. It is a myth that the suburbs are heavily Republican. In several state legislatures (e.g., Maryland and Massachusetts), Democrats hold the majority of suburban seats.

Suburban growth has not helped the Republicans dominate the office of governor in the states with large suburban areas. Only eight of the twenty largest states had Republican governors in the mid-1980s.

In addition, Republicans do not control most of the sunbelt seats in the Senate. In fact, Democrats held most of the Senate seats in the sunbelt at the end of the 1980s. In 1988 there were only eleven Republican senators in sunbelt states compared with twenty-seven Democrats.

Furthermore, the GOP has not gained much in Senate elections from the suburban growth. For example, the Republicans' successes in the 1980–84 elections were not based on suburban support. The Republicans gained the Senate majority primarily by winning most of the seats in small states with few suburban areas. The Democrats, on the other hand, won the majority of the seats in the big states.

Contrary to most predictions, Democrats, not Republicans, gained House seats after the decline of the population in older big cities and the enormous expansion of suburban population.[5] Most analysts assumed that since the Democrats controlled almost all the central city seats and Republicans won a high proportion of suburban districts, the Republicans would gain considerably from the city-to-suburb population shift. But the expansion of the suburban areas created a more heterogeneous population that increased support for Democrats. The Democrats did lose seats because of the declining population in the older central cities, but they more than made up for the loss by winning suburban districts, urban-suburban (about half central city and half suburbs) districts, and central city districts in the sunbelt.

A comparison of the party control of metropolitan House districts between the early 1960s and the 1980s shows how the Democrats gained a significant advantage from the population shifts. In 1963 the Republicans held forty-four of the sixty-five (68 percent) suburban seats in House of Representatives. In 1983 the Democrats controlled sixty-six of one hundred fifteen (57 percent) suburban districts. While the Republicans held only five more suburban districts in 1983 than in 1963, Democrats controlled forty-five more suburban districts. Since the number of Democratic central city districts only declined from seventy-seven to sixty-seven, the Democrats gained significantly from the population changes in metropolitan areas.

In addition, the number of Democratic urban-suburban districts increased from sixteen to twenty-three between 1963 and 1983. Some of these districts were created when suburban areas were added to central city districts that had lost population.

Democrats were successful in winning suburban districts during the 1970s and 1980s. They won the majority of the suburban districts in most of the elections during the 1974–88 period. In some of these elections (e.g., 1974 and 1982), Democrats won over 55 percent of the suburban seats.

Most of these suburban Democrats are moderates or liberals. Their average ideological rating by the liberal Americans for Democratic Action is close to the average liberal rating of central city Democrats.

Republicans also failed to increase their strength in the House through the sunbelt-snowbelt shift. After the 1982 election, political analysts concluded that the Democrats gained more from the 1980 reapportionment, which primarily transferred snowbelt seats to the sunbelt, than the Republicans. One study found that the Republicans controlled ten of seventeen seats eliminated in the Midwest and Northeast.[6] Many commentators had predicted that most of the eliminated districts would be held by Democrats because of the large population losses in the heavily-Democratic central cities. In the 1982 election Democrats won ten of the seventeen new districts created by the 1980 reapportionment. So after the 1982 election, the Democrats had a net gain from the 1980 reapportionment because they lost fewer of the eliminated districts and won more of the new districts.[7]

In addition, the Democrats have consistently won a majority of sunbelt seats in the House of Representatives. In the 1980s, the Democrats usually held over 60 percent of the seats in the sunbelt.

The South is the biggest part of the sunbelt, and the Democrats still won about two-thirds of the southern districts. In California, the major sunbelt state, Democrats won the majority of House districts in the 1982–88 elections. In 1988 the Democrats controlled fifty-six of the ninety-one seats (62 percent) in California, Florida, and Texas, the three biggest states of the sunbelt.

A New Era of Party Competition

Some political analysts, while conceding that a party realignment similar to the 1930s did not occur, still argued that a new era in party competition developed in the 1980s. According to these analysts, the 1980s produced a significant change in the party system but not a complete realignment. Cavanaugh and Sundquist presented this point of view after the 1984 election:

> The GOP did not replace the Democrats as a new majority party in the nation, but it appears to have drawn almost even. For the first time since 1934 the country may now have a well-balanced, competitive two-party system at the national level instead of the one-and-one-half party system it has known since the great realignment of the New Deal era. If the Republicans can solidify most of their gains, American politics will have entered an era quite distinct from that of the half century that separated Franklin Roosevelt from Ronald Reagan.[8]

An examination of the records show that this hypotheses cannot be supported. For the 1981–88 period to be considered a new phase of party politics, the election results and other measures of party strength should indicate that this period differed significantly from the 1933–80 era. The 1981–88 period, however, did not differ much at all from other periods during the previous fifty years.

As mentioned earlier, the pattern of competition in the 1980s was similar to previous periods. The Republicans were competitive in presidential elections from 1948 to 1980, but the Democrats dominated below the presidency. This pattern continued in the 1980s.

The Republicans did win three Senate elections in the 1980s, but the Republicans had won congressional elections before (1946 and 1952) in this era. In the previous Republican congressional victories, the GOP gained control of both the House and Senate.

Also, the Democrats' lead in party identification did decline to below ten for some periods of the 1980s. But again, this is nothing new. In fact, according to the Gallup poll, the Republicans even took a lead in party identification for a while in the 1940s. Besides, in 1988 the Democrats had their lead in party identification almost back to the average for the previous fifty years.

Consequently, the basic patterns of party competition continued through the 1981–88 period. Neither a party realignment nor a change to a new phase of the party system occurred during these years.

Gerrymandering and the Alleged Republican Realignment

After some political observers began to realize that the Republicans would not take over the political system in the 1980s, new hypotheses were devised to explain what happened. One hypothesis was that the realignment occurred, but the Republicans could not win control of several key parts of the system because of Democratic gerrymandering. This thesis was used especially to explain why the Democrats kept winning landslide victories in the House of Representatives during what was supposed to be a Republican era during the 1980s. As proof of this thesis, its supporters pointed out that the House Democrats' percentage of the seats was always more and the House Republicans' percentage was always less than their respective parties' share of the national vote.

Blaming the House Democratic majority on gerrymandering practically became the official Republican doctrine. This can be seen in the following statement by Republican National Committee chairman Lee Atwater.

> Gerrymandering is the offensive technique Democrats have used to carve congressional districts to ensure a winning margin for their party. Sure, they must put up a new candidate once in a while because of retirement or death, but the party that has gerrymandered the district wins.

> Gerrymandering, simply put, is a means of predetermining the outcome of legislative races. And it is effective. The Democrats have controlled the House of Representatives for 35 years—the longest stretch of domination by a political party in U.S. history.[9]

The assertion that gerrymandering keeps Democrats in control of legislative bodies during a Republican era is inaccurate. First, no

Republican realignment occurred in the 1980s. Therefore, Democratic gerrymandering could not be the reason why the Republicans never received their rightful gains from a realignment because the realignment never happened. The Republican party loses in the House of Representatives and in most state legislatures simply because GOP candidates received fewer votes, not because of gerrymandering. In the House of Representatives, for example, the Republicans received less than 50 percent of the national vote in every election from 1948 through 1988. If a party realignment had occurred, the Republicans would have won well over 50 percent of the national vote in the 1980s' House elections and the majority of the seats.

Second, the gerrymandering thesis can only be used to try to explain why the Republicans are robbed of their realignment gains in population-apportional legislatures. It does not explain why the Democrats continued to hold the majority of the Senate seats and governorships after the alleged Republican realignment occurred. The argument would only make sense if the Republicans controlled all the parts of the political system except the House and state legislatures. Then, Republicans would be on much stronger ground to make the case that gerrymandering is denying their legislative majorities in a Republican era.

The Democratic victories in the 1986 and 1988 elections dealt a severe blow to the credibility of the gerrymandering thesis. Before the 1986 election, the case was made that gerrymandering cost the Republicans control of the House becuase they had won the presidency and the Senate, which were not affected by gerrymandering. With the Senate Democratic majorities in 1986 and 1988, the gerrymandering argument became much less believable because the Democrats obviously did not win the Senate by changing the boundaries of the states to their advantage.

Third, the part of the argument that relates the percent of a party's popular vote to the party's percent of House seats is nonsense. This relationship between votes and seats often develops in political systems with a plurality electoral system and single-number district legislatures. In a system where the winner in single-number legislative districts is the candidate with the most votes, the party winning the majority of the total popular votes usually wins a higher percentage of the seats in comparison with its percentage of the popular vote. This will especially happen in legislative bodies, such as the House of Representatives, that have fairly equal population redistricting.

This pattern did not just develop in the 1980s. In every House election during the post–World War II period, the percentage of seats received by the winning party always exceeded its percentage of the popular vote. This pattern occurred in all the Democratic victories since 1946 as well as the two Republican victories in 1946 and 1952.

Finally, the contention that Democrats continually control legislatures through gerrymandering is incorrect because it greatly exaggerates the instances and impact of party gerrymandering. The supporters of the Democratic gerrymandering thesis suggest that gerrymandering occurs in many states and affects the outcome of a high proportion of House elections. In the 1980s' redistricting, however, partisan gerrymandering occurred in only a few states and had a significant impact on the outcome of only a small number of House races.

The hypothesis that partisan gerrymandering affected the outcome of a high proportion of House races in the 1980s can be tested by developing operational definitions and measures of party gerrymandering and then examining the results of the 1982 elections.[10] This is the best election to study because it was the first election after the state legislatures redistricted the House seats.

Normally, successful party gerrymandering is assumed to have occurred when one party controls a state government and changes the districts in ways that aid the election of its candidates and/or the defeat of the opposition's candidate. This general assumption can be broken down into five conditions that must be met before a redistricting could be considered a successful party gerrymander.

First, one party must control the state government. Second, the state government must pass the redistricting plan without court intervention. Third, the majority party must significantly change at least one district of the minority party or one open district. This criterion is needed to distinguish between situations where the districts remained basically unchanged after redistricting and redistricting where the majority party did manipulate districts for its advantage. Fourth, the majority party must gain seats and/or the minority party must lose seats. Finally, these gains and losses must be significantly affected by the redistricting changes enacted by the majority party.

This is a minimal set of conditions to define a partisan redistricting. For successful gerrymandering to occur, a party must have control of the state government, and it must make gains in the election from changes made in the districts.

The next step is to provide measures for these five conditions. The party with the governor's office and a majority in both houses of the legislature is considered to be in control of the state government. Court intervention occurs when the court either draws the district boundaries or orders a state legislature to follow certain guidelines in drawing the districts. A significant change in a district is defined as a situation in which the new altered district contains less than 80 percent of the constituency of the old district (pre-1980 redistricting). The gains and losses are measured by election victories and defeats.

The final criterion deals with the measurement of the impact of partisan gerrymandering on the gain or loss of seats. There are four electoral situations to consider in partisan gerrymandering: incumbent districts, open districts, eliminated districts, and new districts. In districts where the incumbent is running for reelection, the majority party (i.e., the party controlling the redistricting) may either attempt to defeat an opposition party member, aid some of its own members, or combine both strategies. The majority party shapes open districts to favor the candidate of its party. In states losing seats because of reapportionment, the majority party attempts to eliminate districts held by the other party. In addition, the majority party draws new districts to help its own candidates.

Partisan gerrymandering, therefore, may affect the election outcome in several ways: defeat of a minority party incumbent; reelection of a majority party incumbent; election of a majority party candidate in an open seat; elimination of a district held by the minority party; and the election of a majority party candidate in a new district. A loss by a minority party incumbent is considered to have been influenced by redistricting if (1) the majority party challenger received a higher voter percentage in the new areas of the district (new from the 1980 redistricting) than the old areas of the district (already in the district during 1970s), and his/her victory margin in the new areas represented at least one-half of the total winning margin; (2) two incumbents of the minority party were forced to face each other in a primary; and (3) a minority party incumbent lost in an election against a majority party incumbent in a district containing more constituents from the majority incumbent's old district than the minority incumbent's old district.

In races where majority incumbents won reelection, redistricting influence is inferred when (1) the incumbent's winning percentage improved from the competitive range (below 55 percent) in 1980 to the safe range (55 percent or over) in 1982 or remained in the competitive range in both elections; (2) the incumbent's district was significantly altered; and (3) the victory margin in the new areas represented at least one-half of his/her total vote margin. In open races in which the district was significantly changed, the victor was either from the opposition party of the previous incumbent or was of the same party as the previous incumbent and the winning percentage increased from the competitive to the safe range.

The other two situations deal with eliminated and new seats. The elimination of a seat is assumed to have been affected by partisan redistricting if the minority party member held the seat in the eliminated district. The influence of partisan gerrymandering is also assumed in races where the majority party won in a new district.

Only twenty states meet the first condition (one-party control of the state government) for a successful party gerrymander. Eight states had no redistricting before the 1982 election (six had only one seat, and Maine and Montana kept the same boundaries), and twenty-two states had divided party control of the houses of the state legislature and the governor's office.

Since the courts intervened in Georgia, Mississippi, and South Carolina, this leaves seventeen states that meet the first and second (no court intervention) conditions. Applying the third condition (significant changes in districts), eliminates seven more states. Only small changes occurred in the districts in Alabama, Connecticut, Hawaii, Maryland, North Carolina, Rhode Island, and West Virginia.

Of the remaining ten states, Florida, Iowa, Kentucky, Massachusetts, and Okalahoma do not meet the fourth condition (party gains in the election). Although the Florida Democrats drew the districts to help their party more than the Republicans, they did not attempt either to unseat the Republican incumbents or to stack all four new districts in their favor. All the Republican incumbents won easily, and the parties each won two of the new districts.

The Iowa Republicans accepted a redistricting plan drawn by the state's Legislative Service Bureau. While this plan changed some districts, it did not significantly alter the partisan composition of the districts. All the incumbents (three of each party) won by at least 55 percent in the 1982 election.

Oklahoma Democrats tried to help some of the Democratic incumbents by placing more Republican territory in the lone Republican incumbent's district. These changes, however, had little impact on the results in the six districts. The Republican incumbent won with about the same high percentage in the 1982 election as he had in the 1980 election. Only one Democratic incumbent (Dave McCurdy) increased his victory percentage from the competitive range (51 percent) to the safe range (65 percent). His enormous winning percentage in comparison with the number of new constituents in the districts indicates that redistricting had only a small effect on the election victory.

Kentucky Democrats significantly altered only one of the three Republican districts. Although Gene Snyder, the Republican incumbent in the altered district, had a much closer race in 1982 than 1980, he still won reelection with 54 percent of the vote.

In Massachusetts the major change in the districts was the elimination of the one district the state lost through reappportionment. Democrats eliminated the seat by combining areas of districts held by Republican Margaret Heckler and Democrat Barney Frank. Surprisingly, the new district contained a much higher proportion of constituents from Heckler's old district compared to Frank's old district. Frank, however, won the election despite the lack of help from his state party colleagues. Although the Republicans lost a seat, the Massachusetts' redistricting did not meet the fourth condition because the new combined district contained a higher proportion of constituents from the minority party incumbent's former district.

This leaves only six states (California, Indiana, New Jersey, New Mexico, Pennsylvania, and Washington) where the redistricting met all five conditions. And even among these states, only the California Democrats were successful in significantly shifting the party balance in their favor.

TABLE 5.6
Impact of Partisan Redistricting in Six States on the Winners and Losers in the 1982 House Elections

Impact	Democratic Redistricting			Republican Redistricting		
	California	New Jersey	New Mexico	Indiana	Pennsylvania	Washington
Minority Party Incumbent Defeats	3	1	0	1	2[a]	0
Majority Party Incumbent Victories	0	0	0	1	1	0
Majority Party Victories in Open Seats	2	0	0	0	0	0
Majority Party Victories in New Seats	4	0	1	1	0	1
Minority Seats Eliminated to Represent Reapportionment Losses	0	1	0	1	2[a]	0

[a]The numbers in these two cells represent the same two Democratic incumbents.

Using a plan devised by Congressman Phillip Burton, the Democrats drastically altered several districts held by retiring and incumbent Republicans and created several new districts designed to elect Democrats. In the 1982 election, the number of Democratic seats increased from twenty-two to twenty-eight, while the Republican delegation declined from twenty-one to seventeen. The gerrymander influenced almost all the victories and defeats involved in the partisan shift of seats.

Although the Indiana Republicans posted some victories against the Democrats with their gerrymandering plan, they fell short of their goal. The Republicans had hoped to obtain a substantial lead over the Democrats with their boundary manipulations, but they had to settle for a five-five split. They eliminated two Democratic seats by carving up the districts of two Democratic incumbents. One of them ran for a statewide office, and the other one lost a primary election after he challenged a Democratic incumbent in another district. A Republican easily won in a new Sixth District. The partisan redistricting also helped to save Representative John Hiler, a Republican incumbent. Hiler won with only 51 percent of the vote in a district redrawn to add Republican voters. He won by a wide margin in one of the new counties placed in the district.

Similar to the Indiana Republicans, the New Jersey Democrats gained limited success in their gerrymander. The Democrats carved up the districts of a departing Republican incumbent to force the state's loss of one seat from reapportionment onto the Republicans. They also helped Democrat Robert Torricelli defeat incumbent Republican Harold Hollenbeck by adding Democratic areas to the district. However, the redistricting plan failed to unseat any other Republican incumbents.

The New Jersey gerrymander had only a minor impact on the Democratic incumbents. Most of them won by large margins in both the 1980 and 1982 elections. One Democratic incumbent moved from a competitive election in 1980 to a landslide in 1982, but his 1982 victory was so large the vote in the new areas added to the district had only a small impact on the victory.

The redistricting in New Mexico met all five conditions because the Democrats controlled the state government and developed a plan which resulted in a Democrat winning the state's new seat from reappportionment. However, the district scheme did not seriously disrupt the political base of the two Republican incumbents. Both Republicans won reelection in 1982 with a high percentage of the vote.

The Republican gerrymander in Pennsylvania also produced mixed results. The plan produced two successes and several failures. It forced the state's two-seat loss from reapportionment onto the Democrats by merging the districts of two sets of Democratic incumbents. Also, the Republican Thomas Ridge's narrow victory (less than 1000 votes) in an open seat was aided by redistricting. Although the district was not targeted in the gerrymander and changed only slightly, Ridge's margin of victory in the new area added to the district was larger than the overall victory margin.

On the other hand, three incumbent Republicans lost and all the remaining Democratic incumbents won. The gerrymandering scheme's biggest failure occurred in the Fourth District where a Democratic challenger defeated a Republican incumbent by a 60-to-39 percent margin in a district altered to help the incumbent.

A Republican candidate won in the Seventeenth District which had been altered to increase the Republican advantage in this open seat. However, an analysis of the votes in the old and new sections of the district indicates that redistricting had only a small impact on his victory margin of over 20,000 votes.

Republicans drew the district boundaries in Washington. Although the plan had only a small impact on the seven old districts, it helped a Republican win the new Eighth District.

Consequently, the data indicates support for the proposition that partisan redistricting has had little effect on House elections. Although gerrymandering had some impact on the 1982 election, the number of party gains and losses affected by it was small. Only twenty victories and defeats (twelve helped Democrats, eight helped Republicans) in the 1982 election were significantly influenced by partisan gerrymandering. This amounts to under 5 percent of all House races. In addition, the redistricting in only six states met the minimal conditions to be categorized as partisan gerrymanders. Even in these states, only the California Democrats were successful in producing a large shift in the party balance of the state delegation.

Therefore, the Democrats did not maintain control of the House of Representatives through partisan gerrymandering in the 1980s.

They continued to win House elections because they received greater voter support than the Republicans.

Other research has also indicated that partisan redistricting has had little effect on House elections. Erikson discovered that northern Republicans were overrepresented in the House before the mid-1960s.[11] He tested the hypothesis that partisan gerrymandering created this pro-Republican bias. The findings revealed that partisan gerrymandering had little impact on the party distribution of House seats.

In another study of House elections in the 1960s, Noragon compared party turnover in seats among states with partisan, bipartisan, and individual gerrymanders.[12] Although the dominant party in partisan gerrymanders did make some gains, the relationship between partisan control of redistricting and partisan gains in seats was rather weak.

In addition, Born divided districting plans into Democratic, Republican, and bipartisan for House elections between 1952 to 1982.[13] He then used a time series analysis to examine the relationship between seats and votes after the different partisan redistricting plans went into effect. Before the mid-1960s a modest relationship was discovered between partisan gerrymandering and seats gained by the party controlling the redistricting. But for the elections after the mid-1960s, even the small relationship largely disappeared.

Conclusion

In 1988 Democrats controlled a majority of Senate seats, House seats, state legislatures, and governorships. They also dominated the governments of the major cities and many other local governments. They continued to hold the lead in party registration in many states. They also held a fourteen-point lead over the Republicans in the Gallup poll's measure of party identification. This almost matched their average lead over the Republicans for the past fifty years.

The Republicans controlled only eight state legislatures in 1989. This was one of the lowest totals for either party in the post–World War II period. The GOP held the office of governor in only sixteen states during the mid-1980s. The Democrats continued to win House elections through the 1980s, and they usually posted landslide victories. The Republicans have not won a House election since 1952.

Where was the Reagan revolution? Where was the party realignment? In this situation, how could any political analyst proclaim the Republicans replaced the Democrats as the number one party in the country?

Obviously, no party realignment occurred in the 1980s. The Republicans did dominate presidential elections during the past twenty years, but unquestionably the Democratic party remained the top political party in the overall political system during the 1980s.

A new phase of party competition did not develop in the 1980s. The pattern of party competition in the 1980s was similar to the patterns of the previous four decades.

The obsession of the media and many political commentators with the presidency is a major reason why this illusion of a party realignment developed. So much attention is given to the president that the rest of the political system is often ignored. Consequently, most discussions and analyses of party strength concentrate far too much on presidential elections. This concentration on presidential elections led many analysts to erroneously assume that either a party realignment occurred or the party system moved into a new phase.

Presidential elections are a poor measure of party strength. These elections provide a snapshot of voter support for one day every four years. Voting for president usually allows voters a choice of just two major candidates. The vote heavily reflects the conditions, especially the state of the economy, which exists at the time of the vote.

Political analysts should examine party strength throughout the political system, not just in presidential elections. The other elections occur at many points in time and cover a large number of offices. In addition, the voters in these elections often rely more on party identification than in presidential elections because they have less knowledge of candidates and issues.

Notes

1. *The Gallup Report,* September 1988, 5–7.
2. U.S. Bureau of the Census, *Statistical Abstract of the United States:*

1989, (Washington, D.C.: U. S. Government Printing Office, 1989), 242.

3. Kevin Phillips, *The Emerging Republican Majority* (New York: Doubleday, 1969), 466.
4. The sunbelt is defined as all the southern states plus California, New Mexico, Nevada, Arizona, and Hawaii.
5. This section is based on my research presented in Larry M. Schwab, *The Impact of Congressional Reapportionment and Redistricting,* (Lanham, Mass.: University Press of America, 1988).
6. Larry M. Schwab, "The Impact of the 1980 Reapportionment in the United States," *Political Geography Quarterly* 4 (April 1985): 141–158.
7. Ibid.
8. Thomas E. Cavanagh and James L. Sundquist, "The New Two-Party System," in *The New Direction of American Politics,* ed. John E. Chubb and Paul E. Peterson, (Washington, D.C.: Brookings Institution, 1985), 34.
9. Lee Atwater, "Predetermined Elections Must End," *First Monday* 19 (Fall 1989): 2.
10. This section is based on my research presented in Schwab, *The Impact of Congressional Reapportionment and Redistricting;* and Schwab, "The Impact of the 1980 Reapportionment in the United States."
11. Robert S. Erickson, "Malapportionment, Gerrymandering, and Party Fortunes in Congressional Elections," *American Political Science Review* 66 (December 1972): 1234–45.
12. Jack L. Noragon, "Redistricting, Political Outcomes, and Gerrymandering in the 1960s," in *Democratic Representation and Apportionment,* ed. Lee Papaganopoulos. Special issue of the *Annals of the New York Academy of Sciences* 219: 314–333.
13. Richard Born, "Partisan Intentions and Election Day Realities in the Congressional Redistricting Process," *American Political Science Review* 79 (June 1985): 305–19.

6

No Fundamental Conservative Change in Public Policies

According to the Reagan revolution thesis, fundamental conservative changes occurred in public policies during the 1980s. After nearly fifty years of a liberal trend in policies, an enormous conservative policy shift supposedly developed in the 1980s. The Reagan revolution was allegedly responsible for a fundamental conservative shift in policies and government programs similar to the fundamental liberal shift produced by the New Deal in the 1930s. As Chubb and Peterson stated:

> Among the major elements of the political system—voters, parties, institutions, and policy . . . policy has changed in the manner most reminiscent of past political realignments. . . .

> Past major shifts in policy had several characteristics in common: they responded decisively to a major crisis, they offered innovative approaches to long-standing problems, and they established a new agenda of issues for years to come. Developments under the Reagan administration have followed the same pattern. . . . That this is a new policy direction and, equally important, that it will be sustained are evident. . . .[1]

However, an examination of the policy developments shows that no fundamental conservative change happened in the 1980s. In fact, the policy outcomes were often in the opposite direction from what should have happened if a significant conservative shift had occurred. For instance, the size of the federal budget and the national debt increased enormously rather than decreased during the 1980s.

Not only can the assumption of a conservative policy shift be challenged, a case can be made that a conservative policy change could not happen under any circumstances because of the contradictions in conservative ideology. These contradictions make it impossible for public policy outcomes to consistently change in a conservative direction. Since the major parts of conservative ideology contradict other parts, conservative victories on some policies would produce results which directly oppose basic conservative goals.

This problem of conservative contradictions develops primarily in three areas. The first is the conflict between conservatives' support for less government and their support for a huge expansion of military spending. This is such an enormous contradiction because defense spending is by far the largest program in the budget. Obviously, a big increase in the major program of the budget conflicts with the goal of a significant reduction in the size of the federal government. This contradiction became very apparent in the early 1980s when the expansion of the military budget was one of the reasons why federal government spending increased significantly.

A second contradiction is the conflict between conservatives' beliefs on military spending and laissez-faire capitalism. Since the federal government has its biggest impact on the economy through the defense budget, a large expansion of military spending considerably enlarges the government's role in the economy. Therefore, huge increases in military spending move the country more towards a mixed economy and away from laissez-faire economics.

Another conflict develops when a choice must be made between individual freedom and what is perceived by conservatives as the well-being of society. In these situations the liberal usually supports individual freedom, while the conservative supports the well-being of society. In the debate on wiretapping in criminal investigations, for example, the conservative would generally accept more government leeway to use wiretapping so society would benefit by catching more criminals, whereas liberals would oppose this because of its adverse impact on individual rights. Therefore, the conservative ends up supporting an increase in government activities, which contradicts the conservative's belief in less government. This conflict can be seen in many significant policy questions such as abortion, pornography, and drug testing.

Consequently, a fundamental conservative shift never occurred in the 1980s. A policy shift of this type would have been impossible anyway because of the contradictions in conservative ideology. A fundamental policy shift toward the libertarians' beliefs would be possible because of their fairly consistent opposition to governmental activities. A massive conservative shift, however, could not occur because of the conservatives' dilemma of wanting an enormous decline in the role of government yet supporting a major expansion of governmental activities in many areas.

This chapter examines the developments during the 1980s in many public policies and demonstrates why no significant conservative policy change occurred in these areas. To determine whether or not conservative policy changes happened, a definition is needed of conservative policies.

Based on speeches and actions by Ronald Reagan and other conservatives during several decades before the 1980s, several components of modern American conservative ideology can be sketched out. First, government spending, especially federal spending, should be significantly cut back. Second, there should also be an enormous cut in taxes. Third, the federal government should have balanced or surplus budgets. Ronald Reagan made this clear in the 1980 campaign when he complained of the adverse effects of deficits and promised a balanced budget in the second year of his presidency and a $100 billion surplus in the third year.

Fourth, the federal government's role in the economy should be lessened. The economy should return to laissez-faire capitalism. Not only should government spending, taxes, and deficits be reduced, but government regulations should be eased or eliminated in many economic areas. Considerable reductions should occur in government programs such as agriculture, environmental protection, and consumer protection. In addition, free international trade should be promoted by opposing protectionist trade policies.

Fifth, conservatives opposed many of the liberals' initiatives in civil rights. Conservatives, for instance, fought against the Equal Rights Amendment and affirmative action programs. They usually opposed government policies to promote equality.

Sixth, conservatives, especially New Right conservatives, supported various social policies to move the country back to the type of morality that supposedly existed in America before the 1960s. For example, conservatives supported constitutional amendments to ban abortions and to allow prayers in public schools.

Seventh, power should shift from the national government to state and local governments. Government should first be cut back and most of the remaining programs should be administered by the state and local governments.

Eighth, conservatives wanted a large increase in military spending. They believed that the United States had fallen behind the Soviet Union militarily. The U.S. military needed to expand to catch up and eventually surpass the Soviets' strength.

Finally, in foreign policy conservatives wanted to take a stronger stand against the Soviet Union, communism, and terrorism. Reagan and many conservatives were worried about arms control and other aspects of a détente policy with Russia. They also strongly supported governments and insurgent groups in the Third World who fought against leftist regimes or groups which conservatives considered communist.

If the 1980s were a watershed period similar to the 1930s, changes in policy during the 1980s should have been of the same magnitude as changes in the 1930s. Since conservatives opposed most of the policy trends started by the New Deal, a fundamental change in policy would mean the elimination, or at least a significant decline, of the programs and policy outcomes of the previous fifty years. For example, the 1930s produced a historic increase in the size of the federal government. Therefore, a decline in the federal government of similar historic proportions should have occurred for the 1980s to be considered a watershed period in policy. To meet the criteria of fundamental change, a reasonable standard would be to expect overall federal spending to have decreased in the 1980s or to at least have declined considerably as a percent of GNP. Since fundamental changes of this magnitude never happened in federal spending and other policies, there was no conservative Reagan revolution in policy. As the findings in the chapter indicate, the policy results were often just the opposite of what should have happened if the 1980s were a conservative watershed period.

President Bush's policy agenda also shows that no conservative policy revolution occurred in the 1980s. If this revolution in conservative policy had developed, Bush would have presented a clear set of conservative policies in 1988. Then after his election, he would have vigorously pushed this conservative agenda in Congress. What happened, however, was that Bush neither presented a clear conservative agenda in the campaign nor vigorously pursued a broad conservative agenda in Congress.

There are several reasons why Bush never developed a strong conservative agenda. First, as chapter 2 points out, no conservative shift developed in public opinion during the 1980s. Since Bush's campaign strategy was heavily based on the polls, he did not consistently support conservative positions because Americans had not shifted to the right. He did stress the conservative side of issues on which the majority of the public remained conservative in the 1980s, but he also backed liberal positions on several issues for which the polls indicated majority support. For example, he emphasized stronger penalties against criminals and supported a strong environmental program.

Second, the suspicions of many conservative leaders were correct that Bush was not a true down-the-line conservative. Bush had shown moderate tendencies in his congressional career and at other times during his government service. Bush's moderate side came out on several policies stressed in the campaign and during the early part of his first term.

Third, President Bush, along with the rest of the political system, was constrained by the budget deficit. Even if he were so inclined, he was unable to push for large tax cuts and a substantial military buildup. These are two major parts of a conservative agenda that a conservative Republican president would be expected to endorse. These options, however, were not available to President Bush because of their adverse impact on the deficit.

The possibility of supporting large-scale cutbacks in social programs was an option within the deficit's constraints. However, Bush's decision not to take this option shows that a fundamental conservative policy shift never occurred in the 1980s. If a conservative shift had taken place, the polls would have shown overwhelming public support for the elimination of social programs, and Bush's campaign proposals would have included these cutbacks. Instead, Bush did not call for substantial social program cuts and even endorsed the expansion of some programs such as Medicaid.

Agriculture

Agriculture is one of the largest parts of the economy, and the federal government regulates many aspects of it. Hence, President Reagan and congressional conservatives called for a more free-market approach to farming. However, the federal role in agriculture did not decline but expanded enormously from 1981 to 1988. The 1980s witnessed the greatest increase in federal spending on agriculture in the history of the program. From 1980 to 1986, the agriculture budget increased from $8.8 billion to $31.5 (see table 6.1). To say the least, conservatives' actions did not always follow their stated intentions. Superconservative Jesse Helms, for instance, used his position as chairman of the Senate Agriculture Committee to vigorously oppose any attempts to cut back on federal agricultural programs beneficial to North Carolina.

Not only did the Reagan administration end up supporting a huge expansion of most of the existing farm programs, his administration even added new ones. For example, Reagan announced the formation of the Payment-In-Kind (PIK) program in January 1983. Under this program, farmers who had previously agreed to participate in acreage reduction programs would receive surplus crops for not

TABLE 6.1
Agriculture Spending in the Federal Budget, 1976–88
(In billions of dollars)

1976	$ 3.2
1977	6.8
1978	11.4
1979	11.2
1980	8.8
1981	11.3
1982	15.9
1983	22.9
1984	13.6
1985	25.6
1986	31.5
1987	26.6
1988	17.2

Source: Office of Management and Budget, *Historical Tables, Budget of the United States Government FY 1990*

planting the crops in 1983. Instead of lessening the federal government's role in agriculture, the PIK program expanded the policy of the federal government, giving it control of an enormous part of the agricultural economy. PIK was the largest acreage reduction program ever implemented by the government.[2]

In fiscal 1982 the federal government spent a record $12 billion on programs to prop up the income of farmers. This was four times the yearly average for the 1970s. The cost of the price support programs soared to nearly $19 billion in 1983. This was just $3 billion less than had been spent on these programs during the entire period from 1977 to 1980. Moreover, the actual cost of the price support programs was even more because the surplus commodities given away in the PIK program were not included in the calculation of the total cost.[3] The spending on the income and price support programs hit a record of $26 billion in fiscal 1986. Of this total, nearly $13 billion was in the form of direct cash payments.

After consistently failing in his efforts to cut back these price and income support programs in 1981–1984, Reagan tried again in the 1985 farm bill. Just as before, he attacked the price support programs for violating free-market principles. However, the problems of the farm economy ruined the attempts by opponents of agriculture policies to change the price and income support programs. The farm problems put Reagan and the conservatives on the defensive. They had a difficult time trying to explain why farm programs should be eliminated or at least drastically reduced at a time when so many farmers had severe economic problems. Moreover, Senate Republicans were worried about the possible adverse impact of the farm crisis on the party's chances of retaining its Senate majority in the 1986 election. In the end, the Reagan administration and most Senate Republicans from farm states chose political expediency over conservative ideology and supported a continuation of most of the basic agriculture programs in the 1985 farm bill.

If a fundamental conservative change had taken place in the political system, the farm bill would have significantly altered the agriculture economy in a free-market direction. The fact that the Reagan administration and many congressional Republicans ended up supporting the status quo in agriculture policies is another indication of how little the political system changed in the 1980s. The occurrence of a conservative political revolution would have forced the Republicans to wipe out much of the farm program. Instead, many Republicans felt compelled to support the government's role in agriculture to improve their chances in the upcoming election.

Farm policy did not shift from a period of more government involvement to less government involvement in the 1980s. Just the reverse was true. Primarily because of increased exports, more competition developed in agriculture, and government controls lessened during the 1970s. The amount of diverted acreage, for example, dropped considerably during the decade. Then in the 1980s, an enormous policy reversal occurred with the huge expansion of acreage reduction and price support programs.

Sugar

The domestic sugar industry has been protected for much of U.S. history. A sugar tariff was established in 1789 to help a small sugar cane refining industry. The tariff was later used to aid sugar cane growers and the sugar beet industry.

The sugar protection program was altered in the 1930s and 1940s with the passage of the Jones-Costigan Act of 1934 and the Sugar Act of 1948. These laws set up a system of quotas which guaranteed domestic producers a substantial part of the market. Congress first determined the domestic share and then parceled out the rest of the sugar market to several countries. This protected the U.S cane and beet producers against low-cost foreign competitors and kept U.S. sugar prices above world market prices.

The quota system continued with little change until the 1970s. In the 1970–74 period sugar prices increased substantially as sugar consumption increased much faster than production. Reports surfaced of refineries making huge profits as prices doubled and tripled.

In 1974 Congress considered the extension of the Sugar Act in this atmosphere of high sugar prices. Even in this situation, however, most political observers assumed that Congress would simply renew the sugar quotas, but the program was defeated in the House by a margin of 175–209. This was an amazing shift in sugar policy. Since the Senate took no action, the Sugar Act expired and the United States began competing for sugar in an open market.

In 1978 another attempt was made to revive the sugar program. The House and Senate passed bills to set per pound price minimums for sugar producers. Under the provisions of the bills, the price minimums would have been supported by quotas and import fees. The House, however, voted down a conference bill on sugar in the last hours of the 95th Congress.

This set the stage for the debate on the sugar program in 1981. The consideration of the sugar program presented an excellent opportunity to kill a major agriculture program. A coalition of Republicans and northern metropolitan Democrats was available to provide the votes against the sugar program. In fact, the House voted to end the sugar program in one vote in 1981. The election of a conservative Republican president and more conservative Republicans to Congress should have increased the opposition to the sugar program. Also, cuts in social programs gave metropolitan northern Democrats even more reason to oppose sugar price supports. Why should they support protection for the sugar industry when programs important to their constituents had just been cut? Hence, a historic chance was available to eliminate one part of the federal government's involvement in agriculture.

Instead of leading this coalition to victory, the Reagan administration made a deal with southern Democrats and supported the revival of the sugar program. The Senate supported the sugar program and was successful in placing it in the conference bill. With the passage of the conference bill, a new sugar program was created. It required the secretary of agriculture to support sugar prices through various means (e.g., import duties and fees) at a minimum of 17 cents a pound in 1982, rising to 18 cents in 1985.

The program was a disaster. To maintain the price level, the administration could either buy a large amount of sugar or discourage imports. It adopted the latter strategy, and imports dropped significantly. This hurt the economies of developing countries with a large sugar production. Higher domestic sugar prices forced many businesses and consumers to turn to substitutes. Consequently, sugar consumption fell in the 1980s.[4]

The developments in sugar policy during the 1980s were completely contrary to conservative ideology. What happened was the opposite of what should have happened in a fundamental conservative change in policy. First, by supporting the sugar program, the administration helped to revive a federal government program. Second, the administration violated the conservative goal of a domestic free market in agriculture. Third, the sugar program forced the administration to significantly violate the principle of free international trade. Finally, the cutbacks in sugar imports hurt the economies and regimes of several countries backed by the administration.

Tobacco

The tobacco program in 1981 was another example of a farm program which violated laissez-faire principles. The program consisted of government controls on who could grow tobacco and how much they could sell. Also, price support loans nearly guaranteed minimum prices for the producers.

Just as with sugar, the early 1980s offered an excellent opportunity to eliminate the tobacco program. A strong coalition of liberals, conservatives, and moderates had developed in Congress to oppose the program. Many liberals had been trying for years to eliminate the program for health reasons. They were joined by a number of conservatives who wanted to eliminate the program for budget-cutting and deregulation reasons. Many moderates opposed the program for all of these reasons.

The results of the battle over the tobacco program were again just the opposite of what would have been expected of a Reagan revolution. The tobacco program survived during the 1980s, and the federal government continued its controls on many aspects of tobacco farming.

Instead of liberals fighting for more government involvement against the protests of conservatives, the tobacco debate of the 1980s consisted of superconservative Jesse Helms leading the battle for this government program against the antitobacco forces often led by liberals. Since tobacco is a very important crop in North Carolina, Helms used his position as chairman of the Senate Agriculture Committee to keep the program alive and well.

While Helms' chairmanship was a plus for the protobacco forces, the resentment against him was a factor aiding the antitobacco coalition.[5] Some members of Congress are so upset with Helms' abrasive style and right-wing politics that they are happy to oppose the Senator in almost any circumstance. The anti-Helms sentiment was even stronger during the tobacco debate in the early 1980s because of the budget-cutting atmosphere. Many members were angry because of Helms' hypocrisy of attacking the evils of government programs while defending the tobacco program. Also, many representatives and senators questioned Helms' attempt to protect farm programs beneficial to North Carolina and yet to work for cuts in other farm programs.

The Reagan administration missed a golden opportunity in 1981 to work with the antitobacco forces in Congress to eliminate the tobacco program. Reagan aided the continuation of the tobacco program by not playing an active and strong role in the fight against it.

Peanuts

The debate on the peanut program in the early 1980s had several similarities to the debate on the tobacco program.[6] Both crops were heavily controlled by the federal government through what critics called a "feudalistic" system of allotments and quotas. Peanuts were also important to the North Carolina farm economy. Therefore, the Helms factor became part of the debate. Senator Helms defended the peanut program while he continued to work against many other government programs. This angered many other members of Congress and increased the opposition to the program.

The peanut program, however, survived with some modification. Just as with the sugar program, the Reagan administration ended up supporting the continuation of the peanut program in a deal to gain support on other legislation. Once again, President Reagan supported the continuation of a government program which significantly departed from the principles of laissez-faire capitalism.

Dairy

In 1949 Congress created a system to regulate dairy farming. Under the program, the federal government buys dairy products at prices that allow processors to pay farmers at least a set price per hundred pounds of milk. The program produces a market tightly controlled by the government, as in most other sectors of farming.

Not only did the dairy price support program survive during the

1980s, the dairy program moved into a new area.[7] President Reagan signed legislation in 1983 which authorized the government to begin paying farmers for producing less milk. Farm bills had for years provided money for farmers to plant less acreage, but this was the first time this principle had been applied to dairy producers. So the man billed as the most conservative president in fifty years accepted a plan which allowed the government to place more restrictions on yet another part of agriculture.

Honey

The federal government even has a price support program for honey.[8] Through the program, the federal government controls much of the honey market just as it does for many other farm commodities. And similar to these other commodities, the honey program survived and the cost expanded enormously during the 1980s. The program's cost increased from $8 million in 1981 to $90 million in 1984. By 1985 the program had become a disaster. The support price had climbed above the market price. Under the law, the government was forced to buy most of the domestic honey. Therefore, foreign producers moved in to supply much of the domestic market. So the domestic honey producers got large subsidies, the federal government ended up with large amounts of honey, and foreign suppliers took over the domestic honey market.

A new marketing payment plan initiated in the 1985 farm bill helped the honey situation. More domestic honey was sold in the market, imports dropped, and the cost to the taxpayer lessened. However, the government still had a price support program which significantly affected the market and cost millions of dollars.

Wheat, Feed Grains, and Soybeans

The price and income-support programs continued in the 1980s for wheat, feed grains, and soybeans.[9] The 1985 farm bill maintained the crop loan and deficiency payment programs for wheat and feed grains. The crop loans allow farmers to repay loans or default and keep the principle. In the loan defaults, the government takes possession of the crop. The deficiency payments provide cash for the difference between a national average market price and a target price for the crops. The soybean provisions set up a loan rate for price supports for 1986 and 1987 at $5.02 a bushel.

Cotton and Rice

Similar to other crops, the cotton subsidy program continued through the 1980s and expanded substantially. During the decade the program's cost increased from $336 million to a record $2.5 billion. In 1989 a near-record nine million bales of cotton were left in warehouses.[10]

For a while after the passage of the 1985 farm bill, the prospects for the cotton program looked bright. The cotton program appeared to be a model for other farm programs. The main part of the cotton subsidy had been a marketing loan program that provided cash payments to allow farmers to lower prices without losing profits. The cotton industry was healthy in the mid-1980s as exports soared. But when exports leveled off, the cotton program got into big trouble. The cost of the cotton subsidies increased dramatically as the United States' portion of the world cotton trade dropped from 30 percent in the early 1980s to about 20 percent in 1989.

The 1985 farm law extended the rice program.[11] The loan rate was set at $7.20 per hundred pounds for 1986. The rate was set for the 1987–90 period using a formula based on market prices for previous years. The bill also continued provisions for acreage reductions.

Farm Credit and Drought Relief

Two major aspects of the farm crisis in the 1980s were credit problems and a devastating drought that hit many farming areas. Since many farmers had difficulty paying off loans, a number of financial institutions faced difficult times. The credit problems of farmers were exacerbated by the bad weather.

Conservative laissez-faire ideology would suggest that the government would handle these problems by not intervening and thus allow the capitalist system to work on its own. The farmers and people in related businesses would be allowed to sink or swim without government intervention. However, the Reagan administration was unable to move farm policy in this direction. Multi-billion dollar programs were enacted to help the agricultural economy handle these problems. Credit relief bills were passed and Congress enacted a $3.9 billion drought relief law. A $4 billion bailout of the Farm Credit System was also passed.

Budget

Most of the major aspects of the federal budget changed in the opposite direction from what should have happened in a conservative policy revolution. Based on the conservative tenets outlined in the beginning of the chapter, a fundamental conservative shift in the federal budget would mean an enormous cut in overall spending; a decrease in the deficit, national debt, and interest cost on the debt through balanced and surplus budgets; a substantial cut in taxes; a considerable increase in the defense budget; and the elimination of most social programs in the human resources budget. (Human resources is a superfunction budget category which contains most of the social programs.)

At the end of the 1970s (see tables 6.2–6.4) several key budget figures were at the following levels: total federal spending, $503.5 billion (21 percent of GNP); total federal revenues, $463.3 billion (18.9 percent of GNP); national debt, $828.9 billion (34 percent of GNP); deficit, $40.2 billion (1.6 percent of GNP); net interest on the debt, $42.6 billion (1.7 percent of GNP); human resources programs, $267.5 billion (10.9 percent of GNP); and defense spending, $116.3 billion (4.8 percent of GNP). If a historic conservative policy change occurred in the 1980s, it would be reasonable to expect a drop to about 15 percent of GNP in total federal spending; a decline to about 15 percent in federal taxes; an increase in defense spending back to the 1960 level of about 10 percent of GNP; a decline of several hundred billion dollars in the national debt; a decrease to about 1 percent of GNP in the deficit; and a decline to 6 or 7 percent of GNP in human resources spending. As the rest of the section will point out, however, the budget figures generally moved in the opposite direction from a fundamental conservative shift.

Total Federal Spending

A historic increase in federal spending developed in the 1980s rather than a historic decrease. Federal spending hit 24.3 percent of GNP in 1983 (see table 6.2), which was the highest level since 1946. The federal budgets were much larger in the 1980s than in several previous decades. From the 1960s to the 1970s, federal outlays, as measured by the average (mean) yearly percent of GNP, only increased from 19 to 20.5, while the percent jumped to 23 in the 1980s. Federal budget outlays soared to over a trillion dollars a year by the late 1980s. Hence, the 1980s produced the first trillion

TABLE 6.2
Federal Government Spending, 1960–88

Year	Outlays in Millions of Dollars	% of GNP
1960	92,191	18.2
1961	97,723	18.9
1962	106,821	19.2
1963	111,316	18.9
1964	118,528	18.8
1965	118,228	17.6
1966	134,532	18.2
1967	157,464	19.8
1968	178,134	21.0
1969	183,640	19.8
1970	195,649	19.8
1971	210,172	19.9
1972	230,681	20.0
1973	245,707	19.2
1974	269,359	19.0
1975	332,332	21.8
1976	371,779	21.9
1977	409,203	21.2
1978	458,729	21.1
1979	503,464	20.6
1980	590,920	22.1
1981	678,209	22.7
1982	745,706	23.8
1983	808,327	24.3
1984	851,781	23.1
1985	946,316	23.9
1986	990,258	23.7
1987	1,003,830	22.6
1988	1,064,044	22.3

Source: Office of Management and Budget.

dollar budget and the biggest federal budgets in history. Spending by the national government set several records in the wrong direction compared to what should have happened in a conservative era.

These spending records make it difficult to understand how anyone could claim that a conservative Reagan revolution occurred. The central theme of conservative ideology is support for less government, primarily less federal government. Reagan said government was the problem, not the solution. How could anyone conclude that the 1980s represented a historic watershed period in government decline when the federal government was spending over $500 billion more in 1987 than it had in 1979, and federal spending increased from less than 21 percent to about 24 percent of GNP between 1979 and the mid-1980s?

The Reagan revolution thesis presents the idea that the 1980s were a historic conservative period in history mainly because of enormous cutbacks in the federal government. The increase in the size of the federal government, according to the thesis, began with Franklin Roosevelt and the New Deal and continued through the following decades with a significant boost by Lyndon Johnson and the Great Society. Ronald Reagan is presented as the historic figure who led a counter-revolution that turned this around and cut federal spending back to the levels of previous eras.

The actual budget figures, however, present a different picture. The 1980s were not a counterrevolution in federal spending, but a continuation of the trend toward bigger federal budgets. The 1980s should be seen as a major period in the twentieth century in which the federal government expanded. By the 1970s domestic and military programs had pushed federal spending to 20–22 percent of GNP. Then in the 1980s, the federal budget moved to a higher level.

Instead of history viewing Ronald Reagan as a leader of a counterrevolution against spending, he should be seen as just the opposite. Rather than considering Reagan a counterhistorical figure to FDR and LBJ in federal spending, he should be seen along with them as presidents who led the country to major increases in the federal budget.

Moreover, this budget increase in the 1980s was not just the result of more military spending. Nondefense spending was higher in the 1980s than previous decades. Spending on the nondefense areas of the budget increased from 10.1 percent of GNP in 1965 to

17.5 percent in 1985. This expansion of nondefense spending to record levels during the early and mid-1980s occurred while Reagan was president and the Republicans had a majority in the Senate.

Also, the rise of spending during the 1980s developed during peacetime. The federal budgets during the mid-to-late 1960s and the early 1970s were bolstered considerably by spending on the Viet Nam War. In the middle of this war, federal spending was about 20 percent of GNP, whereas during the peacetime year of 1985 federal spending was close to 25 percent of GNP.

In addition, the high levels of spending in the mid-1980s occurred in an economic recovery, not during a recession. So without a war or a recession, federal spending during the mid-1980s moved to a level, as measured by current dollars and as a percent of GNP, well above the levels of the 1950s, 1960s, and 1970s.

If a liberal Democrat had been president during the 1980s with the same high rate of federal spending, political analysts would have probably called the decade a period of government expansion. And this liberal Democratic president would have been considered in the tradition of Roosevelt, Truman, Kennedy, and Johnson. Instead, because Reagan was a conservative Republican, many political commentators focused on cutbacks and ignored the fact that federal spending overall expanded enormously during the 1980s.

Certainly, cutbacks in some programs occurred during the decade, but spending increased so much in other areas that by the mid-1980s, federal spending was higher in relation to the economy than it had been since the end of World War II.

Budget Deficits

The belief in balanced and surplus budgets has been one of the major principles of conservatives' political ideology. They blame the deficits of the federal government on the spending policies of liberals. Ronald Reagan strongly supported this traditional conservative view and claimed that many economic problems were caused by liberals' deficits. According to Reagan, deficits were a major reason why government was not the solution but part of the problem.

Based on these beliefs, Reagan and his advisors presented a fiscal plan which promised balanced and surplus budgets. During the 1980 campaign, Reagan stated that the program would produce a balanced budget in the second year and a $100 billion surplus in the third year. This was revised after the election to a balanced budget in the third year and a $100 billion surplus in the fourth year.

What happened, of course, was that the federal government ended up with record deficits instead of balanced budgets and record surpluses. Deficits skyrocketed from about $40 billion in 1979 to over $221 billion in 1986 (see table 6.3). Most of the deficits in the 1980s were two to three times larger than the highest previous deficits.

The national debt soared during the 1980s to record levels. Incredibly, the national debt nearly tripled during the decade. Almost two-thirds of the entire debt accumulated in the 1980–89 period.

Moreover, the deficit was declining in the late 1970s before the enormous increase in the 1980s. As table 6.3 shows, the deficit had declined in the 1977–80 period to below 3 percent of GNP after the decade high of 4.3 percent in 1976. The deficit fell all the way to 1.6 percent of GNP in 1979.

As the data indicate, the 1980s' deficits were way beyond the deficits of the previous twenty years measured not only in current dollars but also as a percent of GNP. Deficits from 1960 to 1974 were usually below 1 percent of GNP and rarely above 2 percent. In the 1980s the deficit climbed to over 5 percent of GNP for four straight years. It hit an unbelievable 6.3 percent of GNP in 1983.

Reagan and many of his ardent supporters claimed that Congress caused the deficits and the spending increases. This assertion can easily be proven inaccurate by examining the budget records. A president has complete control over his budget recommendation. While Congress has the power to significantly alter the president's budget requests, the president has control over his proposals. If Congress caused the deficits, therefore, a pattern should be discernible in which President Reagan proposed budgets to Congress with relatively low spending levels and balanced budgets, and Congress substantially increased the spending to produce the huge deficits. An analysis of the record shows that this was not the budget pattern during the 1980s. Year after year Reagan would propose a budget, which if passed without any changes, would produce enormous

TABLE 6.3
Surpluses or Deficits in the Federal Budget, 1960–88

Year	Millions of Dollars	% of GNP
1960	301	.1
1961	− 3,335	− .6
1962	− 7,146	− 1.3
1963	− 4,756	− .8
1964	− 5,915	− .9
1965	− 1,411	− .2
1966	− 3,698	− .5
1967	− 8,643	− 1.1
1968	− 25,161	− 3.0
1969	3,242	0.3
1970	− 2,842	− .3
1971	− 23,033	− 2.2
1972	− 23,373	− 2.0
1973	− 14,908	− 1.2
1974	− 6,135	− .4
1975	− 53,242	− 3.5
1976	− 73,719	− 4.3
1977	− 53,644	− 2.8
1978	− 59,168	− 2.7
1979	− 40,162	− 1.6
1980	− 73,808	− 2.8
1981	− 78,936	− 2.6
1982	− 127,940	− 4.1
1983	− 207,764	− 6.3
1984	− 185,324	− 5.0
1985	− 212,260	− 5.4
1986	− 221,167	− 5.3
1987	− 149,687	− 3.4
1988	− 155,090	− 3.2

Source: Office of Management and Budget.

deficits. If Congress had passed Reagan's budgets without altera-
tions, the resulting deficits would have been similar to the actual
deficits accumulated during the 1980s.

Another problem with the Reagan administration placing all the
blame for the deficits on Congress is the fact that the Republicans
had a Senate majority during the period of the major deficit buildup.
Therefore, Reagan was implying that the Senate Republicans, many
of whom are conservatives, played a big role in causing the deficits.

It is interesting to note that the budget deficits were falling as a percent of GNP in the late 1970s with a Democratic president and Democratic majorities in the House and Senate. The deficits then skyrocketed with a conservative Republican president and a fairly conservative Republican majority in the Senate. Finally, the deficits started to decline again in 1987 and 1988 after the Democrats won back control of the Senate. This completely contradicts the pattern which should have developed during a conservative policy shift. If a conservative Reagan revolution had occurred, the deficits should have soared to over 6 percent of GNP in the late 1970s, then dropped to the 1-to-3 percent range in the 1981–86 period, and climbed a little above this in 1987–88.

Finally, two assertions about the deficit and the Reagan revolution must be adressed. The first is the claim by Senator Daniel Patrick Moynihan and others that the Reagan administration deliberately created the deficits as a means to eliminate much of the nondefense part of the budget. This hypothesis, however, is certainly incorrect. It is more likely that the budget goals of President Reagan and his advisors were close to what they had actually stated. Reagan's goal was to have both surplus budgets and cutbacks on social programs from less waste, fraud, and abuse. Why would Reagan want to go down in history as leading the country into the greatest deficits of all time? Reagan's prediction that a $100 billion budget surplus could be achieved, even though taxes would be cut and defense spending would be doubled within a few years, was obviously foolish and inaccurate. But Reagan probably thought it would work. It is difficult to imagine that in 1980 and early 1981, Reagan and his advisors were secretly plotting to develop deficits of $200 billion dollars a year so they could put restraints on social programs.

The second assertion is a claim that the budget deficits institutionalized the Reagan revolution. Supposedly, the pressure of the deficits helped President Reagan and the conservatives achieve their budget goals in the 1980s. The continuation of the deficits after Reagan will keep the Reagan revolution alive for many years in the future.

While the deficit has restrained federal spending to some degree, the overall claim that the deficit instituted a conservative Reagan revolution is nonsense. In the first place, this hypothesis is illogical because it contains major contradictions. Since conservatives traditionally proposed balanced and surplus budgets, the deficits violate their ideological beliefs. The existence of the huge deficits is irrefutable evidence that no fundamental conservative change happened in all aspects of policy in the 1980s. Therefore, it is absurd to argue that a policy outcome that contradicts conservative beliefs instituted a fundamental conservative policy shift.

In addition, the deficits worked against several conservative budget goals. First, the deficits produced an enormous increase in spending through the added costs to finance the national debt. Debt financing was the major growth area of the budget during the 1980s. While a deficit placed some restraints on spending, it also produced enormous increases in spending.

Second, the deficit played a major role in the cutback in military spending which started in the mid-1980s. Deficits were certainly a major reason why Congress shifted from supporting large increases in military spending in the early 1980s to supporting almost no increases in the late 1980s. Moreover, the deficits put more restraint on defense spending than on social spending. The deficits placed very little restraint on Social Security, the largest social program. The increases in Social Security taxes in the late 1970s and early 1980s allowed Social Security spending to continue increasing steadily during the decade. By 1989 the Social Security fund had a huge surplus. Also the Gramm-Rudman-Hollings law, which was passed to eliminate deficits, put more pressure on defense spending than on social spending. The law exempts Social Security and several other social programs from automatic cuts, while it forces half the overall cuts to be taken from the defense budget.

Third, the deficits made large-scale tax cuts impossible and produced pressure for tax increases. Because of the deficits, Reagan was unable to propose any more large tax cuts, and he was forced to support several tax increases. The pressure for tax increases remains as the deficits continue into the 1990s. This pressure could be seen when President Bush violated his no-new-taxes pledge in 1990 by agreeing to support a tax increase.

Consequently, the deficit failed to institutionalize the Reagan revolution. If this had occurred, the deficit should have pushed the budget policy toward more defense spending, large tax cuts, and less nondefense spending. What happened was that the deficit forced defense spending to decline as a percent of GNP, increased taxes, made large tax cuts impossible, and pushed spending on debt financing up substantially to make it the third largest part of the budget. The only aspect of the conservatives' budget agenda the deficit did help was cutting the growth of some nondefense programs. Even here, the pressure of the deficit did not force the elimination of any of the major social programs. In fact, many of the programs hit the hardest by deficit reduction efforts, such as revenue sharing, were not considered high-priority programs by liberals.

The creation of this huge deficit produced ideological warfare among conservatives. Many traditional economic conservatives strongly criticized the deficits and considered a balanced budget as the number one priority in budget policy. Other conservatives, some of whom were supply-siders, abandoned the old-time religion and suggested that the deficits were not so bad. This group wanted to make tax cuts the top budget priority. President Reagan ended up supporting both sides of this issue. One week he would make a speech on the evils of deficit spending. The next week he would defend his budget proposals, which called for enormous deficits. His budget proposals contained the greatest deficits of all time, yet he continually made speeches supporting balanced budgets and the balanced budget amendment.

If a fundamental conservative change had occurred, balanced budgets and budget surpluses would have been the norm in the 1980s. In addition, conservatives would have agreed that this was good policy. Instead the 1980s saw record deficits and ideological squabbling among conservatives over the deficits.

Taxes

If a fundamental conservative policy shift developed in the 1980s, taxes should have declined considerably. As table 6.4 demonstrates, however, the tax cut of the 1980s is another illusion. Taxes did not drop dramatically during the decade. In 1987 and 1988 federal taxes, as a percent of GNP, were close to the level of 1980. The 1988 tax level (percent of GNP) was higher than in all but two years during the 1960s and 1970s. In fact, taxes in the 1980s were a little higher than in the 1960s and 1970s. The yearly average of

TABLE 6.4
Federal Government Receipts as a Percent of GNP, 1960–88

Year	% of GNP
1960	18.3
1961	18.2
1962	17.9
1963	18.1
1964	17.9
1965	17.4
1966	17.7
1967	18.7
1968	18.0
1969	20.1
1970	19.5
1971	17.7
1972	18.0
1973	18.0
1974	18.6
1975	18.3
1976	17.6
1977	18.4
1978	18.4
1979	18.9
1980	19.4
1981	20.1
1982	19.7
1983	18.1
1984	18.1
1985	18.6
1986	18.4
1987	19.3
1988	19.0

Source: Office of Management and Budget.

federal taxes as a percent of GNP was 18.9 in the 1980s (1981–88) compared with 18.2 for the 1960s and 18.3 for the 1970s. The 1981 tax bill did cut taxes, but taxes were raised several times during the decade. The tax increases more than offset the tax cut.

Spending Priorities

The distribution patterns of federal spending among the major government functions is another aspect of budget policy that must be examined. Traditional conservatives supported more spending for defense and less spending for many other programs, especially social programs. Since they supported balanced and surplus budgets, they wanted to be able to cut the costs for financing the debt. Based on these beliefs, a conservative Reagan revolution should have produced an enormous shift in spending from the social programs and deficit financing toward defense spending.

An overall shift toward conservative spending priorities did not happen in the 1980s. The enormous increase in the cost of financing the debt was the biggest change in spending patterns. Net interest costs soared from $52.5 billion in 1980 to $151.7 billion in 1988. While total federal outlays in 1988 were nearly double the outlays in 1980, net interest costs nearly tripled during this period. Net interest costs jumped from 8.9 percent of the total budget in 1980 to 14.3 percent in 1988.

Contrary to the conventional view, overall social spending did not suffer huge cuts. Spending on human resources, the superfunction budget category containing most of the social programs (e.g., education, health, and Social Security), increased from $313.4 billion in 1980 to $533.4 billion in 1988. Human resources spending even increased as a percent of GNP during the early 1980s, but by the end of the decade, spending was about the same percent of GNP as it had been in 1980. Moreover, spending on human resources programs was much higher in the late 1980s that it had been in the 1960s and early 1970s. Human resources spending was 11.2 percent of GNP in 1988 but only 5.4 percent in 1965 and 7.6 percent in 1970. The rate of growth for several social programs, such as housing, was cut, but for others, such as health, the rate increased substantially.

The defense budget did expand, but the mid-to-late 1980s began a historic decline rather than a historic increase in military spending. The defense budget grew at a very small rate from 1987 to 1989. While the defense budget expanded rapidly at the end of the 1970s (28 percent increase from 1978 to 1980), military spending grew slowly in the late 1980s.

Furthermore, the increase in the defense budget from 1980 to 1985 is much less significant when the high rate of growth of the late 1970s is taken into consideration. Reagan and the congressional conservatives were not reversing a trend toward a decline in the military, but were simply continuing the higher rate of growth which had already begun in the late 1970s. If the defense budget had continued growing in the 1980s at the same rate as it was in the late 1970s, 1985 defense outlays would have been simliar to what was actually spent that year.

One of the major battles in the budget war is the competition for dollars between Social Security and defense. These are the two titans of the federal budget. The two programs comprise about 50 percent of the budget. Since these two programs are so large and financial resources are limited, a competition for funding between the two is inevitable. This competition has been dubbed the battle of guns versus canes.

The results of the guns versus canes battle is an excellent test of whether a conservative Reagan revolution replaced the New Deal–Great Society as the dominant policy framework in the political system. If the Reagan revolution won, the military budget should have been over $500 billion a year and soaring at the end of the 1980s. Also, Social Security should have been eliminated or at least significantly reduced.

Clearly, the New Deal won out over the Reagan revolution. The defense budget was under $300 billion and dropping in early 1990. While defense cutbacks of historic proportions were being planned by the Bush administration and Congress, Social Security, the major New Deal program, was thriving.

The two biggest domestic issues in Washington in early 1990—the peace dividend and the Social Security surplus funds—illustrate the weakness of defense spending and the financial strength of the Social Security program. By 1990, tax increases enacted in the late 1970s and early 1980s were producing surpluses in the Social Security fund of about $40 billion a year. A major debate developed over how to count these funds in relation to the deficit and how to preserve these extra funds for future generations of retirees. The situation with defense spending, however, was just the opposite. Rather than arguing over what to do with surplus defense funds, the debate was over the peace dividend—where to spend the billions of dollars to be cut from the defense budget.

Business

The Reagan administration pursued a pro-business, laissez-faire economic policy. President Reagan supported conservatives' goals of less business taxes, less government regulation of business, and less restriction on international trade. The results of Reagan's policies, however, were mixed. While some business policy moved in a conservative direction, no historic conservative shift occurred in this policy area.

This section examines five aspects of business policy: deregulation, international trade, borrowing and finance, business taxes, and antitrust.

Deregulation

The deregulation efforts of the Reagan administration and congressional conservatives largely ended in failure. Very little business deregulation occurred in the 1980s. This limited amount of deregulation during the 1980s was in sharp contrast to the numerous business deregulation successes of the 1970s. During the 1975–80 period, for example, deregulation actions dealing with stockbrokers' commissions, deposit interest rate ceilings, airlines, trucking companies, and railroads were begun.[12] About the only business deregulation measures developed during the 1980s dealt with buses and financial institutions. So instead of being a landmark period in business deregulation, the decade witnessed a considerable decline in deregulation activity in comparison to the 1970s.

Another aspect of deregulation deals with cutting back government regulations on business in areas such as the environment, health, safety, and consumer protection. While the Reagan administration had more success in this type of deregulation, the victories here, however, were limited. The Reagan administration usually placed individuals who shared a strong conservative deregulation philosophy into key bureaucratic positions. In the early 1980s these individuals vigorously assaulted the government regulations with some degree of success. But in several areas, a backlash developed that forced them to significantly curtail their activities. The attempts to lessen government restrictions in environmental programs is a good example of this pattern. After some gains in lessening the enforcement of the environmental laws, outcries from the public and Congress forced the Environmental Protection Agency (EPA) and the Interior Department to abandon several of the previous practices of the Reagan conservatives.

Even the limited success of the Reagan administration against this social type of regulation on business will probably not have a long-term impact. First, these regulations will continue because almost all the basic laws on the environment, health, safety, and consumer protection remain intact. Reagan was unable to persuade Congress to eliminate these laws or fundamentally change them. Therefore, future administrations will be constrained by these laws.

Second, the people filling the key positions will probably have different views than the people Reagan appointed. This change can already be seen in the Bush administration. For example, the new chairman of the Federal Trade Commission (FTC) supported stronger enforcement of the laws in several areas.[13] President Bush did not appoint a cadre of committed conservative ideologues to the key regulatory positions. The shift away from hard-line conservatives in regulatory positions was evident even during the Reagan administration. William Ruckelshaus becoming the head of the EPA is a good example.

Third, the backlash against the Reagan administration's attempts to lessen enforcement of many protective laws will also limit any long-range effects. Future Republican administrations will think twice about following Reagan's deregulation strategy because of possible adverse political repercussions. The Bush administration did not attempt to follow Reagan's course in this area.

International Trade

An advocate of laissez-faire capitalism should strongly support free international trade. President Reagan made speeches supporting free trade and criticizing protectionist trade policies. In practice, however, the Reagan administration often followed the protectionist policies it supposedly opposed. In one industry after another, Reagan would give in to domestic politics and implement policies to protect U.S. businesses against foreign competition. Reagan did stick to his free-trade philosophy in some areas such as shoe imports. But his record in many areas of trade was not much different than previous presidents—praise free trade in the abstract and then help protect many businesses from foreign competition.

In addition, no significant shift toward free-trade policy developed in Congress. In fact, more demands for trade protection were heard in Congress during the 1980s than before because of the increased trade imbalance, the big recession, and the expanded economic power of Japan. Congressmen acted as they always have by praising free trade and then fighting to protect important businesses in their districts and states. Conservatives engaged in these activities along with their moderate and liberal colleagues.

The sugar program provides one of the best examples of Reagan's protectionist policies. Reagan supported a policy which led to significant restrictions on foreign sugar imports. The 1981 law mandated that sugar producers receive a certain price per pound for sugar. Since restrictions on imported sugar were the main measure used to maintain the sugar price supports, foreign sugar's share of the U.S. market dropped substantially in the 1980s.

The administration's policy on auto imports was mixed. While Reagan opposed domestic-content bills designed to protect domestic automakers, he supported other measures to limit Japanese imports. In the early 1980s, the administration encouraged the Japanese to continue voluntary restrictions.[14]

In addition, many conservative Republicans in Congress joined Democrats in proposing measures to curtail auto imports. For example, House Minority Leader Robert Michel introduced a resolution to set quotas on auto imports until the trade balance improved between the U.S. and Japan.

Similarly, on steel imports, Reagan did not follow a consistent free-trade approach. Steel executives claimed that the U.S. steel industry had many problems in the early 1980s. Steelmakers had lost several billion dollars in 1982 and 1983. They blamed many of their problems on foreign competition. In 1983 Reagan agreed to raise tariffs and to set quotas on some steel imports. The following year he opposed the efforts to expand steel tariffs and quotas, but promised to seek voluntary agreements with other countries to limit foreign imports.[15]

This mixed pattern can also be seen in other parts of Reagan's trade policies. On some occasions he supported free trade, at other times he supported protectionist measure. Certainly no historic movement toward free trade developed during the 1980s. Pressures for the protection of domestic industries were even higher in the 1980s than in several previous decades.

Banking and Finance

While the role of the federal government decreased in some aspects of banking and finance during the 1980s, it increased in others. Overall, no major shift toward laissez-faire capitalism developed in this area.

Some measures passed that lessened government regulation in the banking industry. This was one of the few successes in the economic deregulation efforts of the 1980s. Also, the Securities and Exchange Commission (SEC) cut back on its oversight activities.

On the other hand, governmental influence expanded in several financial sectors. One of the major changes in the financial markets of the 1980s was the federal government's increased borrowing to finance the massive increase in the budget deficits. This significantly expanded the impact of the government on financial markets. So President Reagan, by leading the government into these huge deficits, increased the government's influence in capital markets. The deficits forced businesses into greater competition with the federal government for capital resources.

In addition, the savings and loan crisis and the accompanying scandal created a demand for greater government involvement. The savings and loan bailout will cost taxpayers an enormous amount of money. The bailout plan created more regulations for the industry and authorized a new agency to begin grappling with the problem of how to handle the insolvent savings and loans. It became one of the largest financial institutions in the country.

The savings and loan crisis also had an impact on public opinion. It increased support among Americans for more regulation of financial institutions rather than a laissez-faire approach.

Similarly, the public mood moved toward more acceptance of government regulation of the stock market. The stock market scandals and 1987 stock market crash angered many Americans. Again, the public mood shifted toward greater acceptance of government regulations, not less. These events on Wall Street provided a great deal of ammunition for the critics of the laisse-faire policies of the SEC.

Business Taxes

The Economic Recovery Tax Act of 1981 provided for significant cuts in business taxes. To put this tax in proper perspective, however, several preceding and succeeding developments must be considered.[16]

First, support for some type of business tax relief had developed by 1980. Several measures were being considered to counteract the impact of inflation. A business tax cut might have passed if Jimmy Carter has won the 1980 presidential election.

Second, later tax laws substantially altered the 1981 law. The Tax Equity and Fiscal Responsibility Act of 1982 was in response to fears of the projected deficits. It tightened many of the generous depreciation allowance provisions of the 1981 law and significantly reduced the business tax cut.

The Tax Reform Act of 1986 also lessened the tax preferences for business. Surprisingly, many businesses were losers in this tax reform law. Taxes on businesses increased under the new law. Corporate income taxes' share of total federal government receipts increased after 1986.

Antitrust

The Reagan administration successfully eased restrictions on antitrust policy. The administration made little effort to try to break up large companies. Also, few attempts were made to slow down the pace of business mergers in the 1980s.[17]

This success in achieving several goals in antitrust policy, however, did not produce a fundamental change in this policy area. First, the Reagan administration's antitrust policy was not a sharp break with previous policy. A new consensus on antitrust policy began developing during the 1970s. The emerging international economy forced many political leaders to question past antitrust policy. They wondered if the United States could compete with Japan and Western Europe with policies limiting mergers and the growth of the largest corporations. Therefore, Reagan's antitrust policy was not a new policy initiative, but a continuation of a policy course started in the 1970s.

Second, as the Reagan administration backed off from antitrust enforcement, many state officials moved in to fill the void.[18] During the 1980s, aggressive state attorneys general increased their efforts to bring cases against companies on antitrust grounds. For example, twenty-two states challenged Texaco's purchase of Getty Oil after federal regulators refused to prevent the merger. The states became a counterweight to the FTC and the Department of Justice's Antitrust Division.

Third, the Reagan administration's antitrust policy did not have a long-term impact. The Bush administration changed direction and began tightening up on antitrust policy. Many of Bush's key antitrust regulators hold different views than Reagan's administrators.

Civil Rights and Liberties

An examination of the civil rights record of the 1980s shows that the decade was not a period of landmark conservative changes. Certainly conservatives won some victories and slowed the progress of the liberals' civil rights movement, but liberals still won several important victories and conservatives failed to overturn the major liberal civil rights achievements such as the Voting Rights Act. The 1980s demonstrated that the momentum of the liberal civil rights movement could be slowed, but it could not be overturned or reversed.

Furthermore, the Reagan administration's policies on civil rights and liberties provides an excellent example of why a fundamental conservative policy change would be impossible because of the contradictions in American conservative ideology. In many instances in civil rights and liberties, adoption of conservatives' policies would result in a considerable increase of government influence in people's lives. Conservatives, for instance, want to force many groups to take drug tests. Expanded drug testing increases the government's control over individual freedom. In many aspects of the rights of the accused, conservatives support policies which allow the police and prosecutors more flexibility in investigating and prosecuting criminal cases. Again, this increases the government's role in citizens' lives. Therefore, many of the conservative policy gains in civil rights and liberties in the 1980s violated the conservative belief that government should be significantly reduced.

This section examines black civil rights, First Amendment freedoms, and several other civil rights and liberties topics. A few additional individual and group rights' issues will be examined in the section on social policy.

Black Civil Rights

During the 1980s, black civil rights leaders bitterly attacked the actions of the Reagan administration, conservative judges, and conservative members of Congress. They believed that significant advances in black civil rights were being erased. While they had reason to be concerned, the 1980s did not wipe out all the gains of previous decades. The 1980s represented more of a detour for the black civil rights movement than a complete policy reversal.

First, not one of the landmark court decisions and laws on black civil rights was overturned in the 1980s. For example, the 1964 Civil Rights Act, the 1965 Voting Rights Act, and *Brown v. Board of Education of Topeka* easily survived the decade. Since many conservatives had opposed the landmark black civil rights laws and court decisions, a conservative Reagan revolution should have produced a reversal of these acts. The survival of these historic policy decisions on black civil rights provides evidence that no fundamental conservative change happened in the 1980s.

Second, liberals won several significant victories during the 1980s. Probably the most important black civil rights issue of the 1980s was the extension of the 1965 Voting Rights Act. Voting obviously represents a big element of civil rights and liberties in a democracy.

One of the major goals of the black civil rights movement in the 1950s was to end the discriminatory practices against blacks' right to vote. Black leaders won one of their major victories with the passage of the 1965 Voting Rights Act and the resulting increase in black voters and black elected officials.

Since Reagan and other conservatives opposed many of the black civil rights laws of the 1960s, the battle in the early 1980s over the extension of the 1965 Voting Rights Act provided an excellent test of the Reagan revolution thesis. Which was more powerful—the political momentum of past policies or the alleged conservative mood of the 1980s? The overwhelming victory of the liberal forces demonstrated that the policy momentum of the past had more power.

The Reagan administration opposed several aspects of the proposed bill and worked for changes in it. Within Congress, Senator Orrin Hatch and several other conservatives attempted to weaken the bill. In the end, liberals won much of what they wanted since a strong voting rights bill emerged in Congress. The bill received overwhelming support on the House and Senate floors. Even in the Senate with its Republican majority, the bill passed by a vote of 85–8.[19]

The voting patterns of southern senators and representatives showed gains for the liberal rather than the conservative position on black civil rights. While many southerners voted against the 1965 Voting Rights, most southern members of Congress supported the extension of the law in 1982.

The new law extended the enforcement section by requiring several areas of the country to get Justice Department acceptance of election law changes. It also made challenges to election activities easier by specifying certain violations.

The black civil rights movement also won a big victory when Congress designated Martin Luther King, Jr.'s birthday as a national holiday. President Reagan had reservations about the holiday. And Jesse Helms, along with many other conservatives, strongly opposed it. In the end, liberals garnered enough votes to easily win on the House and Senate floors.

Congress also debated an important fair housing bill in the 1980s. Again Reagan and many conservatives opposed the bill, but liberals gained enough support to get the bill passed by lopsided votes in 1988. Liberals had to accept a compromise, but they got much of what they wanted.[20]

The law amended the 1968 Fair Housing Act. The purpose of the bill was to improve enforcement procedures in housing discrimination cases. The new law set up a two-track system which would be used when mediation failed to resolve the problems. The cases could be handled either by administrative judges within HUD or trials in federal courts.

The new fair housing law was another good test of the Reagan revolution thesis because it involved a political battle related to a previous liberal policy victory. Similar to the extension of the Voting Rights Act, the fair housing bill forced a showdown to determine if past liberal victories could survive the alleged conservative mood of the 1980s. The results on fair housing again indicated the triumph of a past liberal policy and the weakness of the assertion of a fundamental conservative change.

Black civil rights leaders won another big victory in the Bob Jones University case on racial discrimination in private schools and colleges. The Reagan administration stirred up a political hornets' nest by trying to reverse the Internal Revenue Service's (IRS) policy of denying tax-exempt status to private educational institutions involved in racial discrimination. In an 8–1 decision, the Supreme Court opposed Reagan's position and upheld the right of the IRS to deny tax exemption to racially discriminatory schools.

Grove City College Civil Rights Law

Another big liberal triumph in the 1980s was the passage of the "Grove City" civil rights bill.[21] This law not only aided the rights of blacks but also the rights of women, the handicapped, and others.

The conflict developed over the Supreme Court's decision in *Grove City College v. Bell* that held that only the program of the organizational unit receiving federal aid was covered by antidiscrimination laws and not the whole institution. The case grew out of the refusal of Grove City College to comply with antidiscrimination laws. The college received no federal assistance except that some students received financial aid. The Court ruled that the college did receive federal assistance, but only the financial aid program was covered by the antidiscrimination law. The new law overturned the Grove City decision by making certain that the whole institution must not discriminate if any program within the institution receives federal aid.

The Grove City law provides another good example of the strength of the liberal civil rights forces over the conservative forces. President Reagan strongly opposed the bill and worked against it. Reagan and many conservatives argued that it would significantly expand the scope of the federal government into many individuals' lives. Despite their objections, the House and Senate voted overwhelmingly for the bill. President Reagan then vetoed the bill. In the override vote, Reagan was soundly defeated by a vote of 292–133 in the House and 73–24 in the Senate. Almost half of the Republican senators (21 of 45) opposed Reagan's position.

Defeat of Judge Bork's Nomination

Liberals also won a big civil rights victory by defeating Robert Bork's nomination for the Supreme Court. The Bork nomination battle provides another excellent measure of the validity of the Reagan revolution thesis. Many conservatives admired Judge Bork because of his ideological position opposing many liberal civil rights policies. Bork wanted to turn the direction of civil rights cases around in several areas. Liberal civil rights advocates were alarmed by Bork's past decisions and mounted a nationwide campaign to defeat him. His sound defeat in the Senate again shows the strength of liberal forces in the 1980s. If landmark conservative changes had occurred, Judge Bork would have been approved by a wide margin in the Senate.

Not only did Judge Bork lose in the Senate, but he even modified his views during the hearings toward more acceptance of liberal views. This made the liberal victory even more significant. Judge Bork, for example, had stated previously that he did not believe the Fourteenth Amendment should be used to incorporate and apply the Bill of Rights to the states. In the Senate hearings, however, Bork said he fully accepted the incorporation doctrine. Bruce Fein, a conservative legal scholar from the Heritage Foundation, was quoted as saying about Bork's testimony: "This week has been a magnificent triumph for liberals. The basic message sent by the hearings so far is that the courts are about where they should be, that no great changes are needed. Bork is bending his views to improve his confirmation chances, and it's a shame."[22] If a conservative Reagan revolution developed in the 1980s, Bork would have stressed his devotion to conservative judicial philosophies rather than attempting to move to the center on some policies.

Cases on the Rights of the Accused

The majority on the Supreme Court generally ruled on the conservative side in criminal cases in the 1980s. For example, the Court's majority often decided in favor of the police and prosecutors in cases dealing with search and seizures and also the exclusionary rule. But the 1980s' Court did not overturn the landmark cases of the Warren Court on the rights of the accused. Also, the Court supported the liberal position in some important criminal cases. In 1981, for instance, the Burger Court reaffirmed the *Miranda* decision. In *Estelle v. Smith* the Court ruled that the requirements for police to tell suspects about their rights must be extended to defendants in psychiatric interviews ordered by courts. The case had added significance because Chief Justice Burger, who as a federal appeals court judge criticized the original *Miranda* ruling, wrote the Court's opinion.[23]

First Amendment Cases

Debates on the Establishment Clause produced many cases during the 1980s.[24] The conservatives won an important victory in *Lynch v. Donnelly*.[25] In a 5–4 decision, the Court upheld the right of the city of Pawtucket to display a Nativity scene. On the other hand, the Court ruled in favor of the wall of separation between religion and government in many other cases. The Court in 1982, for instance, struck down a Minnesota law that exempted only religious organizations from the privisions of a charitable solicitation statute.[26] During the same year, the Court ruled against a Massachusetts' law that allowed churches' governing bodies the power to stop the issuance of liquor licenses in areas close to the churches.[27]

In addition, liberals won in major cases on prayers in public schools and teaching "creation science." The Court decided in 1985 that the Alabama law that provided for a one-minute period of silence in public schools violated the religion clauses because it advanced religion.[28] In 1987 the Court overturned Louisiana's "Creation Act."[29] The law stipulated that the theory of creation science must accompany any instruction on the theory of evolution. Accrding to the Court's majority, the law had a religious bias.

One of the big cases on the Free Exercise Clause during the 1980s was *Goldman v. Weinberger*.[30] The case involved the claim of an Air Force officer, who was a rabbi, that the Air Force's requirement of not wearing headgear indoors violated his religious freedom. He wanted to wear a yarmulke indoors. The Court upheld the regulation in a 5–4 decision. Congress, however, passed a law the next year that allowed members of the armed services, under certain circumstances, to wear religious apparel indoors.

The decisions in cases on free speech did not indicate that the Supreme Court followed a consistent conservative pattern in the 1980s. The Court ruled on what would generally be considered the liberal side in numerous cases. For example, the Court overturned the dismissal of a government employee who had made a controversial remark about the attempted assassination of President Reagan.[31] In one of the most publicized cases of the 1980s, the Court ruled against the conviction of a young man on flag desecration charges.[32] The Court considered the conviction of an American citizen for burning a flag during a protest as a violation of the First Amendment.

The liberal point of view also triumphed in *Bolger v. Youngs Drug Products Corp.*[33] This was a significant case not only in free speech but also privacy rights. The Supreme Court unanimously voted to strike down a federal law that prohibited individuals or companies from sending unsolicited advertisements for contraceptives in the mail.

Jerry Falwell, a major figure in the New Right movement, was involved in one of the key freedom of press cases.[34] Falwell had received a $200,000 award for damages from a parody that appeared in Hustler magazine. In a unanimous decision, the court ruled that the award of the damages in the case violated the First Amendment.

Voting Rights Cases

One of the major problems in voting rights has been the discrimination against black Americans. The Supreme Court issued several rulings during previous decades that aided the struggle for black voting rights. The Court during the 1980s continued to support this trend toward greater equality for black voters. In one decision, for instance, the Court made it easier for blacks to challenge multimember electoral districts.

Malapportionment was another pre-1960s voting rights problem. The size of districts in the U.S. House of Representatives and many state legislatures varied enormously. These population differences favored rural areas in most states. Rural areas were usually over-represented, while metropolitan areas were often underrepresented in these legislative bodies. Urban political leaders fought these districting patterns on the grounds that the malapportionment violated the rights of citizens living in metropolitan areas. Urban liberals usually battled rural conservatives in the malapportionment controversy. The urban factions finally won with the Supreme Court's decision in *Baker v. Carr.*[35] Based on this case and several related decisions, the Court ordered the states to redraw all the seats in the state legislatures and the U.S. House along equal-population, "one person, one vote" guidelines.

The Supreme Court in the 1980s continued to support the one person, one vote concept in the districting decisions. The Court never seriously considered returning legislative bodies to their previous malapportionment condition, which many conservatives had fought to maintain in the pre-*Baker v. Carr* period.

Defense

From the perspective of the whole decade, a major military buildup did not happen in the 1980s. Reagan's military buildup is another illusion. The 1980s were not a period of historic expansion in the U.S. military, but the decade that started the most significant military cutback in the post–World War II era. By the end of the 1980s, the defense budget was growing at a very low rate. Military spending began dropping as a percent of GNP.

If a conservative Reagan revolution had taken place in the 1980s, the decade should have ended with the defense spending (as a percent of GNP) soaring toward record levels. A major debate in Washington should have been over how much money each part of the military would receive in the skyrocketing defense budget. The reality, however, was just the opposite. In 1989 and early 1990, major debates developed on how to cut the defense budget and on where to spend the "peace dividend." The debate was not on how to spend the extra new billions for defense, but on how best to spend the many billions cut from the Pentagon budget.

Reasons for the Decline in the Defense Budget

President Reagan and congressional conservatives shot themselves in the feet on defense spending. Their plan to greatly increase military spending appeared at first to be a huge success, but ended up with disastrous consequences for the defense budget.

One mistake was to push for too large an increase in the early 1980s. The huge expansion of the defense budget early in the decade came back to haunt conservatives in later years. This military spending increase hurt the chances for continued growth in the defense budget in two ways. First, it contributed to the deficit problem by significantly increasing the biggest program in the federal budget. Spending soared as Reagan was unable to push nondefense spending cuts through Congress to offset the mililtary gains. Spending also skyrocketed because of the increased costs of financing the deficit.

The budget deficit was a major cause of the turnaround in defense spending, which started in the mid-1980s. The deficit restrained spending especially on defense, the biggest budget program. Consequently, Reagan's early defense budget success contributed to the deficit problem that later constrained the growth of military spending.

Second, the early defense spending increases also hurt the defense budget's long-term prospects because of the adverse impact on public opinion. The news stories of massive defense spending and Pentagon fraud and mismanagement (e.g., incredible costs of items such as hammers and toilet seats) contributed to the huge decline in public support for defense spending growth. In addition, the large defense increase in the late 1970s and early 1980s led many Americans and members of Congress to conclude that any alleged problem with U.S. military weakness had been solved, or at least significantly reduced. Moreover, the high military growth and cuts in some nondefense areas in the 1981–82 period created a fairness and equity problem for conservatives. Many Americans questioned the morality of a policy that expanded military spending and cut social programs. As indicated in the public opinion chapter, by the mid-1980s the public overwhelmingly opposed huge military increases and social spending cutbacks.

Besides pushing for too much growth in defense spending, conservatives also erred by passing too large an income tax cut. By far the largest portion of the income tax revenues goes to finance the Defense Department. Reagan wanted to double defense spending in five years, yet he also wanted to cut back on the major source of revenue that was needed to finance this expansion.

The income tax cut not only made less money available for defense spending, it also played a role in the creation of the deficit crisis. With spending increasing and taxes cut, the deficit soared to record levels. The recession also hit and increased the deficit and lessened tax revenues needed to fuel military growth.

Consequently, Reagan and the conservatives were left with a military budget shrinking in relation to the GNP. The deficit crisis, fewer income tax revenues, and adverse public opinion severely constrained the growth of the military budget. Reagan would have benefited from a moderate military buildup and a smaller tax cut. These proposals would have produced less public reaction against expanding the defense budget, more tax revenue to finance defense spending, and less constraint on Pentagon spending because of a smaller deficit.

The obvious reason for the increased pressure to cut the military budget in the early 1990s was the easing of the cold war. President Bush had difficulty convincing Congress to pass even small increases in the defense budget after the new policies in the Soviet Union and the demise of the communist regimes in Eastern Europe.

Various Projections on Military Spending

Table 6.5 presents data comparing actual defense spending (outlays) with estimates of defense spending that would have resulted from several projections. The first projection is based on Reagan's proposed defense spending for fiscal years 1981–86, which was presented in the 1981 budget proposals. The figures for 1987–89 were computed by increasing the yearly spending proposals at the same growth rate as the 1981–86 period. The first part of the Carter-Mondale projection consists of President Carter's defense spending proposals for 1981–85. The second part (1986–89) was based on the

TABLE 6.5

Comparison of Actual Defense Spending (Outlays) with Several Defense
Spending Projections for the 1980s

Year	Actual Defense Spending	Reagan Defense Proposals	Carter-Mondale Defense Proposals	Defense Spending of 1979–80 Rate
1981	158	162	146	155
1982	185	189	166	177
1983	210	226	186	202
1984	227	256	207	230
1985	253	304	230	262
1986	273	343	250	299
1987	282	407	271	341
1988	290	483	294	389
1989	295	573	319	443

Source: The Office of Management and Budget is the source for the actual defense
spending and five-year projections for Reagan and Carter.

rate of military growth proposed by Walter Mondale in the 1984
presidential campaign. The third projection is based on the annual
growth rate of defense spending during the late 1970s.

The data demonstrate that there was no significant increase in
military spending in the 1980s. The Reagan military buildup is
another illusion of 1980s' politics. If Congress had spent the money
on defense as proposed by Reagan, a fundamental conservative
change would have occurred in military spending. Note, however,
the enormous difference between what Reagan proposed and the
actual budget outlays. The defense budget at the end of the decade
was only about one half of what it should have been based on
Reagan's proposed rate of growth. This shows how far off the
conventional view is on the Reagan administration's success in
military spending. Instead of securing a historic military buildup,
Reagan failed miserably in obtaining his goals of a massive defense
expansion.

Many political commentators proclaimed a major defense buildup
occurred because of the enormous amount of military spending
during the decade. This is certainly a weak argument. Just stating
that huge amounts of money were spent offers no proof of a
fundamental policy change. To conclude that a historic military

buildup happened in the 1980s, the case must be made that the actual defense spending was significantly higher than would have been spent anyway.

As the data in table 6.5 indicate, almost as much money would probably have been spent on the military if the Democrats had won the White House and maintained majorities in the House and Senate during the 1980s. By the end of the 1980s, the Carter-Mondale projected defense budgets were even higher than the actual budgets. With a Democratic president and Congress from 1977 to 1981, the defense budget was growing at an annual rate of over 12 percent. It is highly probable that the military budget would have continued to grow at a fairly high rate in the early 1980s if Democrats had controlled the White House and Congress. This seems likely since the defense budget was expanding rapidly in 1979 and 1980. Based on the defense spending proposals of Carter and Mondale, about $2.5 trillion dollars would have been spent on the military from 1981 to 1990. This is close to the actual spending for defense during this period.

Much of the military spending of the 1980s consisted of paying for basic costs and programs already in place in 1980. Personnel costs, for instance, comprise a large part of the defense budget. Since there is no indication that the Democrats supported large cutbacks in troop strength in the late 1970s, the huge military personnel costs would have continued each year in the 1980s with an annual increase of several percent if the Democrats had remained in power. Most, if not all, of the planned expansion of the already existing weapon systems would probably have continued into the 1980s.

Even some of the new weapon systems built in the 1980s might have also been approved under Democratic presidents and Democratic majorities in Congress. President Carter, for example, proposed an enormous MX missile system in the late 1970s.

Year-By-Year Analysis

The conventional view of military spending politics in the 1980s was that President Reagan and his conservative allies won virtually everything they wanted. A year-by-year analysis of defense budget politics, however, reveals many inaccuracies in this view.

The first year (1981) was the most successful for Reagan and the conservatives. The defense budget increased by almost $30 billion from fiscal years 1981 to 1982.[36] This represented nearly an 18 percent expansion of military spending. But even in the first year, the restraint of the deficits began to appear on the defense budget. In the summer of 1981, budget data started to show how far off the Reagan administration was on the deficit. Several White House advisors, including Office of Management and Budget (OMB) Director David Stockman, called for cuts of nearly $30 billion from what Reagan had originally proposed for 1982–84 defense budget. Reagan announced in September that he would cut $13 billion from his defense requests for that period.

Moreover, the increase in military spending for the 1982 fiscal year did not represent a radical departure from the previous few years. The Pentagon's budget expanded by 14 to 15 percent a year at the end of the 1970s.

In addition, Reagan's defense program in 1981 did not completely satisfy many of the most hawkish conservatives. Many conservative defense analysts expected a more radical departure from the defense programs of recent administrations. Several of the controversial proposals of Reagan's defense transition team were not part of the final administration plan.

Congress' massive cutbacks in Reagan's defense proposals began in 1982. Congress trimmed a whopping $19 billion dollars in budget authority from the President's request. Not only was the administration losing the votes of moderate and liberal Democrats on many key defense votes, but also a number of Republicans and conservative Democrats began opposing some aspects of Reagan's defense plans. By the end of the 1982, Congress had already cut an unprecedented $27 billion from Reagan's original five-year defense proposal.

Many members of Congress questioned Reagan's military plans. Even many Republican congressmen wondered about the fairness and political feasibility of pushing for huge increases in defense spending coupled with cuts in social programs. They also criticized the plan to greatly expand defense spending when the federal government was facing record deficits. In addition, the administration's defense program was being hurt by the growing perception of incompetence. Many political observers believed that Reagan and Secretary of Defense Weinberger lacked the ability to manage an expansion of the military. The buildup was often perceived as being uncoordinated and riddled with mismanagement and abuse.

The pattern continued in 1983 of the administration winning some defense battles (e.g., development of the B-1 bomber), but with congressional majorities significantly cutting the overall amount of Reagan's request. Congress trimmed the president's request by $18 billion. The final increase in the defense budget represented an increase of 5 percent above inflation compared to Reagan's request for 10 percent beyond inflation. The military budget for fiscal year 1984 was over $60 billion below the corresponding amount in Reagan's original plan.

In 1984 Reagan's proposed increase of 13 percent above inflation for defense spending was dead-on-arrival when it hit Congress. Reagan was unable even to gain support for the plan from the Senate Republican leaders. They continually tried to convince Reagan to leave fantasyland and accept reality concerning the deficit and defense spending. Reagan and the Senate Republicans finally compromised on a real increase of 7 percent. House Democrats pushed through a 3 percent real increase. In the final compromise, the House and Senate passed an increase of 5 percent above inflation. Overall, the defense budget expanded by 11 percent between fiscal years 1984 and 1985. This is a lower rate of growth than in the late 1970s.

The results of the 1985 fight over the defense budget marked the beginning of the historic cutback in U.S. military spending. For 1985 and several years afterwards, Reagan had difficulty getting Congress to approve defense budgets with increases to even match the inflation rate. President Reagan reduced his defense request to about a 6 percent real increase. Congress approved a small increase in overall spending that translated into a real decrease of 2 percent.

Secretary Weinberger and Reagan continued to lose credibility on defense spending. Year after year, Reagan would propose an unrealistically high increase in defense spending, yet everyone outside the administration knew Congress would trim the proposal way back. Instead of compromising on the cuts at the beginning of the year, Weinberger would stick with the fantasy figures and refuse to negotiate. Few congressmen were impressed with this stubborn and unrealistic approach.

The pattern was repeated in 1986. Reagan's proposal for a 12 percent increase in the defense budget was again dead-on-arrival in Congress. Congressional majorities cut over $30 billion from Reagan's plan for military spending.

In 1987 President Reagan finally became more realistic in his budget plans by proposing only a small increase in defense spending. As a result of the budget summit at the end of the year, Reagan agreed to small increases in the defense budget for the 1988 and 1989 fiscal years. The agreement meant that the defense budget would continue to decline in inflation-adjusted terms.

Economics

One way to examine economic policy is to analyze policies and programs on a continuum with laissez-faire capitalism and a mixed economy at opposite ends. A hallmark of the political era that began with the Depression of the 1930s was a significant shift toward a mixed economy. The New Deal and later events, such as the military buildup from World War II and the cold war, enormously expanded the federal government's impact on the economy. If a historic fundamental change occurred in economic policy during the 1980s, the economy should have moved significantly back towards the more laissez-faire conditions of the pre-Depression period. This did not happen in the 1980s. In fact, the economy moved closer to the mixed-economy end of the continuum during the decade.

Components of the Mixed Economy

An analysis of the major ways the federal government influences the economy provides a useful method to determine the direction of economic policy in the 1980s. The primary components of the federal government's role in the economy are fiscal policy, spending, taxation, regulation, finance, and foreign trade.

One of the most important changes in economic policy from the New Deal period was the Keynesian approach to using fiscal policy. In the following years, most liberals supported the idea of using federal budget policy as a means to promote a healthy economy. Among the different aspects of Keynesian economic policy, liberals became associated especially with the idea of advocating deficit budgets to help the economy move away from projected recessions. Although some conservatives accepted some aspects of Keynesian fiscal policy, many opposed the theory and argued for balanced federal budgets.

Ronald Reagan made many statements that clearly demonstrated his support for the traditional conservative fiscal policy. According to Reagan, deficit spending was a major economic problem. He advocated that the federal government adopt his program that would supposedly lead to balanced and surplus budgets beginning in the second and third years of his administration.

Instead, what happened in the 1980s was the creation of the greatest deficit of all time. President Reagan proposed, and Congress passed, budgets with gigantic deficits. Consequently, fiscal policy moved just about as far from traditional conservative beliefs on fiscal policy as possible.

Another important aspect of the government's role in the economy is the economic impact of the billions of dollars from the federal budget. The spending of over a trillion dollars a year, which represents more than 20 percent of GNP, significantly influences the major sectors of the U.S. economy. Conservatives advocate large cutbacks in federal spending to decrease government involvement in the economy. Federal spending, however, increased considerably during the 1980s rather than decreased. As mentioned in the budget section, federal outlays skyrocketed from 21 to about 25 percent of GNP between the end of the 1970s to the mid-1980s. Therefore, the federal government's influence on the economy expanded with the sharp rise in federal spending.

Within the budget, the federal government has the most influence on the economy through defense spending. Defense, one of the largest sectors of the economy, is controlled by the government. The military-industrial complex comprises about 10 percent of the U.S. economy. Many companies from major corporations to small businesses depend on military spending. Several of the biggest corporations depend almost completely on the defense budget.

The defense budget has an enormous impact on employment. Many thousands of people either work for the government (i.e., military personnel or civil Department of Defense employees) or have jobs with defense contractors. The military has an important impact on the distribution of jobs in the economy. Employment opportunities in science and engineering, for example, are heavily influenced by defense spending.

Research funding has become one of the key elements in industrial and post-industrial economies. Companies must keep up with and advance the research in their fields to compete in a worldwide market. In the United States, the federal government, through the defense budget, determines the utilization of a considerable amount of research spending.

Military spending also strongly affects the distribution of the other resources in the economy besides research funding. Many raw materials and finished products are directed toward the military and away from the other sectors of the economy.

Since defense spending has such an enormous impact on the economy, the conventional view of conservatives supporting laissez-faire economics is inaccurate. Their support for less government intervention through policies such as deregulation is cancelled by their desire to expand the government's role in the economy through increased defense spending. This is one of the major contradictions in conservatives' ideology. The goals of a greatly expanded military and a significant movement toward laissez-faire capitalism conflict with each other. If Reagan and the conservatives had successfully pushed defense spending up from 5 percent of GNP to about 10 percent, the federal government's role in the economy would have increased enormously. The federal government, through the Defense Department, would have directed much more of the economy's distribution of capital, employment, raw materials, finished products, and research funds.

Political commentators present liberals as advocates of an industrial policy for the federal government, while Reagan and the conservatives are portrayed as opponents of a policy. In reality, the Reagan administration strongly endorsed a government-planned industrial policy through proposals for a massive increase in the military budget.[37] If the military buildup had been enacted and the defense budget had climbed to over $500 billion by 1990, the economy's direction would have been shaped far more by the Defense Department's "industrial policy" than by anything envisioned by liberal Democrats' industrial policy proposals.

Therefore, President Reagan helped move the pendulum toward

the mixed-economy end of the continuum with his leadership in continuing the high rate of military spending growth of the late 1970s into the early 1980s. His greatest contribution to laissez-faire capitalism was his failure to achieve his goals on the expansion of the defense budget. The decline in defense spending as a percent of GNP that developed during the decade decreased the government's role in the economy.

Agriculture is another major sector of the economy that is heavily dependent on federal spending. In contrast to defense policy, conservatives' ideological position on agriculture does not conflict with their laissez-faire economic beliefs, since they advocate less government spending on agriculture. But the contradiction for conservatives and the Reagan administration developed between practice and theory in farm policy. As mentioned earlier, federal spending on agriculture soared in the 1980s. Consequently, the federal government's enormous involvement in agriculture continued and expanded during the 1980s.

Besides supporting less government involvement through lower spending, conservatives also support lower taxes as a way to promote laissez-faire capitalism. According to their beliefs, lower taxes will shift the control of huge amounts of the country's resources from the public sector to the private sector. Here again, the data in the budget section showed that the Reagan administration did not achieve its goals. Federal taxes were not cut significantly in the 1980s. Federal revenues as a percent of GNP remained at about the same level in the 1980s as compared with the 1970s and 1960s. Moreover, the increases in the Social Security tax in 1983 and the corporate tax in 1986 expanded the federal government's impact on business.

Deregulation policy and international trade policy were also discussed in previous sections of this chapter. In both policies the Reagan administration failed to significantly promote laissez-faire capitalism. Very little business deregulation was developed in the 1980s, much less than what occurred in the 1970s. In foreign trade, the administration and congressional conservatives often supported protectionist policies.

Finally, the federal government's involvement in the financial sector of the economy expanded during the 1980s. The greatest change in the public sector's influence on finance was the massive increase in budget deficits. To finance these enormous deficits, the federal government must go into the capital market to borrow funds. This enormous expansion of federal borrowing drastically increased the government's influence on the direction of capital markets. This provided yet another example of how President Reagan's policies conflicted with the ideals of laissez-faire capitalism.

Some deregulation did develop in banking during the 1980s. However, this was more than offset by increased government involvement in financial institutions brought on by the savings and loan crisis and the resulting bailout.

Economic Theories

The media and political commentators often presented the economic developments of the 1980s as following the guidelines of conservative economic theories. However, an examination of what really happened does not support this assumption. The Reaganomics' proposals of 1980 and 1981 were a mixture of traditional conservative and supply-side economic theories. Instead, what actually happened in the economy and in the government's economic policy could not be characterized as either traditional conservative or supply-side.

Traditional conservatives stressed, among other policies, the need to lessen the federal government's economic influence through balanced budgets and less government spending. Obviously, Reaganomics did not represent the economic ideals of traditional conservatives, because President Reagan proposed budgets with enormous increases in overall spending and record deficits. The 1980s was the decade of record federal spending and deficits, not record budget decreases and balanced budgets. Herbert Stein, a leading conservative economist who was chairman of the Council of Economic Advisers under Presidents Nixon and Ford, pointed out the considerable differences between the conservative goals and the realities of Reagan's economic policies:

> But there has been no radical Reagan revolution. Total taxes are almost as high as ever, relative to GNP, expenditures are higher, and there is no reasonable prospect of any significant reduction of either for years

ahead. Budget deficits, present and projected, are extraordinarily large. In fact, at the present time the most distinctive feature of Reagan's economic policy—aside from its language—is the size of its budget deficits. The country is as far as ever, possibly farther, from having any agreed-upon rules of fiscal policy that would limit particular spending and taxing decisions.[38]

Supply-side economics called for massive tax cuts and deregulation measures. The enactment of these policies would supposedly lead to substantial growth in savings and productivity. Since none of these developments occurred in the 1980s, the Reagan administration failed to achieve the policy measures and outcome of supply-side economics. Federal taxes did not drop significantly in the 1980s. Huge tax increases offset the 1981 tax cuts. The 1980s had much less business deregulation than the 1970s. Also, the rates of savings and productivity did not increase dramatically during the decade.

Furthermore, the supply-side theory would not support the enormous budget deficits each year. While supply-siders accepted budget deficits more than traditional conservatives, they certainly did not advocate running deficits over $150 billion year after year.

Some have suggested that Ronald Reagan was really a Keynesian because of the deficits. This was true for a few years. During the period around the recession, the Reagan administration blundered into an unplanned Keynesian policy. Reagan's goal was to have balanced and surplus budgets by the early 1980s. However, the huge deficits that actually resulted from Reaganomics and the recession exactly fit the Keynesian prescription of running large deficits to aid in moving the economy out of the recession. The administration stopped following its unplanned Keynesian policy during the recovery period. (Keynesians would not support the continuation of record budget deficits during a recovery period.) Reagan, trapped by the failures of his policies and unwilling to make substantial compromises, continued proposing huge budget deficits that neither corresponded to Keynesian theory nor to any conservative theory he was supposed to support.

Education

Since conservatives fought against most types of federal aid to education during the 1950s and 1960s, a fundamental conservative change in education policy would mean the elimination of the major federal education programs. Not only did the federal education programs survive during the 1980s, but conservatives also failed to achieve almost all of their other educational policy objectives.

Education Spending

The Reagan administration and congressional conservatives won some early battles on federal spending on education, but they eventually lost the war. In the early 1980s, Congress accepted some of Reagan's proposals and cut several education programs. The administration, however, was unable to sustain the support necessary in Congress to continue major cutbacks in education programs. A huge backlash against education cuts developed within a large segment of the American public. The phenomenon of people wanting less government spending, but not in areas important to them, was a significant part of this backlash. For example, many middle-class parents, who had voted for President Reagan and other Republicans, were upset when they heard of the cuts in college student aid programs.

A pattern began that continued through Reagan's second term in which the administration would propose cuts in the education budget each year, and majorities in Congress would reject most of them. Even the administration seemed to be affected by the backlash from cuts in education spending. In 1983 the administration substantially increased the budget proposal for the Education Department.[39]

The five-year renewal of the Higher Education Act, which passed in 1986, illustrates the turnabout in education spending.[40] Reagan had again proposed cuts in the college programs. But a bipartisan coalition in each house overwhelmingly rejected the administration's attempts to trim the programs. The bill extended funding of all the major college aid programs into the 1990s.

With Democratic majorities in the House and Senate, supporters of federal aid to education went on the offensive in 1987 and 1988. They easily won approval for an expansion of existing programs and even added new federal programs. For instance, Even Start was established to provide services for very young children and their parents.[41]

The political battle over federal education programs is a good example of the legitimacy factor in domestic policies. In the long run, federal education programs came out of the 1980s in a strong position despite the cuts in the growth of some programs. The fact that the Reagan administration failed either to eliminate any of the major programs or to deeply cut these programs enhanced the long-term legitimacy of these programs. The size of the bipartisan coalition that formed in Congress to stop the Reagan administration from dismantling the federal education programs demonstrated how much support existed for these programs. Reagan's defeats on education spending will send a message to future Republican leaders about the political feasibility of attempting to make substantial cuts in federal education programs.

President Bush's policies demonstrate that no conservative Reagan revolution occurred in education policy. If a historic conservative change had developed in the 1980s, President Bush would have been proposing plans to Congress for the final elimination of a few remaining federal education programs. Instead, Bush claimed during the 1988 campaign that he would be the "Education President" if elected. He certainly did not advocate the dismantling of the federal education programs. While President Bush has not called for either massive new education programs or considerably larger increases in the education budget, he has supported the continuation of the basic federal programs with small annual increases. These policies are supported by many Republicans in Congress. Therefore, the opponents of federal aid to education won a few battles in the early 1980s, but eventually lost the war as the legitimacy of federal education programs was strengthened during the 1980s.

The budget for the Department of Education increased from $13 billion in 1979 to nearly $22 billion in 1989. This represents an increase of about 70 percent during the decade. With an increase of this size, it is difficult to accept the assertion that federal educational funding underwent a radical conservative change in the 1980s. Granted, the spending patterns represented a decline in the rate of growth in these programs compared to the late 1970s, but the fact that the education programs' growth rate declined somewhat in the 1980s does not support the assertion of a historic conservative policy change.

Elimination of the Department of Education

One of Ronald Reagan's many education proposals was a pledge to eliminate the Department of Education. Since conservatives believed public education should be controlled primarily by state and local governments, they opposed the establishment of a Department of Education on the federal level. Reagan wanted to cancel the liberals' victory in this debate by wiping out the Department.

The outcome of this debate provides another excellent test of the Reagan revolution thesis. The establishment of the Department of Education exemplifies the type of policy that fits the trend toward greater federal involvement in domestic programs. The fact that the Education Department easily survived shows again the much greater strength of the legacy of the New Deal and Great Society programs in relation to Reagan's conservative policies.

The support for Reagan's proposal to eliminate the Department was so weak that it never received serious consideration in Congress. The president could not even get the backing of the key Senate Republicans on his proposal to change the Education Department into a foundation. Neither Senator Howard Baker, the majority leader, nor Senator William Roth, the chairman of the Governmental Affairs Committee, provided much assistance to the administration on the proposal.[42] Roth's committee handled proposals on the reorganization of the executive branch.

The plan had even less chance to pass in the House. With the Democrats in the majority, the department-to-foundation plan was dead-on-arrival in the House. Moreover, Roth's counterpart in the House, Jack Brooks, the chairman of the Government Operations Committee, strongly opposed the plan.

Not only did the Education Department easily survive, it gained added prominence and attention during the 1980s. William Bennett, the secretary of education during the last years of the Reagan administration, became an effective spokesman for conservative educational policy. He was able to develop into one of the stars in the administration even though the position of education secretary was never considered a major cabinet post. Bennett's prominence and media attention both helped and hurt conservatives' ideological goals. On the one hand, he effectively advocated the conservative position on many educational issues. His effective advocacy, however, made more people aware of the Education Department and the federal government's role in education, and lessened the attention given to state and local education. An unintended consequence of Bennett's performance was to expand the federal government's impact on education. With Bennett gaining so much attention by suggesting standards, making awards, proposing reforms, and criticizing public education, the U.S. Department of Education began to appear more like the powerful education ministries in some European countries.

School Prayer, Vouchers, Tuition Tax Credits, and
School Desegregation

The Reagan administration and conservatives also failed to make significant progress in several other policy objectives. They lost repeatedly in their effort to pass the constitutional amendment to allow organized prayers in public schools. They also failed to gain enough support to start a constitutional amendment to end large-scale school desegregation programs.

Also, conservatives had only limited success in convincing school officials and the American public to adopt the voucher system. In a voucher system, parents are given a voucher worth the equivalent of a year's education for each child. Depending on which plan a school district or state adopted, the parents could use the voucher either at any appropriate school in the local area or at any public school in the district.

Finally, Congress never passed a bill providing for tuition tax credits. The proposed bills provided for tax credits to parents of college students. Some proposals also included tuition credits for parents with children in elementary and secondary schools.

This was a particularly difficult defeat for the Reagan administration and conservatives because the prospects for the bill seemed so bright. A tuition tax credit bill had passed the House and Senate in 1978, but the House later rejected the conference committee's compromise bill. So if a tuition tax credit bill could pass both houses at a time of Democratic control, it appeared a similar bill should pass with a Republican president and a Republican majority in the Senate. Opponents of the bill, however, easily thwarted the efforts of President Reagan and the congressional supporters of tuition tax credits.

Energy

While the role of the federal government continued to decline in energy production during the 1980s, a fundamental conservative shift never developed in energy policy. The Reagan administration persuaded Congress to decrease the government's involvement in several energy programs. In addition, no new government programs were created to help solve energy problems. However, the administration failed to achieve several major goals. Also, very little energy deregulation took place in the 1980s. The major market-oriented energy policies had been enacted in the 1970s.

Deregulation

The major debates on private versus public control of energy in recent decades developed over price controls on oil and natural gas. Congress passed the basic legislation to decontrol oil and natural gas prices in the 1970s. In energy as in several other sectors of the economy, the major deregulation activities took place during the 1970s. The pace of energy deregulation slowed considerably in the 1980s. The oil and natural gas price control policies in the 1980s largely followed the guidelines set down in the 1970s.

Furthermore, conservatives failed to end all price controls in the early 1980s. The Natural Gas Policy Act of 1978 set up a plan to gradually phase out price controls on natural gas. In 1981 many natural gas producers lobbied the administration and Congress to scrap the gradual phase-out plan and implement a program for immediate decontrol. However, critics of decontrol beat back all efforts in the early 1980s for quick deregulation. The rising cost of natural gas to consumers created a political environment in which the majority in Congress would not support any effort to immediately decontrol natural gas prices.

Elimination of the Energy Department

To show conservatives' disdain for government involvement in energy, President Reagan called for the end of the Department of

Energy. He wanted to put the remaining energy agencies in the Commerce Department. But his plan was never enacted by Congress. Similar to his proposal to eliminate the Education Department, Reagan's plan for the Energy Department was so unpopular that he could not get Congress to seriously consider the bill. When the bill was first proposed in 1982, the administration received almost no support from key senators. In the House, Reagan had a difficult time finding anyone to sponsor the bill. Finally, after several months of trying, the administration found two Republican representatives willing to introduce the bill. The bill went nowhere and was dead soon after it was introduced. Even the administration conceded that it had very little chance of passage. Toward the end of 1982, Energy Secretary Donald Hodel told a Senate committee that the administration no longer considered the elimination of the department a high priority because of the lack of support in Congress.[43]

Nuclear Energy

The position of conservatives on nuclear energy provides another example of a contradiction in their political ideology. Conservatives generally oppose government involvement in the development of various forms of energy except nuclear energy. For some reason, they support government promotion of nuclear energy, but not other competing energy sources. Moreover, the government has more control over nuclear energy than any other form of energy. An expansion of nuclear energy would mean more government involvement in energy policy. Consequently, conservatives' support for nuclear energy conflicts with their goal of less government.

Besides their ideological problems with nuclear energy, conservatives suffered many defeats in their efforts to greatly expand the use of nuclear energy. The 1980s was a disaster for the nuclear energy industry.[44] The construction of new nuclear power plants virtually came to a standstill. Most of the orders placed in the 1970s for these plants were cancelled. Many studies concluded that nuclear electric power costs more per kilowatt than electricity generated by coal. The struggle in Congress over where and how to dispose of nuclear waste focused attention on another major problem for the nuclear industry. The Chernobyl disaster in the Soviet

Union and continued shutdowns of U.S nuclear power plants raised many new questions about the safety of nuclear energy. As a result, public support for nuclear energy declined substantially in the 1980s. While the majority of Americans, according to national polls, favored the construction of new nuclear plants in the 1970s, the majority opposed it in the 1980s.

The nuclear power industry did win some victories during the late 1980s. Congress made some progress on the waste-storage problem and reauthorized the Price-Anderson Act, which regulates insurance coverage for possible disasters in nuclear energy. These victories, however, did not even begin to offset the numerous negative trends associated with nuclear energy during the decade. In the battle between liberals and conservatives over nuclear energy, liberals won a decisive victory.

Energy versus Environment

An important ideological debate between liberals and conservatives relates to the conflict between economic development and environmental protection. Both sides claim support for both policy goals. But when a conflict exists between them, generally liberals favor environmental protection and conservatives support economic development.

Events in the 1980s favored the environmental side of the debate over the economic side in energy policy. The decline in oil prices, the elimination of long lines at the gas pumps, and the demise of OPEC ended the perception that the United States faced a great energy crisis. Without the threat of an energy crisis, many fewer Americans were willing to sacrifice environmental protection for the expansion of energy production.

Furthermore, the inept and sometimes illegal activities of the Reagan administration discredited conservatives' attempts to favor energy development over environmental protection. Many Americans opposed the attempts by members of the Reagan administration to allow companies to speed up energy production with little regard for the environmental consequences.

Finally, the Alaskan oil spill from an Exxon tanker, which was by far the most publicized energy-versus-environment event of the 1980s, also shifted public opinion toward the environmental protection side of the debate. When questions of environmental protection develop in the future, many Americans, including public opinion leaders, will still have the TV images in their minds of the Alaskan environmental disaster that resulted from the oil spill. They will also remember the widespread criticism of how Exxon handled its tankers and the clean-up effort. Proponents of expanding energy production in environmentally-sensitive areas had a much more difficult time making their case after the environmental disaster in Alaska.

Environment

Contrary to the conventional wisdom, the 1980s was a very good decade for the liberal environmental movement. The decade was a setback for conservatives' environmental policy rather than a period of a victorious Reagan revolution.

The environmentalists gained in three major ways. First, the threat presented by the Reagan administration and its assault on the environmental laws in the early 1980s put new life into the environmental movement. By the late 1970s, the progress of the environmental movement had slowed down. The movement needed something to arouse the troops and create new enthusiasm. President Reagan, Interior Secretary James Watt, and several other members of the administration provided the perfect solution to the problem. Membership and funding for environmental groups expanded in the early 1980s in response to the threat posed by the Reagan administration. Instead of crippling the environmental movement, Reagan and Watt greatly helped it. The environmental groups battled through the 1980s with more fervor and support than they would have had if Carter and the Democrats had won the White House and the Senate in 1980. A new adversary or the perception of an increased threat from an old adversary provides interest groups with the opportunity to rally their rank-and-file and gain more support among the public.

Second, the blunders, scandals, and defeats of the Reagan administration's environmental policy discredited the conservatives' approach to this issue. The success of the bipartisan coalition in Congress, which formed to counter the administration, greatly enhanced the legitimacy of the environmental laws, the environmental movement, and the liberals' position on environmental questions. On the other hand, the legitimacy of the conservative point of view on the environment was severely damaged.

As Paul Portney points out, the conservative ideologues in the Reagan administration made drastic mistakes in their strategic planning on environmental policy.[45] The administration had a good plan for conservative reform from a transition group, the Task Force on the Environment. This blueprint stressed regulatory reforms such as using more market-oriented techniques in implementing environmental laws. In the early 1980s, the zealous conservatives in key environmental administrative positions ignored many of these reform proposals. Instead, they pushed for policies such as regulatory relief, severe budget cuts, and huge expansions of mineral and energy exploration in wilderness areas. These policies led to controversy and chaos. Rather than being perceived as administrators with sensible proposals for reform based on their conservative ideology, the Reaganites were perceived as uncompromising ideologues who were willing to bend or even to break the law to achieve their objectives.

Third, not only were liberals able to blunt the attack of the Reagan administration, but they also won several key victories in environmental policy. The authorization of the superfund and the passage of the Clean Water Act over President Reagan's veto are two good examples of how strong the environmentalist forces were in Congress during the 1980s.

In environmental policy, just as in several other policy areas, the Reagan administration won several battles early in the 1980s but lost the war by the end of the decade. In 1981 Reagan persuaded Congress to cut the funding for several environmental programs. The administration also had some success in altering how certain environmental programs had previously been implemented. James Watt, for example, shifted resources in the Interior Department away from preservation of public lands and toward economic development in these areas.

By 1982 environmentalists and their supporters in Congress had enough strength to begin turning the environmental policy battle around. The House voted to cite EPA administrator Anne Gorsuch for contempt of Congress. She had refused to hand over documents related to the enforcement of the hazardous waste law.[46] Administration critics continued their attack on James Watt. In addition, Congress rejected the major spending cuts proposed by the Reagan administration for environmental programs. Funding stayed at about the same level.

The administration's assault on the environmental laws suffered a significant blow in 1983 with the resignation of Watt and Anne Burford (formerly Anne Gorsuch). Also, Rita Lavelle, an EPA official, was convicted of lying under oath before congressional subcommittees. These developments were important victories for the environmentalists, as several of the major figures involved in the formulation and implementation of the administration's environmental policies were forced out.

If a significant conservative change had taken place in environmental policy, Watt and Burford would have kept their positions and successfully led an attack on the environmental laws. Instead, they were forced out and Congress blocked their initiatives in many areas such as coal leasing, offshore leasing, and hazardous waste administration.

The fact that many congressional Republicans put pressure on the administration to mend its ways showed how much of a political liability Reagan's environmental policy had become for the GOP. These congressional Republicans clearly perceived that public opinion had not shifted in a conservative direction on environmental issues.

Reagan was forced to reassure the American public on environmental issues by nominating replacements for Watt and Burford who would promise to properly carry out the laws. William Ruckelshaus replaced Burford, and William Clark replaced Watt.

By 1984 environmentalists not only had blunted the conservatives' attack, but they had begun to take the initiative on environmental policy. Because of the election year, Reagan and congressional Republicans tried to distance themselves from the policies of the Watt-Burford period. This provided liberals with the opportunity to push for their environmental agenda. It was impossible for conservatives to mount an offensive against environmental laws after the public outcry against the Reagan administration's policies. The debate shifted from how to ease restrictions on industries to how much to strengthen the environmental laws.

Environmentalists won many major victories during the 1986–

1990 period. In fact, this period ranks as one of the most successful periods for the environmentalist forces during the entire history of the environmental movement.

George Bush's position on environmental issues certainly does not support the conservative revolution thesis. Bush ran as an environmentalist candidate for president. William Reilly, the former president of the World Wildlife Fund, was chosen by Bush to head the Environmental Protection Agency. Reilly was the first head of an environmental group to become EPA director. Bush's environmental policy proposals (e.g., acid rain and air pollution programs in general) significantly differed from the environmental program of the Reagan administration. Environmental groups criticized several aspects of Bush's environmental policies, but they conceded that his approach was much more acceptable to them than Reagan's.

Clearly, Bush and his advisers correctly perceived that U.S. public opinion had not shifted toward the conservative position on environmental issues. Rather than embracing the Reagan environmental program, Bush ran from it because of its political liabilities. This is just the opposite of what should have happened if a significant conservative policy and public opinion shift had taken place. If a Reagan revolution had occurred, Bush would have overwhelmingly supported the environmental policies of the Reagan administration.

Clean Water

Liberal environmentalists won a stunning victory over the conservative environmental policies of the Reagan administration with the passage of the Water Quality Act of 1987. The law authorized over $20 billion through 1990 for programs to improve water quality under the Clean Water Act.[47]

The passage of the law meant that President Reagan's environmental program had suffered yet another devastating defeat. Reagan's proposal to cut the funding in the original bill from $18 billion to $6 billion received almost no support in Congress. Since Reagan had so little success in shaping the bill, he vetoed it. Congress easily overrode the president's veto in early 1987. Many Republicans joined the Democrats in the vote to override. Reagan could not even convince his fellow Republicans to support his position.

If a fundamental conservative shift had happened in the 1980s, the funding for the clean-water projects would have been closer to the $6 billion in Reagan's proposal. Where was the conservative Reagan revolution?

Congress also strengthened the guidelines for the protection of drinking water through the reauthorization of the 1974 Safe Drinking Water Act. The law established standards to regulate contaminants in water supplies and set criminal penalties for tampering with water supplies. It also provided for the protection of underground water supplies.

Again Congress largely ignored the objections of the Reagan administration and passed the measure by an overwhelming vote. Despite his reservations, Reagan signed the bill.

Superfund

The passage of the superfund bill dealt another blow to Reagan's environmental policy. Just as with the Water Quality Act, Congress largely ignored the Reagan administration's proposals. Reagan called for less spending and objected to many key aspects of the congressional bill. The president threatened to veto the bill, but he reluctantly signed it. He probably signed the bill because members of Congress made it clear that sufficient votes were available to override a Reagan veto. Again, many congressional Republicans abandoned Reagan's environmental program. The vote in both houses was nearly unanimous for the bill.[48]

The new law substantially increased funding for toxic cleanups and strengthened several provisions of the original act. It allowed people a longer time to sue in cases of toxic dumping. Companies were required to provide information to local communities on their use of chemicals. The measure also contained strict requirements for toxic cleanups.

Clean Air

Congress spent a great deal of time during the 1980s attempting to overhaul the Clean Air Act. A compromise was difficult to achieve because of the need to overcome the strong differences on many provisions. The debate featured such divisions as liberal versus conservative, environmentalists versus industry, and region versus region.

A major breakthrough came in 1990 when the Senate passed a bill to extend the Clean Air Act. It ended many years of struggle and compromise in the Senate. The bill certainly did not represent a victory by conservatives who supported the Reagan environmental philosophy. Majority Leader George Mitchell, well known for his liberal environmental views, played a key role in forging compromises and steering the bill through the Senate. President Bush took a much different approach to the issue than President Reagan. This was another example of how Bush distanced himself from Reagan's unpopular environmental policies. On the acid rain controversy, for instance, Bush stated that he was willing to work with Congress to develop a plan to deal with this problem. Reagan, on the other hand, spent much of his administration attempting to stall any serious consideration of the issue.

Land Use

One of the major environmental issues on land use during the 1980s dealt with the utilization of western public lands.[49] James Watt led the Reagan administration's drive to sell off western public lands and to significantly increase economic development activities on these lands. Environmentalists strongly opposed these plans because of possible harm to the environment.

The result of the battle was a clear-cut victory for the opponents of the Reagan-Watt policy. The administration failed to even come close to achieving its goals. No pattern of widespread sales of public western lands occurred in the 1980s, and no significant increase in economic development happened on these lands. Environmental groups successfully sponsored lawsuits and lobbied Congress and state legislatures. The administration's plan suffered a significant defeat when Watt, the plan's major architect, was forced out. The controversy surrounding Watt discredited the policies he was pursuing.

The opponents defeated the administration on many fronts. For instance, they stopped public land sales with lawsuits. The Forest

Service issued guidelines to limit timber operations in national forests. Congress delayed leases for strip-mining western coal to examine the administration's leasing program. Many dam and water projects were cut back in western areas.[50]

Where was the Reagan revolution? This defeat on land use in western public lands offers another useful test of the Reagan revolution thesis. If a historic conservative policy change had happened in the 1980s, massive areas of the western public lands should have been sold and economic development activities should have increased substantially.

Global Environmental Issues

Just as with domestic environmental policies, environmental groups were not satisfied with the Reagan administration's environmental policies on the international scene. However, they generally conceded that the administration's global environmental policies were less objectionable than its domestic policies. In addition, they noted substantial improvement in global environmental policy from the administration after Reagan's first term.[51]

The policy of the Reagan administration on international environmental issues certainly did not represent a triumph for the Watt-Gorsuch philosophy. For example, Secretary of State George Shultz forced the administration to support a strong treaty to reduce the production of chlorofluorocarbons. Also, Treasury Secretary James A. Baker III became more supportive of including environmental-impact considerations in the analysis of projects sponsored by the U.S. Agency for International Development and the World Bank.

Foreign Policy

No historic shift toward the conservative position on foreign policy happened during the 1980s. In fact, just the opposite occurred. The developments in the Soviet Union and Eastern Europe at the end of the decade crippled conservatives' foreign policy. Super anticommunism was the centerpiece of conservatives' foreign policy beliefs during the post–World War II era. This shaped not only their ideas about U.S. relations with the Soviet Union and

China, but with most of the rest of the world as well. They attacked liberals for being soft on communism and claimed that they could better handle the communist menace. The end of communist regimes in Eastern Europe and the demise of the Communist party in the Soviet Union significantly decreased hard-line conservatives' power in making U.S. foreign policy.

Instead of entering the 1990s dominating U.S. foreign policy, hard-line anticommunist groups faced the new decade in a weakened position.[52] Most of these groups faced the grim prospects of declining membership, decreasing resources, and fewer Americans willing to listen to their message. The demise of the American Security Council (ASC) illustrates the plight of these conservative groups. The ASC is a grass-roots organization specializing in the promotion of the conservative position on foreign and military issues. It was forced to initiate a series of major cutbacks in the late 1980s because of declining support, which resulted from the thaw in the cold war. They scrapped plans for a national computer network that would have allowed the ASC to contact its members concerning impending votes in Congress. Dwindling resources forced the ASC to end its Political Action Committee (PAC) which just five years before had spent over $200,000 on campaigns. Furthermore, from 1985 to 1989, ASC's membership decreased substantially from about three hundred thousand to around one hundred and fifty thousand.[53]

With the power of conservatives sapped by the easing of U.S.– Soviet relations, they were having difficulty selling their anticommunist message. In early 1990 Defense Secretary Richard Cheney received a cool reception in Congress when he presented the Bush administration's plans to increase the defense budget by only a few percent. Senate Armed Services Chairman Sam Nunn, who has a hawkish reputation, told Cheney and President Bush that their plan would not receive much support in Congress. According to Nunn, the administration had to rethink its position and reduce its military spending goals considerably because of the cold war thaw. Even some conservative Republicans (e.g., Senator John McCain) criticized the Bush administration for its unrealistically high proposals for defense spending.

The Reagan administration did follow a conservative course in many aspects of foreign policy and had some success in promoting these conservative policies. In some areas such as arms control, however, President Reagan reversed his position and did not follow the staunchly conservative line. In several other areas (e.g., U.S. policy toward South Africa) liberals defeated Reagan's policies in Congress. So, overall, the foreign policy results of the 1980s were a mixed bag of conservative victories, liberal victories, moderate compromises, and developments (e.g., fall of communism in Eastern Europe) that almost everyone supported. No consistent pattern of conservative triumphs can be found in the foreign policy record of the 1980s.

Soviet Union

Liberals, especially since the 1960s, stressed the need for peaceful coexistence with the Soviet Union. They not only strongly opposed the communist regime in the Soviet Union and most of its foreign policy, but they also emphasized the need for easing tensions through agreements such as arms control pacts. Conservatives, especially the right-wing faction of the Republican party represented by Ronald Reagan, attacked liberals for what they considered to be a soft and naive approach to the U.S.S.R. They wanted the United States to stand up and take an even stronger stand against the Soviet Union. Reagan and many of his supporters were skeptical of agreements signed with the Soviet Union, even those negotiated by Republican presidents. According to Reagan, these agreements only served to strengthen the U.S.S.R.

President Reagan followed his staunchly anticommunist position early in his administration. He made speeches, such as the famous "evil empire" speech, in which he strongly denounced the Soviet government and its activities throughout the world. The administration issued a policy on arms control that stressed Reagan's skepticism about the possibility of obtaining arms pacts with the Soviet Union that would be in the best interest of the United States. The Reagan administration's arms control statements set a policy course that differed significantly from the policies of recent administrations. In addition, President Reagan lobbied Congress for an unprecedented defense buildup to counter the military power of the Soviet Union.

Then, in one of the most amazing and significant policy reversals in modern American politics, Ronald Reagan made a 180 degree turn and started to follow the liberals' policies. He pursued a policy of easing U.S.–Soviet tensions. He met with Mikhail Gorbachev several times and sought agreements to improve relations. He even praised Gorbachev and made speeches about the Soviet Union with a substantially different tone than the "evil empire" speech.

And finally, President Reagan signed, and the Senate approved, a treaty with the Soviet Union to ban intermediate-range nuclear force (INF) missiles. The INF treaty represented an almost complete reversal of the Reagan administration's previous stance on nuclear arms control.

Leaders of several major conservative groups vehemently attacked Reagan for signing the treaty. Howard Phillips, president of the Conservative Caucus, was quoted as calling President Reagan a "useful idiot for Soviet propaganda."[54] These conservative leaders denounced the treaty because they believed it helped the Soviets and harmed the U.S. military and foreign policy position. Their criticisms were similar to Reagan's critical statements in past years about previous arms control agreements with the Soviet Union.

President Reagan also had difficulty gaining support for the treaty from conservative Republican senators. As a result of this strange turn of events, Reagan's major Senate opposition to the INF treaty came from conservative Republicans. Liberal Democrats, on the other hand, were among the strongest supporters. The President had to try to convince these conservative Republican senators to ignore what the old Ronald Reagan had said about arms control and U.S.–Soviet relations. Several conservative Republican senators remained disappointed with the new liberal Reagan policies and continued their fight against the INF treaty.

This staunch opposition by conservative groups and several congressional conservatives to the INF treaty and Reagan's general policy toward the Soviet Union is one of the best pieces of evidence to disprove the conservative Reagan revolution thesis. The INF treaty was the most important development in U.S.–Soviet relations during the Reagan administration. Therefore, a fundamental conservative change in U.S. foreign policy did not occur because many conservatives staunchly opposed Reagan's actions on this key policy development.

If a historic conservative policy shift had happened, conservatives such as Howard Phillips and Jesse Helms would have been praising the Reagan administration for its hard-line policy against the Soviet Union. Instead, these conservatives were attacking President Reagan in the late 1980s for supporting a key aspect of the liberals' foreign policy agenda.

China

Before the improvement of U.S.–Chinese relations, liberals and conservatives differed on their proposals for American policy toward China. Many liberals wanted to recognize the communist regime and try to ease tensions between the two countries, while conservatives favored the continuation of a hard-line policy against the communist government. The détente policy of the Nixon administration toward China created controversy within the conservative movement. Some conservatives reluctantly accepted the policy, whereas others remained skeptical.

Ronald Reagan was one of the conservatives who remained skeptical about several aspects of U.S. policy that had developed toward China in the 1970s. In the early 1980s the Reagan administration considered recognizing the government of Taiwan. This would have greatly angered the communist leaders in China, but it would have struck a blow for the past policies of conservatives.

The administration never followed through on this policy. President Reagan basically continued the policy of détente toward China. No fundamental conservative shift developed in U.S.–Chinese relations.

This is another example of Reagan and the legitimacy factor. By not attempting to significantly change the détente policy toward China, Reagan put his mark of approval on this policy. In the future, conservative Republican presidents will have great difficulty trying to reverse U.S. détente policy with China.

U.S.–China relations during the first part of the Bush administration also showed that no historic conservative change had developed. President Bush followed the outlines of the policy established in the 1970s. In fact, Democrats turned the tables on Bush by charging that his administration did not take a hard enough stand against China's communist government. Many Democrats called for stronger measures than Bush advocated against the Chinese regime when it crushed the prodemocracy movement. Democrats also criticized Bush for sending a secret delegation to China too soon after the prodemocracy crackdown and for opposing a bill in Congress designed to protect Chinese students in this country.

Africa

The two issues in Africa which gained the most attention in the United States during the 1980s were the poverty and starvation in several parts of Africa and racial politics in South Africa. In both situations, liberal Democrats took the offensive and denied the Reagan administration the opportunity to pursue a new conservative policy course in Africa.

In U.S. relations with Third World countries, liberals often focus on economic and humanitarian aid, while conservatives often stress the containment policy and military aid. In the 1980s, the widespread economic problems and starvation in several African countries favored the implementation of the liberal approach. With Americans seeing starving African children on the evening news night after night, liberals could focus American policy toward Africa on the need for humanitarian and general economic aid. President Reagan was forced to go along with the congressional initiatives on African aid. Under these circumstances, any administration policy of substantially shifting the emphasis toward military aid was unlikely.

The Reagan administration did try to follow a more conservative policy in its relations with South Africa. The administration embarked on a policy of quiet diplomacy and less confrontation with the South African government. Also, some comments by President Reagan indicated that his administration planned a significant shift in policy toward more acceptance of the government's policies and less support for the blacks' cause.

A battle developed over South African policy as liberals criticized Reagan's approach. The controversy ended up in Congress and reached its peak in the debates on U.S. sanctions. In 1986 Congress passed a bill outlining economic sanctions against South Africa. President Reagan vetoed the bill because he believed the sanctions were counterproductive. In a stunning defeat, Congress easily overrode the president's veto. Even several conservative Republicans voted against Reagan. Therefore, the administration was unable to change U.S. policy toward South Africa. Liberals demonstrated that Reagan's conservative approach was out step with public opinion, Congress, and even many Republicans.

Middle East

During the 1980s, very little changed in the Israeli-Arab conflict as their stalemate continued. President Reagan supported the broad outline of U.S.–Middle East policy. His administration continued to support Israel and to encourage both sides in the conflict to move toward a peace settlement. In the late 1980s, the administration made some attempt to tilt U.S. policy a little more toward the Arab side with discussions about recognizing the Palestine Liberation Organization (PLO). This initiative, however, ended up having only a small impact on Middle East policy. So in 1989, President Bush and the Democratic Congrss inherited the U.S. policy toward the Israeli-Arab conflict, which was in the same basic form as it had been in 1980.

Besides the overall Israeli-Arab confrontation, U.S. policy in the Middle East also focused on Lebanon during the 1980s. Reagan's policy suffered a major setback here. The President sent Marines into Lebanon and stationed ships offshore as part of a peacekeeping mission. These actions ended in disaster, as 241 Marines died in a bombing at a barracks. Although Reagan claimed the United States would keep its military presence in Lebanon, the troops were removed and the ships moved from the offshore positions.

This humiliating defeat harmed Reagan's militaristic, hard-line conservative foreign policy. It brought into question the ability of the United States to use military force as an effective tool of foreign policy. The episode also tarnished Reagan's image as a swashbuckling, macho commander-in-chief. Critics charged that the Reagan administration placed the Marines in a situation where they had one arm tied behind their backs because of unclear military plans and objectives.

Antiterrorism was another key part of the Reagan administration's Middle East policy. President Reagan called for a conservative antiterrorism policy of no negotiations or deals and strong retaliation in most cases. This approach could presumably be differentiated from the liberals' weak and ineffective policy of deals and capitulations.

Despite some success with this policy, especially in relation to Libya, the administration's antiterrorism policy ended in shambles because of the Iran-Contra scandal. After all of the statments supporting a hard-line against terrorism, Reagan almost completely lost his credibility on this issue by trying to make a deal with Iran to free American hostages. Reagan looked like a fool and a hypocrite as he practiced completely the opposite of what he had preached on terrorism. He had said that allowing terrorists to make gains through negotiations would only encourage more terrorist acts, yet he attempted to provide aid to terrorists through negotiations. Certainly Reagan's actions did encourage many terrorist groups to step up their activities. Antiterrorism is another example where Reagan's actions discredited conservative policy.

Latin America

Four of the main aspects of U.S.–Latin American relations dealt with anticommunism, democracy, drugs, and debts. No pattern of historic victories for conservative policy can be found in these four areas.

Despite the huge size of Latin America and the importance of many of its countries, most media attention on U.S. policy in the region was focused on one small country—Nicaragua. The conflict within American politics over Nicaraguan policy overshadowed U.S. relations with the other countries in Latin America.

The outcome of this fierce battle over Nicaraguan policy was not a victory for conservative policy. While the Reagan administration won some important votes in Congress on aid to the Nicaraguan Contras, liberals defeated the administration several times. Liberals restricted U.S. aid to the Contras for several years. Also, public opinion polls showed strong opposition among Americans toward Reagan's policies. The Iran-Contra scandal dealt another blow to the administration's Nicaraguan policy. The revelations of illegal actions by members of the administration severely damaged Reagan's credibility on the issue.

The Contras faced a bleak future in the late 1980s. Conservatives had little chance to build a majority in Congress to support a significant increase in Contra military aid. President Bush and congressional Democrats worked out a deal in 1989 which would lead to an almost certain end to the Contra movement.

Reagan and his conservative Nicaraguan policy gained a little respect from some commentators when Daniel Ortega, the Sandinista leader, was defeated in the 1990 Nicaraguan presidential election. Many conservatives claimed that Reagan's policy produced this election result. On the other hand, liberals claimed success for their policy of supporting the Central American peace process, which had been led by the president of Costa Rica. They argued that the Central American peace process produced the Nicaraguan election result, not Reagan's policy of continued fighting. President Bush emphasized the success of the bipartisan policy of his administration. He did not give all the credit for the election outcome to Reagan's pro-Contra strategy.

Not much change occurred in U.S. policy toward El Salvador during the 1980s. The war between the government and leftist guerrillas continued through the decade. The administration did stress more of an anticommunist theme in U.S. policy toward El Salvador. Reagan was also more willing to accept right-wing parties in the El Salvadoran government than the Carter administration would have. But little changed in the overall policy of supporting the government and seeking peace.

As part of the administration's containment policy, President Reagan proposed a Caribbean Basin Initiative to improve economic conditions in this region. Although the initiative stressed trade and tax credits, the proposed increase in foreign aid made it sound like a proposal of a liberal Democrat. Moreover, Reagan damaged the initiative by supporting a sugar program which led to a considerable decrease in sugar imports.

Reagan followed his conservative ideology and strongly opposed the Cuban government. No major improvements in U.S.–Cuba relations occurred in the 1980s. This opposition to Castro's regime, however, was nothing new. Reagan's Cuban policy certainly fit within the guidelines set by previous administrations since 1961.

Reagan's policy was similar to past administrations on the pro-democracy movements. The 1980s witnessed the successful transition from military governments to elected civilian governments in

several Latin American countries. Reagan praised these developments and supported the new democratic regimes.

If a liberal Democrat had been president rather than Reagan, he/
she would probably have pursued a policy of greater opposition to
the military leaders and more support for the civilian democratic
forces when the military regimes were still in power. But overall, a
liberal Democratic president would have followed the same broad
policy as Reagan of encouraging and supporting civilian democrat-
ically-elected governments in Latin America.

The drug war was another key element of U.S. relations with
several Latin American countries. Hence the administration followed a conservative policy of a supposedly aggressive stance
against drug producers. Reagan talked tough about the need to
deter drug traffic by taking strong action against the flow of drugs
into the United States and aiding anti-drug efforts in drug-producing
countries.

Rather than showing the effectiveness of conservative drug policy, the Reagan administration's approach raised many questions
about the adequacy of conservative policies. When Reagan left
office, the consensus in the country was that the drug war was
being lost. Despite the efforts of the Reagan administration to
substantially curtail the drug traffic, massive amounts of illegal
drugs continued to pour into the United States. Many Americans
saw Reagan's conservative drug policies in Latin America as a
tremendous failure.

President Reagan's anticommunist policies and drug policies led
to the bizarre situation that developed in Panama during the late
1980s. The CIA had paid Panamanian dictator Manual Noriega to
provide the U.S. with help in pursuing its containment policies in
Central America, even though Noriega was a suspected drug dealer.
Reagan sustained a humiliating defeat when his administration
failed to oust Noriega and try him on drug charges.

Finally, the Reagan administration's policy on Latin American
debt did not represent a landmark shift in a conservative direction.
The United States and many Latin American countries faced the
enormous problem of deciding how to handle the incredible amount
of loans countries in the region were unable to pay off. At one end
of the spectrum of policy alternatives were proposals to force
draconian measures onto these countries so the U.S. could receive

at least some of its money back from the loans. At the other end were proposals to largely forget much of the debt so Latin American countries would not have to suffer the horrendous economic consequences of the debt payments. The Reagan administration followed a moderate course and not a conservative hard-line policy. Reagan's Treasury secretaries sought to negotiate with U.S. banks and Latin American countries to establish more realistic payment schedules.

Europe

Since U.S. policy toward Western Europe remained largely unchanged during the 1980s, no fundamental shift toward either the liberal or conservative direction could be found. The Reagan administration continued U.S. support for the democratic governments in Western Europe and for the maintenance of NATO to prevent a Soviet takeover of Europe. Reagan did not develop policy proposals that would significantly change the previous patterns of U.S.–Western European relations that had existed during the post–World War II era.

Economic affairs largely dominated the relationship between the United States and Western Europe. Ironically, two of the major complaints Western European leaders had against Reagan's economic policies involved situations in which the administration violated conservative economic principles. First, Europeans criticized the Reagan administration on several occasions for violating free trade by restricting their imports into the United States. Second, Western European leaders repeatedly criticized the U.S. government about the huge budget deficit. They believed that the U.S. deficits were detrimental to the European and world economies. An absolutely incredible foreign policy exchange developed in which Western European officials would attack President Reagan's budget policies, which were completely contrary to his stated beliefs. Reagan would then respond by defending these deficit policies even though he stated many times, pre- and post-1981, that he opposed deficit spending and supported balanced budgets.

Of course the main development in Eastern Europe during the decade was the decline of communism in 1989. This was not a triumph of American conservatives over liberals since everyone in the political mainstream favored the demise of communist govern- ments and Soviet influence in Eastern Europe. U.S. conservatives may have made some short-term gains because a Republican presi- dent was in office during the fall of these communist governments. But as mentioned earlier, the decline of communism will have a devastating impact on conservatives' role in making U.S. foreign policy. They must adjust to the new political environment in which anticommunism, their main concern in international relations, is no longer the major aspect of U.S. foreign policy.

The movement toward the reunification of Germany was another extremely significant development in Europe at the end of the 1980s. Since President Bush and the Democratic leadership ac- cepted German reunification, there was no sharp partisan or ideo- logical debate on this development. Therefore, it did not represent a significant conservative policy victory over liberal policy.

Japan

U.S relations with Japan during the 1980s had some similarities to relations with Western Europe. First, no significant conservative changes developed in the policies that make up the relationship. Second, economic issues dominated the relationship during the decade.

Just as with Western European leaders, the Japanese leadership criticized several American economic policies. The huge budget deficit was a major target of their criticism. On the other hand, many U.S. leaders and interest groups complained about Japanese economic policies, especially their trade policy. The president and Congress faced enormous pressure to restrict the growing Japanese influence on the U.S. economy. President Reagan followed his free- trade philosophy on some Japanese trade issues, but supported trade restrictions on others.

Social Policy

Most of the conservatives' social policy goals are related to the New Right's social agenda. New Right conservatives concentrate on issues such as pornography, women's rights, minority rights, and prayers in public schools. They are disturbed by the moral and social direction in which the country has been heading since the 1960s. They believe the United States needs to return to the morality of earlier periods.

An examination of government policy and major social trends indicates that the United States did not experience a New Right revolution during the 1980s. While New Right conservatives won some victories, they failed to enact the major parts of their agenda. Most importantly, liberals defeated every constitutional amendment proposed by the New Right. In addition, New Right conservatives failed to significantly alter the social trends they so strongly opposed.

Level of Morality

When Ronald Reagan entered office, he and Mrs. Reagan made pledges about leading the country into a new period of higher morality. This new era of morality was to be based on principles, such as integrity, that were proclaimed by New Right.

The unprecedented number of scandals in the Reagan administration made President Reagan look like a hypocrite. The many questionable and outright illegal activities of high officials in the Reagan administration convinced many Americans that the level of morality in the country was declining, not elevating, to a new golden age. Officials at the White House, the EPA, Defense Department, Interior Department, and many other places were involved in scandals. The Iran-Contra investigations even raised serious questions about whether President Reagan engaged in illegal and unconstitutional activities. Incredibly, the revelations of scandalous behavior in the Reagan administration continued even after Reagan left office. Investigations uncovered a massive amount of fraud and abuse in the Department of Housing and Urban Development. Furthermore, the continuation into 1989 and 1990 of the trials stemming from the Iran-Contra scandal tarnished the reputation of the Reagan administration even more.

These scandals not only weakened Reagan's role as moral leader, but harmed the whole New Right agenda. With these scandals, conservatives had difficulty taking the moral high ground in debates on social issues.

Religious Values

The Religious Right is a major component of the New Right movement. It is primarily made up of Christians in several conservative Protestant churches. They believe Americans need a religious revival to counter the immoral societal trends which have swept the country since the beginning of the 1960s.

One of the New Right's primary policy goals is to enact a constitutional amendment to allow prayers in public schools. They believe that bringing organized prayers and other religious activities back into public schools will help to increase the influence of religious values among America's youth.

In one of the devastating defeats for the New Right, Congress repeatedly refused to adopt the constitutional amendment on school prayers. The New Right conservatives could not even get over the first hurdle of a two-thirds vote in Congress. Certainly if a conservative Reagan revolution had taken place, the school-prayer amendment should have swept through Congress and three fourths of the state legislatures within the first few years of the 1980s. The New Right also lost a key court decision when the Supreme Court struck down the Alabama law on a moment of silence in schools.[55]

In the 1980s, the Religious Right pursued another religious-educational policy goal by attacking the teaching of evolution in schools. They developed a method to present the biblical explanation of creation through their creation science teachings. They wanted schools to teach the biblical explanation as a substitute or alternative to the theory of evolution. Whereas the Religious Right won a few victories in some states, their attack on the theory of evolution suffered a major defeat when the Supreme Court ruled against the Louisiana law that provided for the teaching of creation science.[56]

Besides these defeats, the Religious Right movement was damaged by the enormous media attention given the scandals involving several television evangelists. Television preachers are the most famous members of the Religious Right. The shocking revelations about several of the most prominent TV preachers tarnished the image of the Religious Right. The movement had more difficulty receiving serious attention for its proposals when these preachers, who were perceived as important leaders of the movement, were discredited and became the target of numerous jokes.

Overall, the Religious Right did not become a major political force in the 1980s, as many political analysts had predicted after the 1980 election. Election studies indicate that Ronald Reagan and George Bush won their elections for reasons other than support from the Religious Right. Also, religious conservatives failed miserably in their attempts to influence congressional elections. They successfully influenced the outcome of only a handful of congressional races during the 1980s. These few successes must be balanced against the races in which the winning candidate used the Religious Right's support of the opposing candidate to his/her advantage. David Price, for example, fought off a Religious Right attack to win North Carolina's Fourth District in the 1986 House election.[57]

The crushing defeat of Pat Robertson in the 1988 presidential race also demonstrated the weakness of the Religious Right's political power. National polls showed that Robertson had very little support in the country. Studies done on his positive and negative ratings indicated that he had almost the highest amount of negative ratings among all the Republican and Democratic candidates. And, according to these polls, much of this negative reaction developed from Robertson's policies and religious connections.

Women's Rights

The New Right conservatives oppose the policies of feminist groups and support a return to a more traditional role for women in society. They oppose many of the efforts by women's rights groups to significantly expand women's influence in American society.

An analysis of numerous social, political, and economic indicators demonstrates that New Right conservatives failed to reverse the trend toward greater equality for women. The 1980s were not a period of historic change in which women's rights returned to the conditions of several decades ago. There was no significant reversal of the trend of more women attending college, graduate school, and professional schools. Many more women continued to enter the workforce outside the home. More women than ever before moved into prestigious jobs such as lawyers, doctors, and business executives. No reversal can be found in women's participation in government, as more women sought public office.

Women's rights' advocates were upset with many of the policies supported by the Reagan administration and congressional conservatives. They also wanted the pace of change toward greater equality for women to speed up. However, they would still have to admit that the 1980s could not be seen as a decade in which the New Right successfully moved the role of women back to what it had been several decades ago.

As the survey research data in chapter 2 pointed out, no shift in public opinion occurred in the 1980s toward the New Right's position on women's role in society. In fact, a comparison of public opinion polls from the 1960s and 1980s indicates a significant shift toward the liberal position on most women's rights issues.

More, not less, attention was paid to women voters in the 1980s. Reports of increased voter turnout among women compared to men encouraged both parties to design strategies to gain more votes from women. Both parties also paid more attention because of the gender gap. The gender gap discussions began when public opinion studies found a small shift of women towards the Democrats and of men towards the Republicans. With the gender gap, Republicans began to worry about how to stop their losses among women, while Democrats plotted how to exploit their new gain.

Granted, the Equal Rights Amendment (ERA) died in the early 1980s. This defeat, however, was not caused by a fundamental conservative shift in the political climate in the 1980s. Public opinion studies continued to show overwhelming support for the ERA during the 1980s.

In addition, the ERA proponents also had trouble winning in the last few state legislatures in the 1970s. Therefore, the ERA's problems in the early 1980s were a continuation of the problems it encountered in the 1970s.

Moreover, the main reason why the ERA lost is because of the high proportion of votes needed to pass an amendment. This is the main reason why most amendments fail. The constitutional framers created an amendment process that is very difficult to successfully complete. The primary way amendments have been considered requires a two-thirds vote in Congress to propose an amendment and then the acceptance by three-fourths of the state legislatures to ratify it. Such a difficult process gives the opponents of an amendment a big advantage, since they need to win just a small minority of either Congress or the state legislatures. The ERA received an enormous amount of support by winning over two-thirds of the vote in Congress and about two-thirds of the state legislatures. The ERA opponents were able to defeat the amendment with only limited support because the playing field is set up to greatly favor opponents of amendments.

The Family and Child Care

To the disappointment of the New Right, the proportion of families made up of traditional families (i.e., a father with a job, a mother at home, and children) continued to decline during th 1980s. This trend focused media attention on the many families with single women as the head of household and families with two wage earners. It also focused attention on issues related to this new era of family patterns. This new attention given to the problems of nontraditional families aided feminist groups in their battle against the New Right. For instance, the changing family patterns forced policymakers to consider government programs to help families obtain adequate child care when the parents worked. Both parties scrambled to formulate child-care proposals to attract voter support. Even conservative Republicans who have been leaders of New Right causes (e.g., Senator Orrin Hatch) reluctantly accepted the need for childcare legislation. Child care was one of the major issues in the 1988 presidential election. George Bush and Michael Dukakis presented different approaches to providing child-care options for Americans.

The prominence of child care as an issue provides another excellent illustration to show that no fundamental conservative policy change happened in the 1980s. A New Right revolution would have produced a political climate in which liberals would not have been able to force the political system to consider increasing the government's role in child care.

Abortion

Conservatives' views on abortion provide another good example of the contradictions in their ideology. The government's role in society would expand enormously if abortions were to become illegal again. This obviously conflicts with conservatives' belief in less government. The government would need to initiate a massive effort to stop an activity that has the approval of a majority of Americans either in all or some cases. In addition, the government would need to develop an organized network to stop the importation of the new European abortion pill.

Banning abortions has been one of the most important goals of the New Right. If the 1980s had witnessed a conservative Reagan revolution, the New Right would have had enough power to make abortions illegal within the first few years of the decade. Instead, the pro-choice movement showed that they had more strength than the abortion foes by keeping abortion legal throughout the decade. Just as with the school-prayer amendment, the New Right conservatives did not even gain enough support to get their proposed constitutional amendment to ban abortions through Congress.

During the 1981–88 period the Supreme Court allowed some restrictions on abortion, but continued to uphold the right of women to have abortions. The court continued to support the basic principles of the *Roe v. Wade* decision.[58] A conservative Reagan revolution certainly should have produced a Supreme Court decision overturning *Roe v. Wade* during Reagan's presidency.

In 1989 the Supreme Court changed course somewhat on abortion in the *Webster* case.[59] Although the case did not overturn *Roe v. Wade,* it did add important new governmental restrictions on abortion.

Political commentators generally thought that the *Webster* decision would greatly help conservatives, Republicans, and the antiabortion movement, and substantially hurt liberals, Democrats, and the pro-choice movement. Certainly the decision did provide some gains for the antiabortion forces. What happened during the rest of 1989 and into 1990, however, did not follow most of the earlier predictions. Liberals, Democrats, and the pro-choice movement staged a comeback on the abortion issue. The threat posed by the *Webster* decision invigorated the pro-choice movement with a new spirit and more resources and support. Previously, the media often presented the abortion issue as a battle with the antiabortion groups on offense and the pro-choice groups on defense. Pro-choice was often portrayed as a relatively weak movement scrambling to fight the powerful advances of the opposition. But after *Webster,* the media portrayed the pro-choice movement more as a political force that had acquired new strength and had changed from defense to offense.

Contrary to most predictions, the post-*Webster* abortion debate in 1989 and 1990 created more problems for the Republicans than the Democrats. Many moderate Republicans warned of impending disaster if their party did not change its antiabortion stance. Their statements heated up the intraparty battle between the moderates and conservatives. As an indication of the shift in support toward the pro-choice view, President Bush and national party chairman Lee Atwater emphasized that both sides in the debate were welcome in the party.

Instead of running from the pro-choice position, many Democrats adopted it as a major part of their platform and effectively used it against their Republican opponents. In the 1989 governor's race in Virginia, for example, L. Douglas Wilder, the Democratic candidate, strongly endorsed the pro-choice position and often criticized his Republican opponent for his antiabortion views. Believing his abortion position was hurting his campaign, the Republican candidate tried to modify his position. A number of political analysts concluded that Wilder's handling of the abortion issue was an important factor contributing to his election victory. This successful use of the pro-choice position occurred in a fairly conservative southern state. Granted, Virginia in 1989 was not as conservative as it had been several decades before, but still Virginia is not a hotbed of liberalism. If a substantial conservative shift in public opinion occurred during the 1980s, a gubernatorial candidate in Virginia would not have been able to gain support with a pro-choice strategy.

The new power of the pro-choice movement could also be seen in the 1990 gubernatorial races. Many candidates adopted pro-choice positions. For example, five Democratic candidates, all leading in the polls for their party's nomination, switched to the abortion-rights position.[60]

Sexual Behavior

The New Right was unable to initiate a sexual counterrevolution in the 1980s. Studies on sexual behavior did not indicate that a drastic shift in either sexual beliefs or practices occurred in the 1980s.

The AIDS epidemic was one of the major developments to affect sexual behavior in the 1980s. In one aspect, the disease, by focusing attention on the possible harmful effects of promiscuous sexual behavior, helped the Religious Rights' efforts in social policy. In other ways, however, the attention given to AIDS helped their opponents. With the AIDS crisis, health officials stressed the need for sex education. Surgeon General C. Everett Koop shocked the Religious Right and the whole conservative movement when he made a strong plea for sex education in the schools. He even stated that it should start at the lowest grade possible.[61] Here was the Surgeon General in the Reagan administration promoting an activity that many conservatives considered a menace to society. Where was the conservative Reagan revolution?

The New Right received another shock when many health officials began advising people to use "safe sex" practices to combat AIDS. Public service advertisements began to appear with messages about the benefits of certain types of sexual practices and the risks of others. Advertisements promoting the use of condoms were aired. Without the AIDS epidemic, media executives would have been afraid to air announcements of this type.

Sexually-Explicit Presentations

Another major part of the New Right's social agenda is the effort to reverse the trend toward more sexually-explicit presentations in books, movies, records, and on television. New Right conservatives wanted more restrictive obscenity laws and stronger enforcement of these laws.

The position of conservatives on obscenity is another illustration of why a fundamental conservative policy change would be impossible. Here again, New Right conservatives want to greatly expand the role of government in society. If the government passed and strongly enforced obscenity laws that were much more restrictive than the present ones, governmental units at all levels would need to significantly increase their resources devoted to implementing this type of law. Much more manpower and other resources would have to be allocated to monitor what people write, read, hear, and see. And then after Americans' activities had been monitored, the court systems would need to expand so the people arrested for violating the new pornography laws could be prosecuted. Finally, the government would need to enlarge the prison capacity to handle the influx of Americans convicted under the new laws. These citizens jailed for violating the new pornography laws would join those convicted of antiabortion laws as well as other new laws the New Right would have passed to regulate objectionable behavior. Obviously, the expanded influence of government in American society produced by more restrictive obscenity laws would conflict with the ideal of having less government.

In the 1980s the New Right movement failed to lead the country into a historic conservative shift in how sexual activities are portrayed. The trend toward more explicit discussions and presentations of sex was not reversed during the decade. No nationwide network of censorship boards was established to ban books, TV shows, plays, movies, and records. Magazines with nude pictures, R- and X-rated movies, books with "four letter words" and highly-detailed descriptions of sexual activities continued. Popular prime-time TV shows, such as "thirtysomething" and "L.A. Law," showed more explicit sex scenes than shows of previous decades. Soap operas competed for viewers with sexy promotional ads. The expansion of cable television provided Americans with more opportunities to see more programs considered offensive by the New Right. Many teenagers and preteens watched sexy record videos on MTV. The enormous expansion of VCRs in homes allowed many people to see and hear all parts of movies rather than missing the words and scenes censored by the television networks.

The Supreme Court did not make any landmark decisions in the 1980s significantly restricting the presentation of sexual activities. The major obscenity case of the past twenty years was *Miller v. California*.[62] In this 1973 decision, the Court set down three guidelines to define obscenity. Rather than moving in a new direction in the 1980s, the Court modified the *Miller* standards in sexual cases. In *Pope v. Illinois*, for instance, the Court ruled that the third *Miller* standard—whether a work has artistic, political, literary or scientific value—need not obtain the approval of a majority under "contemporary community standards" to receive protection.[63]

Opponents of the Court's obscenity rulings made some progress, as a few state courts refused to accept the *Miller* guidelines.[64] For example, the Oregon Supreme Court opposed the prosecution of people in the state on standards that it considered vague and deviating from Oregon's social and political culture.[65]

The New Right had some limited success in Congress. Some members of Congress attempted to end telephone services that provide callers with sexually-explicit messages by passing a ban on "dial-a-porn." The Supreme Court, however, ruled that the statute had not been drawn up in a sufficiently narrow manner.[66]

During the 1980s, Congress also strengthened the laws against child pornography. However, this was not a significant triumph for the New Right conservatives because their opponents generally accept many aspects of these laws. Critics of obscenity laws are concerned with attempts to limit freedom of speech and press for adults.

Social Programs

A major feature of the New Deal and post–New Deal eras has been the proliferation of federal social programs. Several hundred billion dollars are spent on these programs each year. If a fundamental conservative policy change happened in the 1980s, most of these programs should have been eliminated, or at least drastically curtailed. However, this did not happen. All of the major social programs survived and the spending on these programs increased enormously. As mentioned in the budget section, the social programs, in relation to the overall economy, even increased in the early 1980s.

Supporters of the Reagan revolution thesis pointed out that cuts were made in the funding of several social programs. While this is true, several points need to be made to put this into perspective.

First, the cutbacks in most social programs produced only cuts in the rate of growth. The budgets of almost all of these programs increased from year to year. After the news stories of the spending cuts in 1981, many Americans had the impression that the spending was drastically lower in these programs from one year to the next. In reality, most of the federal programs expanded by billions of dollars, and some social programs increased at a faster rate than the economy and the overall federal budget.

Second, the fact that some social programs in the 1980s grew at a slower rate compared to previous periods hardly constitutes sufficient evidence to proclaim that a historic fundamental change occurred in public policy. For the political system to enter a new era of conservative policy, it would be reasonable to expect that most of these programs would have been wiped out.

Third, the decline in the growth rate of social programs began in the 1970s. This trend did not start in the 1980s, but continued from previous years. The federal social programs grew rapidly in the late 1960s and early 1970s. The rate of growth then started decreasing in the last half of the 1970s. This trend toward a lower growth rate continued into the 1980s.

Even at a lower rate of growth, spending on the human resources programs, as measured by the percent of GNP, remained above the 1979 level for all the 1980s. In addition, spending on social programs was much higher in the 1980s than in the 1960s. Human resources spending was 7.1 percent of GNP in 1969 and 11.9 percent in 1985. How could a landmark conservative change have taken place when spending on social programs was much higher in the 1980s than in the supposedly liberal 1960s?

A declining growth rate for the federal social programs was inevitable. The economy was not expanding fast enough to provide sufficient wealth to fund a high growth rate for these programs. The economic problems of the 1970s and early 1980s made the situation even worse. Furthermore, many of the major programs cost much more than most analysts had predicted.

In addition, the continual expansion of Social Security spending lessened the possibility that other social programs would continue to enjoy high growth rates. The Social Security program is so large that its growth puts pressure on spending in other parts of the budget. Its growth lowers the growth potential of other spending areas because both cutting Social Security and significantly increasing taxes are politically difficult.

This decline in the growth rate of social programs was not the result of a conservative shift in the country. Public opinion polls showed strong support for most of these programs during the 1970s and 1980s. Much of the problem for these programs was that liberals were victims of their own success. Liberals passed many new social programs in the 1960s; enough resources were available to fund a high growth rate for a few years. But eventually the federal budget plate became overcrowded, and Congress had to slow the spending increases for many social programs.

Fourth, the assault on social spending by the Reagan administration and conservatives damaged the programs in the short run, but aided their long-term prospects. Similar to the environmental programs, President Reagan won some early battles but lost the war. The ability to survive the conservative onslaught improved the chances that federal social programs will survive and prosper in future decades.

This is another excellent example of the legitimacy factor. President Eisenhower enhanced the legitimacy of the New Deal programs. Preident Reagan continued to aid the legitimacy of the New Deal, but also added the Great Society programs. The social programs survived and even grew by many billions of dollars, despite eight years of a conservative president fighting for social spending cuts and six years of a Republican-controlled Senate. This fact increased the perception with the public and within the political system that these programs have a legitimate place in the federal budget and American society.[67]

The legitimacy and long-term prospects of the programs were improved in several ways. In the first place, Reagan never proposed eliminating the social programs. His proposals called for maintaining a "social safety net," which meant a continuation of most social programs, but in a scaled-back form.

In addition, Reagan's defeats in Congress on spending cuts helped the social programs' legitimacy. After 1981, congressional majorities developed to stop Reagan from making further cuts in social programs. Each year, the president would send a list of proposals to make more cuts, and Congress would usually ignore the requests. Public opinion polls showing majority support for the social programs and the congressional opposition to further cuts demonstrated the depth of the support for the programs.

Furthermore, Reagan and congressional conservatives became victims of their own success. The survivability and long-term prospects of the federal social programs were improved by the cutbacks in the early 1980s. By successfully passing new restrictions and eligibility standards, conservatives weakened their chance of getting even greater cutbacks. Conservatives had claimed that cuts were needed because of the waste and abuse in the social programs. With the passage of more restrictive standards, however, fewer people would buy the conservatives' case for more cutbacks, because it was assumed that much of the waste and abuse had been eliminated from the programs.

Finally, the long-term prospects of the federal social programs were enhanced because the failures of Reagan's social-welfare plans raised serious questions about the effectiveness of the conservative approach. President Reagan promised that the country's basic social-welfare needs could be met even with cutbacks in govern- ment programs. Since Reagan and many conservatives assumed that much of the social programs' budgets was wasted on inefficient administration and abuse, a policy of better management could produce even better services for the needy at lower costs. There- fore, the administration promised less government along with an adequate social safety net.

A greater role for volunteerism and nonprofit groups was another part of the plan. After the government's role declined, Reagan and his conservative allies expected a massive increase in the activities of private groups to help those less fortunate.

The developments of the 1980s proved Reagan and his conserva- tive philosophy wrong on both counts. First, Reagan and congres- sional conservatives were unable to reduce costs drastically by just cutting the fat out of the social programs. A policy lesson of the 1980s is that cutting basic benefits is the only way to make signifi- cant cutbacks in social programs. Waste and fraud are difficult to eliminate and make up only a small portion of the programs costs. Most practitioners and policy analysts knew this before the 1980s, but many conservatives refused to believe it.

Second, a huge increase in actions by private groups to combat social problems never developed in the 1980s. In fact, one major study found that Reagan's policies hurt the efforts of private-sector groups dealing with social needs.[68] Lester Salamon concluded:

> By emphasizing the importance of private sector initiatives and volun- tary action, the Reagan administration has put the philanthropic sector on the agenda of American politics in a forceful way. But by pursuing a serious assault on a broad range of domestic programs that help to sustain the sector financially, without accompanying this with a positive

program of action, the administration may have set back its own private-sector agenda for some time to come and discredited voluntarism further as a serious policy alternative.[69]

Social Security

Social Security is the major program of the New Deal and by far the largest social program in the federal government. If a conservative Reagan revolution replaced the New Deal–Great Society era, the Social Security program should have been eliminated, or at least altered significantly. However, just the opposite happened. Presidents Reagan and Bush and most congressional Republicans not only approved of the continuation of the program, but even tried to convince the public that Republicans supported the Social Security program even more than the Democrats.

In the 1970s, Ronald Reagan made statements indicating support for cutbacks in the Social Security program. During the 1980 campaign, Reagan tried to distance himself from his past position and pledged support for Social Security. Then in 1981, Reagan changed direction again by proposing some cutbacks in the Social Security program. Congress approved some cuts, particularly the elimination of the minimum benefit. Reagan also proposed a larger plan for scaling back Social Security spending that primarily involved changes in provisions for early retirement. These Social Security cuts and proposed cuts proved to be some of the administration's biggest mistakes of the first term. A public outcry arose against the Social Security cuts. Democrats went on the offensive and effectively used the issue against the Republicans. Congress restored the minimum benefit. And even before Reagan sent his proposal on the early retirement provisions to Congress, the Senate effectively killed it by unanimously passing a resolution against it.

Also, in 1982 the debate began on how to save the Social Security system. The Social Security fund had supposedly been repaired for the next several decades with the large Social Security tax increase of 1977. However, economic problems had created new difficulties for the fund. Many analysts predicted that within a few years the fund's income would not be large enough to pay the Social Security checks for eligible recipients.

After months of discussion, negotiations, political posturing, and partisan conflict, a compromise was reached in 1983 to solve the Social Security crisis.[70] A compromise was delayed primarily by Reagan's unwillingness to accept the inevitability of a tax increase. Finally, Reagan did accept the compromise plan, which contained a large tax increase. This increase in the Social Security tax was one of the largest tax increases in U.S. history. The final plan did include some small cuts such as a delay in a cost of living increase for six months, but the tax increase was the key aspect to ease the funding crisis. The tax was set so high that the Social Security fund was running nearly a $50 billion surplus in the early 1990s.

So rather than eliminating Social Security or making drastic cutbacks in the program, President Reagan and the majority of congressional Republicans agreed to significantly increase the Social Security tax. This tax increase should provide enough revenue for the program to expand well into the next century.

The outcome of the Social Security crisis of the early 1980s provides another excellent test of the Reagan revolution thesis. The crisis pitted the powers from the legacy of the New Deal against the conservative forces led by President Reagan. In the end, the New Deal won a clear and almost complete victory. The program continued and generated huge surpluses within a few years. The Republicans then went to the American people to beg for forgiveness because they had committed the great political sin of trying to cut Social Security.

Social Security is such a sacred cow in Washington that plans to make drastic changes in the program never even received serious consideration. The outcome in the early 1980s demonstrated that the conservative forces of the 1980s could not even begin to challenge the New Deal's biggest program. It also showed that the Republican Party and the conservative movement in general must support the federal government's largest social program (i.e., Social Security) if they want to remain competitive players in national politics.

Republicans certainly learned this lesson. Ronald Reagan pledged full support for the Social Security program in the 1984 campaign. In addition, most Republican congressional candidates promised to maintain a healthy Social Security system. George Bush also took the Social Security pledge in the 1988 campaign. He even tried to make the Republicans more the "Party of Social Security" than the

Democrats. When Senator Daniel Patrick Moynihan proposed canceling the scheduled increase in the Social Security tax, President Bush spoke out against the plan and argued that Moynihan and other Democrats would ruin the program.

Welfare

The 1980s did not produce a fundamental conservative shift in welfare policy. Although Congress did tighten the eligibility rules on Aid to Families of Dependent Children, food stamps, and other welfare programs in the early 1980s, all the major welfare programs survived and expanded by billions in current dollars. Also, the administration failed to achieve one of its major goals of offsetting benefits from multiple programs. Bowden and Palmer stated:

> . . . the administration was largely unsuccessful in obtaining congressional approval for its numerous proposals to offset the benefits of various means-tested programs against one another. As a consequence, both basic AFDC and SSI benefit levels and multiple program basic benefits for AFDC and SSI recipients have performed better under the Reagan administration than over the 1970s.[71]

In addition, the welfare programs made a comeback after 1981.[72] First, Congress refused to make further cuts and even restored some of the benefits. In 1985, for example, Congress increased spending on food stamps and broadened eligibility. Second, House Democrats won a major victory in the budget battle by including a provision in the Gramm-Rudman-Hollings bill to protect welfare programs. Under the provision, several welfare programs would be exempt from the across-the-board cuts mandated by the law to achieve annual budget reduction goals.

This provision is another piece of evidence to show that no conservative Reagan revolution occurred in the 1970s. While Social Security and welfare programs were protected from cuts under Gramm-Rudman-Hollings, the law mandated that half the automatic cuts must come out of the defense budget. If the 1980s represented a historic conservative era, the provisions in the law should have been just the opposite—protection for the defense budget from automatic cuts and half the reductions mandated for social-welfare programs.

The 1980s will probably not be seen as a conservative turning point in the history of welfare policy. From a longer perspective, the decade will more likely be noted more for the legitimacy factor and the 1988 welfare reform law. The fact that the major welfare programs survived the attack of the Reagan administration should improve the long-term prospects of the programs. In addition, the congressional actions of refusing to accept further cuts, reversing course to increase benefits, and protecting welfare in Gramm-Rudman-Hollings enhanced the legitimacy of the welfare programs.

Compared to the welfare reform bill of 1988, the cutbacks in the welfare programs of the early 1980s were a relatively minor change. The 1988 law represented one of the most important reforms in the history of welfare policy.

This law was not a conservative victory. It was a moderate compromise that resulted from a consensus that developed over years of debate among conservatives and liberals. The law included work requirements, education and training, child care, and contin-ued benefits for welfare recipients. In the final analysis, the new welfare package favored liberals more than conservatives because it increased the legitimacy of the federal government's welfare programs and insured the continuation of the programs for many years in the future.

Child Care

Not only did the social programs survive the 1980s, but the social-welfare state moved into new areas. The developments in child-care policy offer a good example of this trend.

New Right conservatives strongly oppose the government playing a role in child care. They believe in traditional families with mothers staying at home and providing care for children. If the country had experienced a historic conservative change in ideology and policy, the issue of greater government involvement in child care would not have been on the political agenda. Instead, child care became a major policy debate in the 1980s with the continual increase in single-parent homes and mothers working outside the home. As public opinion polls indicated, a substantial portion of the American public in the 1980s wanted the federal government to provide much more assistance with child care. During the 1988 election, child care was one of the key issues. Michael Dukakis and George Bush prominently featured child-care proposals as important components of their platforms. Many congressional candidates also promised support for some type of federal child-care program.

Besides the debates and promises on child care, a major child-care program was enacted in the 1980s. The 1988 welfare reform bill contained a section on child care. It marked a historic step in federal child-care policy. This created the first federal child-care entitlement. This provision of the welfare bill provided child-care assistance for eligible women in welfare programs.

In 1990 Congress passed a landmark child-care law which extended assistance to a large segment of the population. The main debate was not over whether the social-welfare state should move into this new area, but rather the best way to set up a federal child-care program.

Again, where is the Reagan revolution? If the United States had entered a historic conservative era, the possibility of a major federal role in child care could not have gotten serious consideration in Congress, let alone received enough bipartisan support for the enactment of a significant law.

In addition, the House of Representatives passed a parental leave bill in 1990 to allow a parent time off from his/her job to care for a child. Even though President Bush vetoed the bill, the fact that a child-care policy such as this could receive congressional support demonstrates the weakness of the New Right position on family issues among the American public. To reiterate, a fundmamental conservative shift in U.S. policies would not have allowed this type of issue even to be on the political agenda.

The strong support for child-care legislation is another example that demonstrates that the United States remains in the New Deal–Great Society era. With more women in the work force and a shift to more of a service economy, child care provides the next logical step in the growth of the social-welfare state. The political forces supporting the maintenance of federal social programs and the addition of new programs obviously remain much stronger than the power of New Right conservatives.

Health Programs

The high growth rate of the federal government's health programs continued during the 1980s. The spending on these programs soared to record levels. This enormous growth demonstrates that no fundamental conservative change occurred in federal health policy. Just the opposite happened, since the federal government's role in health care expanded in the 1980s.

From 1979 to 1988 the medical care budget category skyrocketed from $48 billion to $128 billion. This is a whopping 167 percent increase! Federal medical care spending expanded from 1.9 to 2.7 percent of GNP. The health programs grew at a much faster rate than overall federal spending and the economy.

Medicare. The Medicare program grew at a phenomenal rate during the 1980s. Outlays increased from $24 billion in 1980 to $85.6 billion in 1989. Here is a program in which the federal government plays a significant role in paying the health costs of senior citizens. A fundamental conservative change in policy would mean a drastic reduction of the federal government's role in this key area of health services. Instead, federal funding skyrocketed for Medicare, and thus the government's influence expanded in health services for the elderly.

Medicare was the major social program passed by Congress since the mid-1960s. A conservative shift away from liberals' social programs should have produced the elimination of such a significant program, or at least a drastic reduction in spending. The enormous increase in Medicare funding is another piece of evidence to show that the New Deal–Great Society era continued through the 1980s.

On several occasions, the Reagan administration proposed spending cuts in the Medicare program. Congress accepted some of the cuts in the early 1980s and generally rejected the proposals later in the decade. Since Medicare spending increased by so much during the decade, the cutbacks had only a limited impact. The major story of Medicare in the 1980s is the huge expansion of the program and not the cutbacks.

The Reagan administration also worked with Congress to devise new administrative procedures to help control the spiraling Medicare costs. In 1983, for instance, Congress changed from a reimbursement system based on costs to a payment system with fixed fees related to particular types of medical problems. The administrative changes probably helped lessen the costs of the program, but increased the federal government's influence in the health care delivery system. If Carter and Mondale had won the presidency in the 1980s, some type of administrative changes and cost-cutting measures would have probably passed anyway. Mondale, for example, presented a plan in the 1984 presidential campaign for a national cap on health expenditures.[73]

Finally, in 1988 Congress expanded the Medicare program significantly by passing the catastrophic health program. This was the largest expansion of the Medicare program in its history. The law set up several provisions to help protect senior citizens from financial disaster as a result of severe illness.

Although Congress rescinded the catastrophic-cost program in 1989, its passage contradicts the Reagan revolution thesis. Congressional Democrats did not pass the bill over the objections of President Reagan. He proposed a catastrophic-cost bill to Congress. So instead of Reagan presiding over the destruction of Medicare, the major health program of the federal government, he proposed a massive increase in the program. President Reagan's proposal of a catastrophic-cost plan was about as far from what should have happened in a conservative policy era as could be imagined.

Medicaid.   Medicaid funding also increased significantly during the 1980s. Medicaid's budget expanded from $13.2 billion in 1980 to $29.0 billion in 1988. A historic conservative policy change would have forced most poor people out of public health programs. Instead, Medicaid spending more than doubled in just eight years.

The Reagan administration and congressional conservatives won a few victories in their attempts to cut Medicaid. In 1981, for example, Congress passed provisions designed to cut nearly a billion dollars a year from the program.

On the other hand, Reagan and his fellow conservatives lost several key congressional fights over Medicaid. The majority in Congress on several occasions refused to accept deeper cuts in the program. In 1981 Congress turned down Reagan's proposal to cap federal contributions to Medicaid. The administration's plan for taking control of the full funding of Medicaid in exchange for the states' assuming responsibility for other welfare programs received very little serious attention. Futhermore, Congress enlarged the Medicaid program in 1986 by expanding coverage to poor pregnant women and their children under the age of one.[74]

AIDS crisis.   The governmental response to the AIDS epidemic provides another illustration of New Deal–Great Society policy extending into the 1980s. Many Americans demanded action by the federal government to help fight this disease. Although Reagan slowly and reluctantly accepted a greater federal role in combating AIDS, he still did propose an expansion of the program. A key feature of the New Deal–Great Society periods has been the assumption by most Americans that federal government officials will propose plans to solve major national problems. Reagan's response showed that he could not ignore this and simply tell the American people to wait for the private sector and state governments to solve the problem.

Moreover, conservatives' response to the AIDS program provides another illustration of the contradiction in conservative ideology. Reagan and many conservatives advocated more mandatory testing for AIDS and more government inspection of health records for AIDS detection. Here again, conservatives advocated more governmental involvement in individual's lives, which violated their belief in less government.

Defense Personnel Costs

Although most political observers do not consider it as such, the billions of dollars spent on the personnel costs of the Defense Department constitute one of the most important social programs. It comprises one of the major aspects of the social-welfare state. The cradle-to-grave programs provided for military personnel are far beyond the scope of most of the regular social programs. In addition, the thousands of civilian employees of the Defense Department receive many government benefits.

This creates another contradiction in conservatives' ideology. Conservatives want to significantly reduce the number of people who receive government services such as housing assistance and medical care, yet they support proposals for substantially expanding the military, which would greatly increase the number of people who depend on the government for social services.

If Congress had increased the defense budget at the growth rate outlined by President Reagan's first five-year budget plan, the amount of social services provided by the federal government would have soared. The government would have provided many billions of dollars in benefits to many thousands of new Defense Department personnel. This increase in social spending on defense personnel would have offset much of the savings gained by the cuts in the growth rates of the several regular social programs.

Tax Policy

Most political commentators portrayed the 1980s as a conservative period in tax policy. Analyses of the 1980s' tax policy outcomes consistently dwelled on the tax cuts for individuals and businesses. This representation of tax policy, however, misses several other important developments that must be considered. An examination of other aspects of tax policy, besides the 1981 tax law, raises serious questions about the conventional view.

First, as the budget section pointed out, the enormous cutback in taxes that supposedly occurred in the 1980s was an illusion. It simply never happened. The overall tax burden on Americans, consisting on federal, state, and local taxes, did not decline significantly during the 1980s. Just the opposite occurred as taxes expanded considerably in current dollars and as a percent of GNP. Total federal, state, and local tax revenue increased from $334 billion (33.7 percent of GNP) in 1970 to $932 billion (34.9 percent of GNP) in 1980 and $1516 billion (36.2 percent of GNP) in 1986.[75] So the 1980s was a period of substantial expansion in taxes, not a historic period of tax reductions.

Even federal taxes increased in the 1980s. The yearly average for federal taxes as a percent of GNP in the 1980s was higher than it was during the 1960s and 1970s.

Second, Congress with the support of the Reagan administration passed several huge tax increases. Federal taxes expanded considerably with the passage of the 1982 tax law and the 1983 Social Security reform package. These tax increases were among the largest in U.S. history. The expanded revenue from these laws offset much of the losses from the 1981 tax bill.

Why did the media and political commentators concentrate on the 1981 tax cuts and portray the 1980s as a low-tax period? Why didn't they emphasize the tax increases and the overall expansion of the tax burden? If reporters and political analysts had presented a more balanced picture of tax cuts and tax increases, this illusion of the low-tax 1980s might not have developed.

Third, several developments in the 1980s' tax policy favored liberal goals. For example, the 1986 tax reform law was one of the major antipoverty measures of recent decades. It took many low-income taxpayers off the tax rolls. In addition, the 1986 law closed many tax loopholes and increased taxes on businesses.

Finally, some type of tax cut would probably have passed in the 1980s anyway if the Democrats had retained control of the White House and the Senate. Members of Congress were discussing the possibility of a tax cut in 1980, and congressional Democrats had often used tax cuts in the past as part of their political strategy to maintain control of Congress. Furthermore, tax cuts would probably have been part of a Democratic fiscal policy to combat the recession of the early 1980s. If a similar recession had hit, a Democratic president and Congress would have followed Keynesian policy and created a large deficit by increasing spending and cutting taxes.

Conclusion

A fundamental conservative policy shift is another illusion of the 1980s. Many of the major policy developments of the decade were the opposite of what should have happened in a conservative era.

Agriculture policy in the 1980s ended up about as far as possible from a conservative policy revolution. Instead of the elimination of the government role in agriculture, or at least significantly cutting it back, most farm programs not only survived but expanded to record levels. While the impact of the federal government had declined in agriculture during the 1970s, the government's influence increased considerably in the 1980s. The cost of price and income supports increased by several times a few years into the 1980s. New farm laws created the first large-scale program to pay dairymen to produce less milk. The Reagan administration initiated the largest acreage reduction program in the history of farm policy. President Reagan also supported the reauthorization of a program to protect domestic sugar producers that had been defeated in Congress in the 1970s. He accepted the continuation of the peanut program, which also was in trouble in Congress. Senator Helms lead the fight to save the tobacco program. In all three of these situations, the Reagan administration missed a historic opportunity to work with the congressional critics of these programs and aid their efforts to significantly lessen the government's role in agriculture. Overall, agriculture policy in the 1980s moved in an opposite direction from what should have happened in a conservative Reagan revolution.

No historic conservative changes developed in the major aspects of the federal budget. In fact, most of the budget trends were in the opposite direction from what traditional conservatives would support. Instead of balanced budgets and budget surpluses, record deficits were created, and the national debt nearly tripled during the decade. Rather than substantial cutbacks in spending, federal outlays skyrocketed to the highest levels, as measured by current dollars and percent of GNP, in the post–World War II period.

Instead of a massive tax cut, federal taxes at the end of the decade were at about the same level as 1979. The yearly average of federal revenues as a percent of GNP was even slightly higher in the 1980s than in the 1970s and 1960s. The overall tax burden expanded enormously during the 1980s.

President Reagan accepted thirteen different tax increases in the 1980s. Some of these laws, especially the increase in the Social Security tax, were among the biggest tax increases in U.S. history. In 1990 President Bush announced his support for a tax increase as part of a budget plan to lower the deficit. He advocated higher taxes even though his most famous pledge in the 1988 campaign was "Read My Lips—No New Taxes!" Bush's flip-flop on taxes demonstrated that Reagan's legacy on tax policy was not lower taxes, but the tactic of gaining support in campaigns by promising lower taxes or no tax increases.

Rather than a dramatic shift in spending away from debt financing and social programs, the costs of debt financing soared and human resources spending increased as a percent of GNP in the early 1980s. Social Security and Medicare, the major social programs, expanded considerably.

Rather than a massive increase in defense spending, the late 1980s began the largest cutback in military spending during the cold war era. Congress cut several hundred billion dollars from Reagan's defense proposals during the decade.

Furthermore, the budget policy outcomes during the 1980s have shown that it is a myth to assume that conservatives support a much smaller federal government. According to their stated position, they want a large cutback in the national government. In practice, however, they support the continuation of a large federal government.

They support as much, if not more, federal spending as liberals. Conservatives want to significantly expand defense, which is the biggest part of the budget. Also, the politics of the 1980s demonstrated that conservative Republicans must support the Social Security program to stay alive politically. These two programs account for about one half of the federal budget. Conservatives must also approve of the 15 percent of the budget that needs to be spent on financing the national debt. Much of the remaining one third of the federal budget consists of programs and functions, such as veterans' benefits and law enforcement, which conservatives also support. Therefore, conservatives actually oppose a relatively small part of the budget.

Liberals, on the other hand, want to trim defense spending. Moreover, they do not support all nondefense sections of the budget. Consequently, it is a myth that liberals support a greatly expanded federal government, while conservatives want a significantly reduced federal government.

Conservative approval of a larger federal budget could be seen in Reagan's budget proposals. While Reagan supported huge cuts in some parts of the budget, he proposed enormous increases in the overall size of the budget. The federal budget would still have expanded to record levels even if Congress had passed Reagan's budget exactly as proposed.

No fundamental conservative shift developed in the 1980s in civil rights and liberties. While the Reagan administration and congressional conservatives were able to slow the progress of the liberal movement in this area, they were unable to reverse this trend. Not one of the landmark liberal victories, such as the 1965 Voting Rights Act, was overturned in the 1980s. In addition, liberals won several notable victories during the decade. The fair housing bill, the 1965 Voting Rights Act extension, the defeat of Judge Bork's nomination, the Grove City civil rights law, and the Supreme Court decision on creation science are examples of how well the liberal view on civil rights and liberties fared during the decade.

No fundamental shift toward conservative economics occurred in the 1980s. It is an illusion to assume that a new era of laissez-faire capitalism developed in the decade.

In many ways, the role of the federal government increased in the economy rather than decreased. The need to finance the soaring deficit substantially increased the federal government's impact on capital markets. The huge increase in federal spending and the enormous expansion of the agriculture program also enlarged the government's influence on the economy.

The contradictions in conservatives' ideology became apparent in economic policy. The defense budget is the major influence the government has on the economy. By continuing the high rate of growth for military spending from the late 1970s into the early 1980s, conservatives increased the government's impact on the economy in the first part of the decade. Ironically, Reagan's greatest contribution to laissez-faire capitalism was his failure to convince Congress to sustain the high rate of military spending throughout the 1980s.

Many commentators portrayed the 1980s as a period of significant cutbacks in government involvement in the economy following the 1970s, which was assumed to be a period of increased government involvements. In many aspects the reverse was true. Through the mid-1970s the government's impact on the economy declined with the cutbacks in the military following the Vietnam War. The federal government's role declined in agriculture during the 1970s. The decade also witnessed some of the major developments in deregulation (e.g., airlines and trucking) in U.S. history. Federal spending had hit a plateau around 20 percent of GNP, and budget deficits, in relation to the overall economy, had started downward in the mid-1970s. Developments in the 1980s, such as the enormous expansion of the deficits and agriculture spending, along with the decline in deregulation, either reversed or slowed these trends in the 1970s toward less government involvement in the economy.

While the emphasis was on more market-oriented energy policies in the 1980s, no conservative revolution in policy occurred. Little deregulation activity developed in the 1980s because Congress passed the major energy deregulation laws in the 1970s. Also, conservatives failed to achieve several important energy goals during the 1980s. For instance, the Reagan administration was unable to eliminate the Energy Department, to obtain a quick end to price controls on natural gas, and to significantly expand the use of nuclear energy. Furthermore, in the environment-versus-energy debate, those favoring environmental protection gained more public approval during the decade than those supporting energy production.

Despite the Reagan administration's efforts, the 1980s proved to be an excellent decade for liberal environmental policy. While Reagan achieved some success through the changes in the implementation of environmental laws, the environmental groups gained many policy victories. Reagan was unable to make any substantial changes in environmental laws. Bipartisan coalitions formed in Congress to reauthorize several major environmental laws. These congressional coalitions largely ignored Reagan's proposals. Moreover, the controversies and scandals that accompanied Reagan's environmental policies discredited the conservative position on the environment. President Bush distanced himself from Reagan's policies and followed a policy course much more acceptable to environmental groups.

The 1980s was not a decade of historic conservative shift in American foreign policy. While the Reagan foreign policy team enjoyed some success in following their conservative policies, they also suffered several defeats. Congress, for example, overturned Reagan's conservative approach to South Africa by overriding the president's veto of a strong sanctions bill. And in Soviet affairs, which is the most important part of U.S. foreign policy, President Reagan reversed his position and began following the liberal agenda. He started to work with Mikhail Gorbachev to ease U.S.–Soviet tensions with agreements such as the INF treaty. In many other parts of the world, few changes occurred in the broad outline of U.S. foreign policies during the Reagan administration.

The New Right failed to achieve most of its goals in social policy. For example, Congress never passed the constitutional amendments to allow organized prayers in public schools and to ban abortions. In addition, the New Right conservatives failed to reverse the major social trends they strongly oppose.

The predictions that the 1990s would be dominated by a conservative policy agenda were almost completely wrong. In early 1990 the major policy debates in Washington concentrated on cutting military spending, finding a new focus other than anticommunism in foreign policy, increasing taxes, spending the peace dividend, handling the surplus in the Social Security fund, regulating the savings-and-loan industry, and passing strong environmental protection laws. These policy developments were all in the opposite direction from what should have happened in a conservative era. The early 1990s appear to be developing into a period of historic decline in conservative policies rather than a continuation of historic conservative victories, as the Reagan revolution thesis would suggest.

Notes

1. John E. Chubb and Paul E. Peterson, "Realignment and Institutionalization," in *The New Direction in American Politics*, ed., John E. Chubb and Paul E. Peterson (Washington, D.C.: Brookings Institution, 1985), 24.
2. "Farm Programs Cut in Reconciliation," *Congressional Quarterly Almanac: 1982* (Washington, D.C.: Congressional Quarterly, 1983), 362.
3. Ibid., 351.
4. Jonathan Rauch, "Sugary Shakedown," *National Journal* 20 (4 April 1988): 1131–34.
5. "Helms Possibly a Factor: Tobacco Subsidy Program Facing Raft of Complaints as New Foes Take It On," *Congressional Quarterly Weekly Report* 39 (5 September 1981): 1675–76.
6. "New Farm Bill Clears by Two-Vote Margin," *Congressional Quarterly Almanac: 1981* (Washington, D.C.: Congressional Quarterly, 1982), 539.
7. "Congress Revises Dairy, Tobacco Programs," *Congressional Quarterly Almanac: 1983* (Washington, D.C.: Congressional Quarterly, 1984), 375.
8. Jonathan Rauch, "Why the Honey Bees Aren't Laughing," *National Journal* 19 (4 July 1987): 1737.
9. "Farm Bill Granted a Limited 'Win' to All Sides," *Congressional Quarterly Almanac: 1985* (Washington, D.C.: Congressional Quarterly, 1986), 319–20.
10. Jonathan Rauch, "Cotton Comes a Cropper," *National Journal* 21 (22 April 1989): 994–96.
11. "Farm Bill Granted a Limited 'Win' to All Sides," 521–22.
12. Perry D. Quick, "Business: Reagan's Industrial Policy," in *The Reagan Record*, ed. John L. Palmer and Isabel V. Sawhill (Cambridge, Mass.: Ballinger Publishing, 1984), 287–316.

13. "Inside Washington," *National Journal* 22 (31 March 1990): 765.
14. Collen McGuiness and Patricia M. Russotto, ed., *U.S. Foreign Policy: The Reagan Imprint* (Washington, D.C.: Congressional Quarterly, 1986), 136–39.
15. Ibid., 140–42.
16. Quick, "Business: Reagan's Industrial Policy."
17. Ibid.
18. W. John More, "New Cops on the Beat," *National Journal* 19 (23 May 1987): 1338–42.
19. "Voting Rights Act Extended, Strengthened," *Congressional Quarterly Almanac: 1982* (Washington, D.C.: Congressional Quarterly, 1983), 373–77.
20. "Compromise Fair-Housing Bill Is Cleared," *Congressional Quarterly Almanac: 1988* (Washington, D.C.: Congressional Quarterly, 1989), 68–74.
21. "Grove City Bill Enacted Over Reagan's Veto," *Congressional Quarterly Almanac: 1988* (Washington, D.C.: Congressional Quarterly, 1989), 63–67.
22. Quoted in Anthony Lewis, "The Bork Surprise," *New York Times* 24 September 1987, p. A27.
23. "Stand-Pat Supreme Court Defers to Others," *Congressional Quarterly Almanac: 1981* (Washington, D.C.: Congressional Quarterly, 1982): 4-A.
24. The source for some of the information about the cases mentioned in this section is Louis Fisher, *Constitutional Rights: Civil Rights and Civil Liberties* (New York: McGraw-Hill, 1990).
25. *Lynch v. Donnelly*, 465 U.S. 668 (1984).
26. *Larson v. Valente*, 456 U.S. 228 (1982).
27. *Larkin v. Grendel's Den, Inc.*, 459 U.S. 116, 125–126 (1982).
28. *Wallace v. Jaffree*, 472 U.S. 38 (1985).
29. *Edwards v. Aquillard*, 482 U.S. 578 (1987).
30. *Goldman v. Weinberger*, 475 U.S. 503, 514 (1986).
31. *Rankin v. McPherson*, 483 U.S. 378 (1987).
32. *Texas v. Johnson*, 109 S. Ct. 2533 (1989).
33. *Bolger v. Youngs Drug Products Corp.*, 463 U.S. 69 (1983).
34. *Hustler Magazine v. Falwell*, 108 S. Ct. 876 (1988).
35. *Baker v. Carr*, 369 U.S. 186 (1962).
36. Much of the discussion in this section is based on the information in the "Defense" articles in the 1981–88 editions of *Congressional Quarterly Almanac* (Washington, D.C.: Congressional Quarterly).
37. For an analysis of the Defense Department's impact on industry, see Bruce Stokes, "Fighting Separate Wars," *National Journal* 19 (14 March 1987): 602–7.
38. Herbert Stein, "The Reagan Revolution That Wasn't," *Harpers*, February 1986), 46.
39. Janet Hook and Elizabeth Wehr, "Health/Education/Welfare," *Con-

gressional Quarterly Almanac: 1983 (Washington, D.C.: Congressional Quarterly, 1984), 390.

40. "Five-Year Higher Education Bill Cleared," *Congressional Quarterly Almanac: 1986* (Washington, D.C.: Congressional Quarterly, 1987), 231.

41. "Congress Clears $8.3 Billion Education Bill," *Congressional Quarterly Almanac: 1988* (Washington, D.C.: Congressional Quarterly, 1989), 330.

42. "ED Dismantlement," *Congressional Quarterly Almanac: 1982* (Washington, D.C.: Congressional Quarterly, 1983), 501.

43. DOE Dismantlement," *Congressional Quarterly Almanac: 1982* (Washington, D.C.: Congressional Quarterly, 1983), 303.

44. Rochelle L. Stanfield, "Regrouping," *National Journal* 19 (3 November 1987): 47.

45. Paul Portney, "Natural Resources and the Environment," in *The Reagan Record*, ed. John L. Palmer and Isabel V. Sawhill (Cambridge, Mass.: Ballinger Publishing, 1984), 141–75.

46. See Richard W. Waterman, "Reagan and the Environmental Protection Agency: Revolution and Counter-Revolution." Paper presented at the 1987 Annual Meeting of the Midwest Political Science Association, Chicago, Illinois.

47. "Congress Overrides Clean-Water Bill Veto," *Congressional Quarterly Almanac: 1987* (Washington, D.C.: Congressional Quarterly, 1988), 291.

48. "Reagan Signs 'Superfund' Waste-Cleanup Bill," *Congressional Quarterly Almanac: 1986* (Washington, D.C.: Congressional Quarterly, 1987), 111.

49. Iver Peterson, "Rising Opposition Stalls U.S. Effort to Develop Federal Lands in West," *New York Times*, 5 March, 1986, p. 10.

50. Ibid.

51. Rochelle L. Stanfield, "Global Guardian," *National Journal* 19 (12 December 1987): 3130–3142.

52. James A. Barnes, "In From The Cold," *National Journal* 21 (11 November 1989): 2746–2749.

53. Ibid.

54. I. M. Destler, "Reagan and the World: An Awesome Stubbornness," in *The Reagan Legacy*, ed. Charles O. Jones (Chatham, N.J.: Chatham House, 1988), 241; and *Washington Post* (5 December 1987).

55. *Wallace v. Jaffree*, 472 U.S. 38 (1985).

56. *Edwards v. Aguillard*, 482 U.S. 578 (1987).

57. Michael Barone and Grant Ujifusa, *Almanac of American Politics 1988* (Washington, D.C.: National Journal, 1987), 887.

58. *Roe v. Wade*, 410 U.S. 113 (1973).

59. *Webster v. Reproductive Health Services*, 109 S. Ct. 3040 (1989).

60. James A. Barnes, "Flip-Flopping," *National Journal* 22 (17 February 1990): 418.

61. Linda E. Demkovich, "Raising the Shades on Sex Education," *National Journal* 19 (31 January 1987): 274–75.
62. *Miller v. California*, 413 U.S. 15 (1973).
63. *Pope v. Illinois*, 481 U.S. 497 (1987).
64. Fisher, *Constitutional Rights: Civil Rights and Civil Liberties*, 633.
65. *State v. Henry*, 732 P. 2d9, 16 (Ore. 1987).
66. Fisher, *Constitutional Rights: Civil Rights and Civil Liberties*, 633.
67. On President Reagan and the long-term legitimacy of the federal social programs, see Hugh Heclo, "Reaganism and the Search for a Public Philosophy," in *Perspectives on the Reagan Years*, ed. John L. Palmer (Washington, D.C.: Urban Institute Press, 1986), 60.
68. Lester M. Salamon, "Non-Profit Organizations: The Lost Opportunity," in *The Reagan Record*, ed. John L. Palmer and Isabel V. Sawhill (Cambridge, Mass.: Ballinger Publishing, 1984), 261–85.
69. Ibid., 284–85.
70. See Paul Light, *Artful Work: The Politics of Social Security Reform* (New York: Random House, 1985).
71. D. Lee Bowden and John L. Palmer, "Social Policy: Challenging the Welfare State," in *The Reagan Record*, ed. John L. Palmer and Isabel V. Sawhill (Cambridge, Mass.: Ballinger Publishing, 1984), 193.
72. See Peter Gottschalk, "Retrenchment in Antipoverty Programs in the United States: Lessons for the Future," in *The Reagan Revolution?*, ed. B. B. Kymlicka and Jean V. Matthews (Chicago: Dorsey Press, 1988), 142–43.
73. Janet Hook and Elizabeth Wehr, "Health/Education/Welfare," *Congressional Quarterly Almanac: 1984* (Washington, D.C.: Congressional Quarterly, 1985), 449.
74. Julie Rovner, "Health/Education/Welfare," *Congressional Quarterly Almanac: 1986*, 229.
75. Computed from data in Office of Management and Budget, *Historical Tables, Budget of the United States Government, 1990* (Washington, D.C.: U.S. Government Printing Office, 1989), 18; and U.S. Bureau of the Census, *Statistical Abstract of the United States: 1989* (Washington, D.C.: U.S. Government Printing Office, 1989), 267.

7

The Illusion of President Reagan's Great Legislative Success

According to the Reagan revolution thesis, many of the landmark conservative changes of the 1980s developed through President Reagan's brilliant successes in influencing Congress. Reagan was often portrayed as setting the congressional agenda and then pushing this agenda through Congress with his dazzling communication and political skills. Supposedly he won on almost every major issue in Congress by arousing public support through the mass media and convincing members of Congress through informal meetings and telephone calls. Congress was seen as a weak institution unable to initiate policy and unable to stop the Reagan onslaught. Some political commentators contended that Ronald Reagan was the most successful president in congressional relations since Franklin D. Roosevelt.

However, an examination of the record of what happened in Congress for the full eight years of the Reagan administration indicates that Reagan was one of the least successful presidents since FDR in achieving legislative goals. Many political analysts concentrate too much on Reagan's victories in 1981 and ignore the many failures during the rest of his administration.

Reagan's Overall Legislative Record

In political science research, an important measure of presidential success in legislative politics in Congressional Quarterly's presidential support scores. This is a measure of the votes in which congressional majorities voted the same as the stated position of the president. If President Reagan was the most successful postwar president in the legislative leadership role, he should have the highest scores in this measure. Instead, Reagan had one of the worst overall records during the 1953–88 period. The yearly average for the presidents was Eisenhower, 72; Kennedy, 85; Johnson, 83; Nixon, 67; Ford, 58; Carter, 76; and Reagan 62.[1] This is yet another example of a significant measure of the developments in the 1980s that is just the opposite of what it should be according to the Reagan revolution thesis.

Reagan compiled record-low scores during the period. He is the only president with scores in the forties. He also recorded half of all the scores below sixty.

The data demonstrates the problem of focusing on Reagan's successes in the early 1980s and ignoring the failures during the last three fourths of his administration. Reagan did post high presidential support scores the first two years, but compiled moderate and low scores during the final six years. Consequently, many political analysts have been so far off the mark on Reagan's legislative record because they characterize the Reagan-congressional relationship during the 1980s by what happened primarily in 1981. An analysis of the entire eight years shows that Reagan had a moderate-to-poor record of success rather than the great success presented by the conventional view.

Reagan's second term was a disaster. Before the 1980s, a presidential support score below sixty was rare. Reagan, however, received a score below sixty for all four years of his second term. His average for these four years was far below the average of any other four-year period from 1953 to 1984.

Many political observers have given Johnson and Reagan high marks in legislative leadership, while the other presidents' performances in the 1953–88 period are often judged somewhere from poor to moderately successful. Carter and Kennedy are especially criticized for their ineffective relationships with Congress. The criticisms of Eisenhower, Nixon, and Ford are tempered somewhat by the fact that they, except for two years of the Eisenhower administration, faced congresses controlled by Democrats.

The data from the presidential support scores raises serious questions about Reagan's ranking in these assessments. Why is

Reagan ranked well above these other presidents, except Johnson, when his overall presidential support scores were below all the others except Ford's? Many political analysts portrayed Carter as a bumbling, incompetent leader in his relationship with Congress, whereas Reagan was presented as a political genius who dominated Congress. Carter's performance was often presented as an example of how not to conduct presidential-congressional relations, in contrast to Reagan's performance, which was mentioned as an illustration of how the relationship should be handled. Yet Carter's presidential support scores were much higher than Reagan's.

Even though Reagan was favorably compared with Johnson in legislature leadership, or even rated above him, his scores were far below Johnson's. Whereas LBJ never scored below seventy-five, Reagan recorded only two of eight ratings above seventy.

Admittedly, the presidential support scores have some weaknesses. For instance, the scores do not take into account party control in Congress. Presidents have an advantage when both houses of Congress have majorities of their party. During the 1953–88 period, presidents always received a score of seventy-five or higher when the president and Congress were controlled by the same party. All the low presidential scores occurred in situations in which one or both chambers were controlled by the opposition party.

Even considering this, however, Reagan's record is still relatively poor. Eisenhower and Nixon each averaged about sixty-seven a year on their scores during the six years they faced Democratic majorities in the House and Senate. Reagan had only a yearly average of sixty-seven during the six years of the Republican majorities in the Senate. If Reagan had been highly effective in his congressional relations, he should have scored much higher than Eisenhower and Nixon during the six-year period because of the advantage of having a Republican-controlled Senate. In addition, Reagan generally received very low scores in the House. In 1986, for example, Reagan recorded a score of only thirty-three.[2] These low scores in the House suggest that if Reagan had faced a Senate and House with Democratic majorities for all eight years, his overall ratings would have been much lower than those of Eisenhower, Nixon, and Ford.

Another problem with the presidential support ratings is the inability to distinguish between important congressional votes and relatively insignificant votes. It provides a broad measure on a large number of votes without differentiating votes on landmark legislation from votes on minor matters. Here again, however, Reagan's performance is not greatly enhanced by taking this into consideration. Reagan often failed to achieve his legislative objectives in major policy areas as well as less important areas. His lack of success on many important policies will be pointed out later in this chapter in the discussion of Reagan-congressional developments in various policy areas.

Other measures and studies also raise questions about Reagan's alleged mastery over Congress. Analyses of congressional voting patterns fail to uncover any substantial "Reagan magic" with Congress. Fleisher and Bond, for example, examined House roll calls in the early 1980s and found little evidence of Reagan being able to sway a significant number of votes toward his position.[3] Edwards compared the support received by Eisenhower, Nixon, Ford, and Reagan in congressional votes. His findings showed a fairly similar pattern of support among these Republican presidents. Therefore, the data did not indicate that Reagan had a superior ability to gain congressional support.[4]

One of the reasons why Reagan had such a poor record in congressional leadership was his limited success in bringing the conservative coalition together after 1981. Since Republicans rarely have majorities in the House and Senate, Republican presidents and Republican congressional leaders must form coalitions with some Democrats, especially southern Democrats, to win on congressional votes. During the 1982–88 period, however, party unity increased among Democrats.[5] The increase developed primarily from a higher rate of party voting by southern Democrats. This led to the near death of the conservative coalition of Republicans and southern Democrats. While the percentage of recorded votes in which the conservative coalition appeared was between 20 and 30 during the 1970s, it dropped to only the 8-to-18 range in the 1980s.[6]

Here again, what happened is just the opposite of what should have happened in a Reagan revolution. If Reagan had been extremely successful in congressional leadership, party unity among Democrats should have plummeted as the conservative coalition formed at a substantially higher rate. Instead, Reagan gained a relatively small amount of congressional support, partly because of southern Democrats turning away from Reagan's conservative appeals and sticking with their own party's majorities at a much higher rate than in several previous decades.

Reagan's Legislative Record in Major Policy Areas

This section divides the developments in Congress into major policy areas and provides an analysis of the Reagan administration's successes and failures. The record again shows that Reagan often failed to obtain his legislative goals.

President Reagan failed almost completely in attaining his legislative goals in agriculture policy. He was unable to persuade the majority in Congress to significantly shift from government programs to a more free market in agriculture. While Reagan pushed a few cuts through in 1981, these cuts become particularly meaningless as the cost of the federal government's agriculture program soared during the 1980s.

The Reagan administration tried again in 1985 to alter agriculture policies, but the president suffered another big defeat. Many members of Congress, including a number of Republicans, largely ignored the White House in the formulation of the 1985 farm bill. Reagan reluctantly signed this bill even though it extended, and in some cases expanded, most of the basic agricultural programs for five years.

Reagan was often portrayed as achieving most of his budgetary goals and dominating Congress in budget policy. This view of budgetary politics is incorrect in both aspects.

First, Reagan certainly did not achieve his budget goals. The budgets passed by Congress created spending patterns about as far from President Reagan's budget goals as could be imagined. Reagan's overall goals were to significantly cut back the federal government and to produce a balanced budget in 1983 and $100-billion-surplus budgets in the following years. Instead, the country ended up with record spending as the federal budget increased from less than 21 percent of GNP in 1979 to over 24 percent in 1985. Rather than budgets with $100 billion surpluses, Congress passed with Reagan's acceptance budgets with $150–$220 billion deficits.

Second, Reagan did not dominate Congress in budgetary politics after 1981. Reagan often had only a limited impact on the budget. After huge deficits developed rather than budget surplus, Reagan retreated to a fantasy world. By not accepting reality and not providing feasible plans for a balanced budget, Reagan lost much of his credibility in budget policy.

The reality was that Reagan's plan for handling the $200 billion deficit was completely unrealistic. Reagan proposed to greatly increase military spending, the biggest part of the budget, block any tax increase, and still make significant progress toward a balanced budget. For this plan to work, Congress would have needed to eliminate a large amount of the nondefense portion of the budget. This, however, was not politically feasible. The Democrats had the votes to stop any attempt to eliminate a large number of major programs. Many congressional Republicans would not support such an approach because they feared voter retaliation in the next election.

As a result, the system ended up in a deadlock. Reagan would make speeches on the evils of deficits and would then propose another budget with an enormous deficit. Many of Reagan's budgets were dead-on-arrival. The President even had trouble gaining support from his own party. In 1987, for example, his budget proposals for the 1988 fiscal year received only twenty-seven votes in the House and eleven votes in the Senate.[7]

While Reagan continued to influence some aspects of budget policy, it was generally a negative influence. He refused to offer a feasible plan, and he threatened to veto any large-scale congressional plans that included tax increases and defense cuts.

In this situation, members of Congress often stepped in to provide leadership in the deficit crisis. In 1982 Reagan's budget plan was so unrealistic that the Senate Budget Committee voted 20–0 against it.[8] The President ended up largely accepting the budget proposals of the Senate Republican leadership as his own. On several occasions, members of the leadership and the tax-writing committees formulated and pushed through tax increases. This was especially surprising since they had to overcome their colleagues' fears of voter backlash and Reagan's threats.

In another major budget development, majorities in the House and Senate began to oppose Reagan's proposals for a huge defense increase. Many members of Congress refused to significantly increase funds for defense, the biggest spending area, when the federal government was running a $200 billion deficit.

Congress also passed the Gramm-Rudman-Hollings law. This plan was formulated by members of Congress, not by the administration. After much debate within the Reagan administration about this plan for a balanced budget, the President signed it.

After the Democratic victory in the 1986 election, Reagan's influence on budget policy declined even more. With majorities in both houses, Democrats were even less inclined to accept Reagan's priorities. In 1987 Speaker Jim Wright set forth a budget plan and aggressively lobbied for it. Congressional Democrats passed the first budget resolution without much regard for the administration's proposals.

Finally, in late 1987, Reagan and the Democratic leaders in Congress agreed to a two-year budget compromise. The plan included provisions for small tax increases and another huge cut in Reagan's defense proposals.

This budget compromise represented another major defeat for President Reagan in budget policy. The key part of the compromise was the enormous defense cutback. By agreeing to this budget compromise, Reagan finally accepted the reality that the growth of the defense budget would be cut significantly rather than increased.

Congressional liberals also defeated the Reagan administration on several key debates on civil rights and liberties policies. Majorities in Congress, for example, largely ignored Reagan's objectives in enacting the extension of the 1965 Voting Rights Act, the Martin Luther King, Jr., holiday bill, and the amendments to the 1968 Fair Housing Act. Congress also overrode Reagan's veto of the Grove City College civil rights law. In addition, the Senate voted down Robert Bork's nomination to the Supreme Court.

Data in chapter 6 point out the enormous difference between what Reagan proposed in defense spending and what Congress passed. Based on the rate of growth Reagan proposed in his initial five-year defense plan, the defense budget would have been over $500 billion a year by the end of the 1980s. The actual budget was a little under $300 billion. So Congress spent several hundred billion dollars less on defense during the 1980s than Reagan had requested. This definitely shows that Congress did not give Reagan everything he wanted on defense. President Reagan failed to achieve his goal on defense spending by a huge amount.

The Reagan administration had a mixed record in Congress on strategic nuclear policy. Congress brought the B-1 bomber program back to life. Although research funds continued for the Strategic Defense Initiative (SDI), the majority in Congress made large cuts in Reagan's SDI spending proposals on several occasions. While the administration did get an MX missile system built, Congress strongly influenced the outcome. Congress rejected several basing plans proposed by the administration before accepting the Scowcroft Commission's plan to put MX missiles in existing silos. But to get this plan through Congress, Reagan had to accept a deal whereby he agreed to take a more flexible position in arms control negotiations with the Soviet Union. In addition, majorities at one point capped the number of MX missiles at fifty rather than the one hundred recommended by the administration. Also, the Midgetman program, the smaller mobile missile that was proposed along with the MX, never made much progress in Congress during the Reagan years.

In economic policy, Reagan failed to get a large-scale plan enacted by Congress to drastically lessen the federal government's role in the economy. Deficits and spending expanded enormously, while taxes remained at about the same level, since the large tax increases offset the 1981 tax cut. The administration had very little success in persuading Congress to pass far-reaching legislation on deregulation and privatization. The amount of major business deregulation legislation declined considerably in the 1980s in comparison to the second half of the 1970s.

After the Reagan administration lost so much public support from James Watt's antics and the EPA scandals, Congress dominated environmental policy. The administration spent much of the time reacting to initiatives from Congress. In most of the major legislative battles, the pro-environmentalist congressmen beat Reagan and the conservatives.

The administration failed in every attempt to significantly change the important laws on the environment. Congress passed the reauthorization of the Endangered Species Act without any major relaxation of the key provisions. Congressional majorities reversed the decline in spending for the EPA and stopped James Watt from carrying out several of his policy proposals. In 1984 a bill was passed to significantly increase federally protected wilderness areas. Over 8 million acres of national forests were protected. The reauthorization of the Resource Conservation and Recovery Act was also passed in 1984. This law regulates the handling of hazardous wastes.[9] Congress enacted the reauthorization of the Safe Drinking Water Act despite strong objections by the Reagan administration to key provisions.

The reauthorization of the superfund program and the Clean Water Act were two of the biggest victories for environmental groups and congressional liberals over the Reagan administration. The administration reluctantly signed the superfund bill, which expanded the program far beyond what Reagan wanted. Reagan strongly opposed the clean water bill (Water Quality Act of 1987) and vetoed it. Congress, however, voted overwhelmingly to override the veto.

While President Reagan won some key foreign policy victories in Congress, he suffered several major defeats. Congress strongly influenced several aspects of U.S. foreign policy. Members of Congress did not just rubber-stamp Reagan's policies. Majorities in Congress, for example, forced a change in U.S. policy toward South Africa by overriding President Reagan's veto of a bill on economic sanctions. This was the first time since the passage of the War Powers Act in 1973 that Congress had overridden a presidential veto on a major foreign policy measure.[10] Congress heavily influenced Nicaraguan policy, as Reagan lost several key votes on aid to the Contras. In 1987 Speaker Jim Wright played a large role in U.S. policy toward Nicaragua by directly participating in discussions with major figures in Central America.

Special congressional committees investigated the Iran-Contra scandal in 1987. The findings from these hearings and the scandal in general considerably lessened Reagan's political clout. Congress had an important impact on trade policy and arms control negotiations. The administration officials had to react, and in some cases modify, their positions in these areas because of congressional initiatives.

The heart of the New Right's legislative agenda on social policy was the proposed constitutional amendments on abortion, prayers in public schools, and school desegregation. The Reagan administration failed to get any of these proposed amendments through Congress.

Reagan successfully persuaded Congress to cut back on the growth of several social-welfare programs. But he failed to get any major social program eliminated, and Congress repeatedly turned down Reagan's attempts to make bigger cuts in many social programs. In fact, congressional majorities even expanded the eligibility of some social programs later in the 1980s. Congress also protected Social Security and welfare programs from the Gramm-Rudman-Hollings cuts.

President Reagan won a small victory in Congress in his efforts to cut the Social Security program but suffered a huge defeat overall. At the request of the administration, Congress made small cuts in Social Security in 1981. However, Reagan was soundly defeated on his proposal to substantially cut benefits. The proposal died after the Senate unanimously passed a resolution against its key parts.

Some political commentators concluded that the 1983 Social Security reform bill, which was enacted to solve the program's financial problems, was a great victory for President Reagan. They also believed that his actions in the policy formulation process showed his outstanding ability as a legislative leader.

Actually, the 1983 Social Security law was a major defeat for Reagan and his conservative agenda. It contained some minor cuts in the program and a large tax increase. The Social Security crisis was solved primarily by a tax increase and not by spending cuts. Reagan agreed to a huge tax increase that allowed the federal government's largest social program to continue its enormous expansion for several more decades.

Reagan largely accepted what most Democrats had supported in the first place—a continuation of the program financed by higher taxes. He could have made a deal with the Democrats long before if he were just going to accept the tax increase. If Reagan had been willing to bargain earlier, the commission that was set up to hammer out a compromise would not have been needed. Rather than demonstrating brilliant leadership skills, the developments involved in the 1983 Social Security bill showed Reagan to be ineffective. He prolonged the struggle and then just accepted the main position of

the opposition. This policy option (i.e., a big tax increase) contradicted his ideological position.

Reagan is often portrayed as having dominated Congress on tax
policy. He supposedly got everything he wanted from Congress.
However, an analysis of what actually happened indicates otherwise. Congress dominated tax policy after 1981. Even though
Reagan continually said he opposed tax increases and bragged
about his record of tax cuts, taxes were increased thirteen different
times during his administration.

Moreover, all the credit for the 1986 tax reform law should not
be given to President Reagan. He certainly deserves some praise,
but the party leadership in Congress and members of the House
Ways and Means Committee and the Senate Finance Committee
should also be given credit. The administration did not initiate these
tax reform proposals, because Congress had been considering tax
reform bills similar to Reagan's for several years before the president submitted his bill. Congress did not just rubber-stamp the
administration's proposal, but it made important changes.

In addition, the bill did not pass just because of Reagan's lobby-
ing persuasion. The leadership of both parties, and the chairmen
and key members of Ways and Means and Finance, played significant roles in convincing their colleagues to accept the bill.

Finally, Congress refused to pass Reagan's major proposal on
federalism. The proposal included a plan to reshuffle the funding
and responsibility for several important social-welfare programs
between the federal and state governments.

Conclusion

Rather than being the most successful president since FDR in
legislative leadership, President Reagan was one of the least successful. One of the main reasons why no fundamental conservative
policy shift occurred in the 1980s was that Reagan had such limited
success in persuading Congress to eliminate liberal policies and
programs and to enact the conservative agenda.

Instead of ranking first in measures of presidential support by
members of Congress, Reagan ranked second to last during the
1953–88 period. His low scores in the Democratic House indicate
that he would have ranked last if the Democrats had had a Senate

majority for all eight years of the Reagan administration. Reagan received four of the eight lowest presidential support scores during this period, including the only ratings below fifty.

Part of Reagan's problem was his inability to build the conservative coalition after 1981. For a Republican president to be successful in a Congress with Democratic majorities in one or both houses, he needs to develop conservative coalitions by holding the support of a high percentage of Republicans and adding the votes of many southern Democrats. Reagan and the Republican congressional leaders had little success in forming conservative coalitions for most of the 1980s. The conservative coalition almost disappeared in the 1980s. The yearly average of conservative coalition votes as a percentage of total votes declined from the mid-twenties in the 1970s to only about ten in the late 1980s.

Where was the conservative Reagan revolution? How could a fundamental conservative change have occurred in the 1980s if the conservative coalition almost vanished from Congress? Obviously, record high levels of conservative coalition voting should have developed in Congress during the decade, rather than record low levels. Southern Democrats in Congress should have become more conservative during the 1980s and voted against Democratic majorities at increasingly higher rates. Instead, southern Democrats became more liberal and voted with their Democratic colleagues at relatively high rates.

While the increased party voting of the southern Democrats was caused by social, political, and economic changes in the South, President Reagan and the politics of the 1980s were also contributing factors. Reagan and the New Right helped to create a divisive and partisan atmosphere in U.S. politics during the 1980s. This atmosphere aided the congressional Democratic leadership in their task of persuading southern Democrats to stay within the fold. Again, just the opposite happened from what the conventional view suggested about the relationship between President Reagan and Congress. Rather than Reagan being a political genius who could consistently form winning coalitions in Congress, the president helped to create a political environment that made the key coalition (i.e., the conservative coalition) much more difficult to create.

President Reagan did not dominate Congress during the 1980s. In fact, members of Congress often took the lead on major policies and forced the administration to react to their initiatives. After 1981 Congress checked Reagan's advances on many policies and moved in new directions. For example, congressional majorities blunted many of the administration's efforts to lessen the impact of the environmental laws. On almost every major environmental area (e.g., superfund, clear water, endangered species), Congress defeated attempts by the administration to weaken the regulatory provisions. In some casese, the funding was expanded and the implementation process was strengthened.

Congressional majorities began cutting back on the growth of the defense budget in the mid-1980s. Congress cut several hundred billion dollars from Reagan's plan for a military buildup. Besides defense cuts, Congress initiated cuts in nondefense spending, increased taxes, and passed the Gramm-Rudman-Hollings law to deal with the budget deficit. President Reagan's impact on the budget policies declined enormously with the mounting deficits. His inability to offer feasible budget plans that would lead to significant reductions in the deficits cost him a great deal of credibility in Congress. He was unable to face the reality that his goal of sharp tax cuts, substantial defense increases, and balanced or surplus budgets could not be attained at the same time.

Majorities in Congress reauthorized several important civil rights laws and generally ignored the Reagan administration's attempt to weaken key provisions. Congress continued the basic farm programs and refused to adopt a more free-market approach to solve the farm crisis. The legislators played an important role in many key foreign policy areas such as South Africa, Nicaragua, and foreign trade.

Moderate and liberal Democrats defeated the New Right conservatives on every one of their proposed constitutional amendments. After 1981 Congress stopped cutting back on several social programs and even expanded eligibility requirements for a few social programs.

After watching President Reagan's influence decline in Congress after 1981, some political analysts rejected the conventional view of Reagan's legislative success. They pointed out that later in the decade Reagan suffered a number of defeats in Congress. Many analysts, however, still cling to the notion that Reagan achieved historic successes in 1981. Louis Fisher, for example, wrote in *The Politics of Shared Power:*

> In 1981, flush from an electrifying triumph in the national elections, President Ronald Reagan put together a series of remarkable legislative victories: the tax cut, the defense buildup, and a major retrenchment of domestic spending. Not since Lyndon Johnson's passage of the Great Society legislation in 1965, or possibly Franklin D. Roosevelt's stunning New Deal programs in 1933, had a president been so dominant over a Congress. . . . In 1981 he was able to build a bipartisan-conservative majority in the House and enjoyed partisan loyalty from the Republican Senate. Within a year, however, he faced stiff opposition from both houses.[11]

While the Reagan administration won important victories in 1981, the significance of these victories has been exaggerated. The percentage increase in the military budget in 1981 was about the same as the increase for 1980. The military buildup started in the late 1970s, not in 1981. Before Reagan arrived, the majority in Congress had already been convinced that the growth of military spending had to be increased. Under these circumstances, getting a large percentage increase in the defense budget through Congress was relatively easy.

Getting the 1981 tax cut enacted was also relatively easy. Persuading legislative bodies to cut taxes is like shooting fish in a barrel. Since citizens do not want to pay taxes, tax cut proposals will always be popular. The temptation always exists for legislators to ignore their responsibilities and to gain public support through the enactment of huge tax reductions. Proposing a tax cut is one of the easiest ways for a president to win a major victory in Congress. Members of the president's party in Congress will want to support such a popular proposal, whereas members of the opposition party will fear a voter backlash if they oppose it.

The significance of the social-welfare cuts in 1981 was not as great as the conventional view suggests. Most of the cuts were in the programs' rate of growth and not in the actual funding. Reagan and the congressional conservatives were unable to eliminate any of the major social-welfare programs.

Furthermore, the historical significance of the 1981 legislative achievements cannot be compared to the legislative success of the

1930s and mid-1960s. The congressional actions during these earlier two periods have had an important long-term impact on public policies and the political system. In contrast, the 1981 developments did not produce long-range conservative changes. After the tax cut, taxes were increased several times to the point that federal taxes as a percent of GNP were higher in the mid-1980s than in 1979. At the end of the 1980s, the military budget was declining in relation to the economy. Congress refused to appropriate the funds for Reagan's planned military buildup. Finally, overall spending on social-welfare programs, as measured by percent of GNP, was higher in the mid-1980s than in the late 1970s.

Notes

1. This analysis is based on data presented in Chuck Alston, "Reagan's Support Index Up—But Not Much," *Congressional Quarterly Weekly Report* 46 (9 November 1988): 3233–3353.
2. "Hill Support for President Drops to 10-Year Low," *Congressional Quarterly Almanac: 1986* (Washington, D.C.: Congressional Quarterly, 1987): 21-C.
3. Richard Fleisher and Jon R. Bond, "Assessing Presidential Support in the House: Lessons from Reagan and Carter," *Journal of Politics* 45 (August 1983): 745–58.
4. George C. Edwards III, *At the Margins* (New Haven, Conn.: Yale University Press, 1989), 182–85.
5. John R. Cranford, "Election-Year Impact: Party Unity Scores Slip in 1988, But Overall Pattern Is Upward," *Congressional Quarterly Weekly Report* 46 (19 November 1988): 3334–42.
6. Macon Morehouse, "Conservative Coalition: Still Alive, But Barely," *Congressional Quarterly Weekly Report* (19 November 1988): 3343–52.
7. David E. Price, "From Outsider to Insider," *Congress Reconsidered*, 4th ed., ed. Lawrence C. Dodd and Bruce I. Oppenheimer (Washington, D.C.: CQ Press, 1989), 432.
8. "First Budget Resolution Becomes Binding," *Congressional Quarterly Almanac: 1982* (Washington, D.C.: Congressional Quarterly, 1983), 187.
9. "Congress Tightens Hazardous Waste Controls," *Congressional Quarterly Almanac: 1984* (Washington, D.C.: Congressional Quarterly, 1985), 305–8.
10. "Hill Overrides Veto of South Africa Sanctions," *Congressional Quarterly Almanac: 1986* (Washington, D.C.: Congressional Quarterly, 1987), 359.
11. Louis Fisher, *The Politics of Shared Power,* 2nd ed. (Washington, D.C.: CQ Press, 1987), ix–x.

8

No Fundamental Change in the
Governmental System

Supposedly, the Reagan administration not only had a long-term impact on politics and policies, but also on how the government functions. According to this assumption, the three branches of the federal government and the relationship between the federal, state, and local governments changed substantially during the 1980s. These changes are supposed to affect the system for many years in the future.

Richard Nathan presented this point of view in relation to the presidency and federalism in his analysis in *Perspectives on the Reagan Years*.

> . . . I believe that President Reagan has been decidedly successful in the domestic policy arena, and that his success has enabled him to make skillful use of—and change—American political institutions. . . . His term in office has demonstrated that the presidency can work effectively; he has brought both a leadership style and strategy to bear that are likely to have a strong influence on future practice. . . . Reagan came to the presidency with a strong and long-standing theory of American federalism, favoring the reduction of the role of the federal government and the enhancement of the role of state governments. . . . I argue that he has been strikingly successful in achieving his intergovernmental reform aims, and that his efforts to realign American federalism are likely to have a lasting effect.[1]

The relevant data and the political developments of the 1980s do not support Nathan's position. No fundamental shift occurred from the federal government to the state and local governments. In

203

addition, future presidents will probably not use Reagan's leadership style as a model for their presidencies. President Bush and the other 1988 presidential candidates clearly indicated that they would not follow Reagan's administrative style.

This chapter also considers the bureaucracy, Congress, and the federal courts. Similarly, no fundamental changes developed in these institutions during the 1980s.

The Presidency

President Reagan differed considerably in his administrative style from most of the other recent presidents. He approached the office as a detached chairman of the board. Reagan had less involvement in the operation of his administration than any president during the past fifty years. In the Reagan administration, the president would set broad policy and then delegate an unprecedented amount of responsibility. The other members of the administration were expected to fill in the details and to carry out policy within Reagan's conservative philosophy.

The events of the last few years indicate that Reagan will indeed influence the administrative style of future presidents. However, the influence will be in a negative manner. Reagan's leadership style became so discredited by the end of his second term that future presidents and presidential candidates will avoid rather than emulate his approach. His administrative failures probably eliminate the detached, hands-off approach as an option that will be seriously considered by future presidents.

The proof of this could be seen in the 1988 presidential election and Bush's presidency. Every Democratic and Republican candidate, except George Bush, rejected Reagan's administrative approach to the presidency.[2] They promised to employ a more hands-on approach with more presidential involvement and less delegation of power. Bush seemed to have a similar opinion, but evidently he did not want to criticize President Reagan while he was still vice-president.

When George Bush became president, he went out of his way to stress that he would not follow Reagan's managerial style. He talked about a hands-on approach, similar to the style outlined by the other presidential candidates. Bush has followed this type of leadership style, because his approach to the office is much different than Reagan's. He delegates less responsibility and is involved at a much lower level of detail than his predecessor. Bush knows much more about what is happening in his administration.

These developments are just the opposite of what should have happened in a Reagan revolution. If Reagan had had a profound impact on the presidency, all the 1988 presidential candidates would have promised to emulate Reagan's approach if they were elected. Also, George Bush would have followed Reagan's example and used the detached hands-off method.

Another important aspect of Reagan's approach to the presidency was his distinctive use of the media. Just as in other administrations, an effort was made in the Reagan administration to emphasize the president's strengths and downplay his weaknesses. Reagan had communication skills because of his acting background, but he had a poor memory and often had difficulty grasping the details of complex issues. Therefore, his advisers tried to maximize the opportunities for Reagan to give speeches to large groups or on television and to generally avoid news conferences and other situations where the president could be asked direct questions.

President Bush has not followed this aspect of the Reagan approach. Bush is more accessible to the media than Reagan. He also is much more willing to participate in question-and-answer sessions with reporters. On the other hand, Bush relies less on using television speeches to increase support for his policies.

Future presidents will probably use a media style similar to Reagan's only if they have similar strengths and weaknesses. The chances are slim that a president would just follow Reagan's style and disregard his/her own abilities.

The Iran-Contra scandal was a major reason why President Reagan ended up with such a poor reputation as an administrator. The hearings and reports on the affair painted a picture of an administration headed by a president who was incredibly uninformed and detached from the basic activities under his control. The Tower Commission, which Reagan appointed to investigate the scandal, was very critical of the president's administrative style.

Reagan's reputation as an administrator was also damaged by books written by top administration officials after they left office. The description of Reagan's administrative style presented by several of these former officials corroborated the findings in the Iran-Contra reports. The revelations in these books portrayed Reagan as a president with little knowledge of complex issues and limited involvement in the operation of his own administration. Columnist David Broder points out how the books by Donald Regan, the White House chief of staff and later treasury secretary in the Reagan administration, and other high administration officials ridiculed Reagan's leadership style.

> This is a total embarrassment, at the tail end of the president's term, something that cannot be erased and is not likely to be forgotten. The picture Regan draws of a domineering First Lady, with her astrological adviser, and a passive president, ostensibly so lacking in initiative that he doesn't even react to a smoking fireplace in his office, is so weird, so far beyond a cartoonist's caricature, that it carries its own built-in credibility. . . .

> What makes it worse is that the wounds Reagan has suffered have been inflicted by his friends, not his enemies. No Democrats and no "liberal reporter" has drawn as unflattering a picture of this president as his chosen associates in government—David Stockman, Alexander Haig, Michael Deaver, Larry Speakes, and now Regan—in their books. The portrait they paint is appalling: a president almost devoid of curiosity, reflectiveness, energy of purpose, a man full of his own preconceptions, yet easily manipulated and fooled by others.[3]

Under these circumstances, it is easy to understand why the presidential candidates in 1988 made a point of stressing that they would adopt an administrative style different from Reagan's. Future presidents with knowledge about the Iran-Contra scandal and the portrayal of the Reagan style outlined in these books will probably shun the Reagan approach.

Another claim by many political analysts is that President Reagan rescued the presidency from a state of significant decline. Supposedly, Reagan's successful leadership after several failed presidencies put new life into the office and restored some of its lost prestige. Again, quoting from Richard Nathan's analysis:

> Ronald Reagan was elected at a time when the presidency was in deep trouble. His predecessors, Presidents Johnson and Nixon had left office in disgrace. Both Presidents Ford and Carter were defeated in their bids for reelection; their administrations were not popular. The executive

office needed resuscitation, and Ronald Reagan, in a way that surprised many observers, has accomplished precisely that.[4]

From the perspective of the late 1980s and the early 1990s, this point of view seems way off the mark. Almost the opposite happened. Reagan damaged the presidency rather than rescuing it from a great decline. Much of the discussion about Reagan restoring confidence in the presidency relates to the perception that he successfully used the office in 1981 to make significant changes. But the damage done to the presidency by developments such as the deadlock on the deficit, the Iran-Contra scandal, the many other investigations of unethical and illegal activities of high administration officials, and the kiss-and-tell books of several top aides, more than offset any increased confidence people had in the office from Reagan's triumphs in 1981.

This can be seen in the actions of the 1988 presidential candidates and President Bush. The presidential candidates in the 1988 campaign and George Bush after he was elected stated that they would follow a different administrative style. They took this position because Reagan had, especially in the Iran-Contra scandal, so tarnished the image of the office. So rather than perceiving that Reagan had restored respect to the presidency, these candidates and President Bush believed that they would need to restore confidence in the office by telling the public that they would handle the presidency in a different manner than President Reagan.

Federal Bureaucracy

Since conservatives often complain about the size of the federal government and its bureaucracy, a conservative Reagan revolution should have produced an enormous reduction in the size of the federal bureaucracy. Ronald Reagan advocated this in the 1980 campaign and during his administration. For example, he called for a hiring freeze in nonmilitary areas and proposed cutting the number of cabinet departments from thirteen to eleven by eliminating the Energy and Education Departments.

Again, as with so many other developments in the 1980s, just the opposite happened from what should have occurred in a fundamental conservative change. Rather than an enormous reduction in personnel, the number of federal civilian employees plus the active duty military personnel increased from 4.9 million in 1980 to 5.3 million in 1987.[5] During this period, the number of civilian employees in the federal government increased by 215,000. This increase marked a departure from the 1970s in which the number of federal civilian employees remained fairly stable.[6]

Instead of decreasing from thirteen to eleven, the number of departments increased to fourteen with the addition of the Department of Veterans' Affairs. President Reagan failed to get the Energy and Education Departments eliminated. In fact Congress never even seriously considered these proposals. Also, Reagan shocked his conservative advisers by announcing his support for the proposed Department of Veterans' Administration. These advisers advocated the standard conservative position of a smaller federal government. They were also worried about the historical implications of the number of departments actually increasing under a conservative Republican president. Reagan ignored their advice and pushed for this expansion of the cabinet departments.

The issue of the bureaucracy's size is another example of a contradiction in conservatives' ideology that makes a fundamental conservative change impossible. Conservatives advocate a cutback in the federal executive branch and a huge expansion of the military. These two goals, however, are impossible to attain together because nearly two thirds of all federal government employees work for the Department of Defense. Military personnel make up by far the largest group on the federal government's payroll. In addition, the civilian employees at the Department of Defense outnumber the federal employees at any other department by a wide margin. Therefore, an enormous expansion of military spending would result in a huge increase among the largest group of federal employees. Under these circumstances, a substantial reduction in federal employment could only be achieved by eliminating a major portion of the federal workers in domestic programs. But as the 1980s proved, the elimination of major domestic programs is not politically feasible. Conservatives would be unable to reduce civilian federal employment in domestic programs enough to match the enormous expansion of Department of Defense personnel that would result from a large military buildup.

If the Reagan administration had achieved its goals in military spending and the defense budget had exceeded $500 billion in 1988, the number of federal employees would have increased substantially during the 1980s. Since the Defense Department has by far the most civilian employees, federal civilian employment would also have expanded considerably.

Just the reverse happened from what could be assumed from the Reagan revolution thesis. President Reagan was unsuccessful in pushing a program through Congress that would have resulted in substantial reductions in federal employment. But by cutting several hundred billion dollars from Reagan's defense plans, moderate and liberal Democrats in Congress kept the rise in the number of federal employees much lower than what would have resulted from a large military buildup.

Congress

During the past forty years, the major changes in the power structure, rules, and behavior patterns in Congress occurred in the late 1960s and the 1970s, not in the 1980s. The 1980s did not usher in a new congressional era. The basic patterns of operation established in the 1970s continued through the 1980s.

Certainly, no historic conservative change occurred in Congress during the 1980s. In fact, the Congresses at the end of the decade were among the most liberal of the postwar period. Liberals in the late 1980s generally had more power in the House and Senate than liberals had during the period from the late 1930s to the early 1960s.

During the 1980s, the Republicans' six-year Senate majority was the only major change in how Congress operates that fit the Reagan revolution thesis. Congress, however, did not enter a new era because of these Senate victories. Republicans had won the majority of seats in the Senate and the House earlier in the post–New Deal era. Furthermore, the Democrats won back the Senate majority in the 1986 and 1988 elections.

Congressional scholars often compare the older textbook Congress with the new reform or postreform Congress.[7] The old congressional era lasted from the 1940s to about the early 1960s, while the new era has continued since the early 1970s.

The old textbook Congress was characterized by a relatively closed system with a fairly centralized power structure dominated by committees and the committee chairmen. Rural and southern Democratic members usually controlled most of the power in the old Congress.

Several congressional reforms, along with numerous political, social, and economic changes in the country, produced the reform Congress. During the 1970s, the media and the public's access to Congress increased through more recorded votes, open hearings, and television coverage. The power structure became more decentralized. Several components of the House, such as the subcommittees, subcommittee chairmen, individual representatives, the Speaker, and the Democratic Caucus gained power. In the Senate, much of the power shifted to the individual senators. The full committees and the committee chairmen remained powerful, but less influential than in the previous congressional era.

In the House, the growth of metropolitan areas and equal-population redistricting shifted many seats from rural to metropolitan areas. Metropolitan representatives replaced their rural colleagues as the dominant group in the House power structure.

In both chambers, the power of southern Democrats finally declined in the late 1960s and the 1970s. Northern Democrats, who were generally more liberal, replaced southern Democrats in many committee and subcommittee chair positions.

The basic patterns of the 1970s continued into the 1980s. Although the deficit crisis concentrated more power in the majority party leadership and the budget-related committees,[8] the decision-making process remained fairly decentralized. Metropolitan northern Democrats continued to dominate the House power structure.

No historic shift toward conservative power occurred in the House during the 1980s. The House was generally more liberal in the 1980s than it was in the period from the 1940s to the mid-1960s. While the conservative coalition was powerful in the previous congressional era, it almost disappeared in the last half of the 1980s. In 1987 the coalition formed in only 8 percent of votes. A key part of the conservative coalition's power in the 1950s was the alliance of conservative southern Democrats and Republicans who controlled the House Rules Committee. This alliance, led by powerful Chairman Howard Smith, would often oppose the policies of moderate and liberal Democrats. In the 1970s and 1980s, the Rules

Committee was dominated by moderate-to-liberal Democrats who worked with the Democratic leadership in the House.

In the late 1980s, a high proportion of the most powerful members of the House were moderate and liberal Democrats, not conservative Republicans and conservative Democrats. This can be seen by first identifying the power elite in the House and then measuring their ideological backgrounds. The most powerful House members are the Speaker, the other Democratic leaders, the Republican leaders, and the committee chairmen. Other representatives, such as key subcommittee chairmen and leaders on national issues, are also powerful members. A useful way to identify a congressional member in the second group is to utilize the list compiled by the *National Journal* of the most influential members of Congress outside of the party leadership and committee chairmen.[9] Including the representatives from the *National Journal*'s list with the party leaders and committee chairmen produces a group of fifty representatives.

The ideological ratings of the liberal Americans for Democratic Action (ADA) and the conservative American Conservative Union (ACU) can be used to divide the representatives into liberals, moderates, and conservatives.[10] Of the fifty representatives in the House's power elite during the late 1980s, thirty-five were liberals, ten were moderates, and only five were conservatives.[11] So liberals dominated the power structure in the House, while only a few conservatives were in the group of the most powerful representatives.

The shift to a more liberal House power elite in the new congressional era can especially be seen in the committee chair positions. In the previous congressional era, conservative southern committee chairmen, such as Howard Smith, dominated the House. In the late 1980s, Sonny Montgomery, the chariman of the Veterans' Affairs Committee, was the only conservative southern chairman, and he was the head of only a minor committee. In the 1980s most of the House chairmen were northern liberals.

In addition, the majority party leadership in the House at the end of the 1980s was one of the most liberal in the past fifty years. Speaker Thomas Foley had an eighty-five percent approval rating from the ADA in 1988, while Majority Leader Richard Gephardt had a rating of seventy-five. William Gray, the majority whip, and

Steny Hoyer, the chairman of the Democratic Caucus, posted ADA scores of ninety-five.

Conservatives were powerful during the six years of Republican control in the Senate (1981–86), but moderates and liberals returned to dominate the Senate after the Democratic victories in 1986 and 1988. Among the party leaders, the committee chairmen, and senators on *National Journal*'s list in 1989 were fifteen liberals, six moderates, and only five conservatives.

George Mitchell became the Senate majority leader in 1989. He is one of the most liberal majority leaders of the past several decades. In 1988 he had an ADA rating of ninety-five and an ACU rating of zero.

Just as in the House, the Senate Democratic committee chairmen were much more liberal in the post-reform era than in the old congressional period. The shift to more liberal chairmen developed from the decline of the conservative southern chairmen who had dominated the Senate. In 1968, for example, there were eight Senate committee chairmen with ADA scores below ten. In 1988 none of the chairmen had an ADA rating below forty, while half of them had ADA ratings of eighty or more.

Once again, just the opposite occurred from what should have happened in a historic conservative era. Rather than the most powerful members of Congress being much more conservative in the late 1980s than in the old congressional era, they were much more liberal.

Another major development in Congress during the past fifteen years has been the shift toward more liberal Democrats being elected to Congress from the South. This is especially important because this ideological shift in the South was one of the main reasons why the power of the conservative coalition declined substantially in Congress and party cohesion among congressional Democrats increased during the 1980s.

Table 8.1 shows the enormous ideological change among southern Democratic senators and representatives. In 1968 most of the southern Democratic senators still had conservative voting records. The majority had ADA ratings of zero. By 1988 conservative southern Democrats had almost disappeared from the Senate. Most southern Democrats had moderate voting records, and a few would generally be considered liberals.

TABLE 8.1
Ideological Changes Among Southern Representatives and
Senators from 1968 to 1988

State	1968 Democratic Senators ADA Rating	1968 Mean ADA Ratings of House Dem.	1988 Democratic Senators ADA Rating	1988 Mean ADA Rating of House Dem.
Alabama				
Hill	7	12		42
Sparkman	0			
Heflin			30	
Shelby			35	
Arkansas				
Fulbright	14	17		72
McClellan	0			
Bumpers			80	
Pryor			75	
Florida				
Holland	0	31		56
Smathers	7			
Chiles			50	
Graham			55	
Georgia				
Russell	0	11		49
Talmadge	0			
Fowler			75	
Nunn			40	
Louisiana				
Ellender	7	25		55
Long	0			
Breaux			50	
Johnston			55	
Mississippi				
Eastland	0	5		58
Stennis	0		45	
North Carolina				
Ervin	0	7		64
Jordan	0			
Sanford			90	
South Carolina				
Hollings	14	13	55	53
Tennessee				
Gore	43	33		
Sasser			75	63
Gore			60	
Texas				
Yarborough	57	36		61
Bentsen			40	
Virginia				
Byrd, Jr.	0	0		63
Spong	29			

Source for ADA ratings: Congressional Quarterly Weekly Report 26 (22 November 1968): 3197; Congressional Quarterly Weekly Report 47 (4 March 1989): 486.

The liberal shift in the Democratic House delegation in most southern states was amazing. For example, the Virginia House Democrats were often very conservative. As the table indicates, all the Virginia Democrats received ADA scores of zero in 1968. In contrast, the 1988 ADA scores among Virginia House Democrats ranged from a low of fifty to a high of seventy-five. The five Mississippi Democrats had ADA scores of 0, 0, 0, 8, and 17 in 1968, while the four Democrats had ADA ratings of 25, 55, 65, and 85 in 1988.

Granted, some of the conservative Democrats were replaced by conservative Republicans. But since the late 1950s, congressional Democrats have more than made up for their losses in the South by winning many northern seats from the Republicans. Since these northern Democrats were usually moderates and liberals, the net effect was to move Congress to the left.

Federal Courts

According to the Reagan revolution thesis, President Reagan fundamentally changed the court system. Supposedly, the Reagan administration produced landmark conservative changes in the federal courts that will last for many years. These changes allegedly developed from placing many conservative judges in the federal courts and successfully pursuing a conservative agenda in court cases.

Certainly President Reagan had an important impact on the federal courts, especially through the appointment of so many conservative judges. But declaring that the 1980s produced a historic conservative shift in the federal courts, which will last well into the next century, greatly exaggerates Reagan's impact.

A new Supereme Court era did not develop in the 1980s. The important Supreme Court change of recent decades occurred in the late 1960s and early 1970s with the shift from the liberal Warren Court to the more conservative Burger Court. The 1980s simply represented a continuation of this more conservative court era. The Burger Court remained largely in place for the first half of the decade. Most of the decision-making patterns of the Burger Court remained during the last part of the decade with the transition to the Rehnquist Court.

One conservative Chief Justice replaced another in the shift from Warren Burger to William Rehnquist. Also, the ideologies of the three new justices coming on the Court in the 1980s were about the same as those of the three justices they replaced. Overall, the ideological backgrounds of Sandra Day O'Connor, Antonin Scalia, and Anthony Kennedy, the three new justices, are probably more conservative than the three former judges, but the difference is not great. The situation would have been different if the Reagan appointees had replaced more liberal justices such as William Brennan and Thurgood Marshall.

In addition, Rehnquist surprised many court observers by moving more to the center after he became Chief Justice. His opinion on cases such as libel, rent control, and entrapment were more liberal than would have been expected from his previous record. This is just the opposite of what should have happened in a conservative era.[12]

The effects of the Reagan changes in the lower federal courts also have been exaggerated by many commentators. There are still many federal court judges who were not appointed by Reagan. Reagan's influence will only last so long because these judges will eventually be replaced by new judges. The early indications from the Bush administration are that the new president will not follow Reagan's policy of appointing almost all conservatives to the federal courts.

Furthermore, there is no guarantee that the Reagan appointees will all consistently follow a hard-line conservative position throughout their careers. The history of the federal courts is filled with examples of judges who ended up with records far different from what the president who nominated them expected.

In addition, the power of the federal courts within the whole political system should be put in perspective. While the U.S. federal courts are more powerful than the courts in most other countries, these courts still significantly influence only a small portion of the major policy areas. The courts have a great deal of influence on civil rights and liberties and on constitutional issues. But the legislative and executive branches dominate most of the major policy areas, such as taxes, defense, foreign affairs, education, environmental protection, Social Security, and welfare. Also, the federal courts are only part of the court system.. The bulk of cases is handled by state and local courts.

The impact of Reagan's appointments to the federal courts is limited, since he appointed only a portion of one part of the governmental system. Compared to the other branches of government, the federal courts significantly influence policy in relatively few major policy areas.

Finally, the Reagan administration had amazingly little success in persuading the Supreme Court to accept its position on cases. The major story about the Supreme Court in the 1980s was not that it moved significantly to the right, but how often the court rebuffed the conservative position of the Reagan administration. A conservative administration should have easily been able to win in a Supreme Court with a conservative majority. However, in a surprising number of cases, from the constitutionality of the independent counsel to civil liberties cases, the court ruled against Reagan's conservative position. Stuart Taylor, Jr., a *New York Times* reporter who covered the Supreme Court, came to this conclusion about the court's decision to uphold the validity of the federal independent counsel law and to make many other decisions against the Reagan administration.

> Whether or not Rehnquist intended it to, the decision also seemed to say something else: that this is the Rehnquist Court—not the Reagan Court. Indeed, on that dramatic day the Court rejected the Administration's position in five cases, while ruling in its favor in only one. . . .

> For seven years, President Reagan, Attorney General Edwin L. Meese 3d and the fervent conservatives who surrounded Meese during his tenure had mounted the most systematic campaign in decades, perhaps in history, to reverse the ideological direction of the Federal judiciary. . . .

> But despite Reagan's elevation of Rehnquist from Associate Justice, and his appointments of Justices Sandra Day O'Connor, Antonin Scalia and Anthony M. Kennedy, his Administration has lost more of the political blockbuster cases than it has won.

> . . . the Court's legacy from the Reagan years is one of continuity. Indeed, in the two areas in which the Adminstration battled most passionately to move the law to the right—abortion and affirmative action—the Court pushed in the opposite direction. . . .[13]

Federalism

Many political observers considered the 1980s as a historic period in the relationship between the federal and state and local governments. Supposedly, the continual movement of power to the national government, which started with the New Deal, finally ended in the 1980s as power significantly shifted back to the state and local governments.

President Reagan and congressional conservatives had some success in federalism policy, especially in cutting federal grants to state and local governments and creating new block grants. However, no fundamental change occurred in the relationship between the federal government and state and local governments during the 1980s. The power relationship remained about the same with the federal government even gaining a little.

Several points can be made to show why no fundamental shift of power to the state and local governments occurred. First, most of the major measures of power do not show that a historic transfer of power happened in the 1980s. The amount of spending is one of the best measures of power in a federal system. Since the 1930s and 1940s produced a shift from a large state and local advantage in spending to comparatively greater spending by the federal government, a fundamental conservative change should have made the state and local government the spending leaders again. But this did not happen in the 1980s. Even though many political commentators proclaimed that power shifted to state and local governments, the federal government's share of total government spending actually expanded during the 1980s. The federal government's share of total spending increased from 62.5 percent in 1970 to 64.4 in 1980 and 65.3 in 1985.[14] So power, as measured by government spending, shifted to the federal government during the 1980s.

Another important aspect of political power in the late twentieth century is media attention. The greater media attention given to Washington is a factor in the national government's dominance in the federal system. The effective use of the media by the Reagan administration plus developments such as the deficit crisis, the conflicts between President Reagan and congressional Democrats, the Iran-Contra scandal, and the rise of Mikhail Gorbachev, helped to maintain the federal government's advantage with the media through the 1980s.

Second, the major part of President Reagan's New Federalism program was not adopted. The plan, which called for swapping the administrative responsibilities and funding between the federal and state levels in several social programs, never even received serious consideration in Congress. This again shows how the power of past policies was so much stronger than the conservative forces of the 1980s. If the decade had been a landmark conservative period, Reagan should have been able to persuade members of Congress and state and local officials to agree to eliminate some major federal programs and shift many others to the state and local level.

Third, as mentioned in the environmental section, the Reagan administration could not implement its plan to transfer federal lands to the state. This proposal was a key part of Reagan's federalism agenda.

Fourth, President Reagan contradicted his conservative position on federalism in several important ways. The most important contradiction concerns the major conflict conservatives have in their beliefs about federalism. This is the conflict between conservatives' support for a smaller federal government and a much larger military as part of an aggressive foreign policy. The enormous expansion of the military and the greater post-1940 foreign policy role of the United States, especially in the containment policy, were the major reasons why power shifted to the federal government. So by emphasizing the need for a greater U.S. military power in the world, conservatives favor an enormous expansion of the federal government in relation to state and local governments, while they proclaim their support for just the opposite power relationship in federalism.

This contradiction was evident in the 1980s. Reagan's support for a massive military buildup and a greater U.S. role in places such as Central America meant that he was advocating a substantial shift of power from the state and local level to the national level. An emphasis on areas such as education and police and fire protection would favor state and local governments because these are policy areas where these governments dominate. However, a focus on military and foreign policy shifts power to the national level because these areas are almost completely controlled by the federal government. If military spending had increased at the rate of growth Reagan advocated in his first five-year budget plan, the federal government would have gained considerably greater power over the state and local governments. The best thing President Reagan did to increase state and local power was to bungle the military buildup. The historic military cutback starting in the mid-1980s was the major factor favoring the state and local side in federalism.

Much of the media and most political analysts mistakenly focus on social programs and government regulations in analyses of federalism. From this focus, they conclude that liberals advocate a large federal government with relatively weak state and local governments, while conservatives are assumed to support the reverse. More focus on military and foreign policy would show that conservatives actually support a big federal government. If Reagan had been able to persuade Congress to increase the defense budget from $158 billion in 1981 to over $500 billion in 1988, the gain in federal power would have been much more than the gain in state and local power through all of the administration's New Federalism proposals.

There also were many other important policy issues where the Reagan administration violated its conservative principles on federalism. For example, the legal center of the Academy for State and Local Government discovered that the federal government opposed the position of state and local governments in at least ten friends-of-the-court briefs with the Supreme Court in just the period from mid-1985 to early 1987.[15] In the Baby Doe controversy, the Reagan administration attempted to regulate states' rights and parents' rights to determine if life-support systems should continue for fatally impaired infants.

Reagan also forgot his conservative principles in the bill on the drinking age. Even though conservatives often complain about laws which set up sanctions against states for noncompliance of federal directives, President Reagan supported the law which required states to increase the drinking age to twenty-one or lose federal funds for highways.[16]

In a debate over the state governors' power over the National Guard troops in their states, which was one of the decade's major constitutional issues on federalism, the Reagan administration again favored federal over state power. The controversy arose over the attempt by several governors to prevent the Defense Department from sending their National Guard troops to Central America for practice exercises. In this constitutional debate, the Reagan administration strongly opposed the rights of the states.

Finally, federal mandates and regulations on state and local governments continued and even expanded in the 1980s.[17] This, coupled with the cuts in funds to the state and local governments, lessened the state and local officials' flexibility on many policies. So instead of gaining more power in the 1980s, state and local governments were restricted even more by federal mandates. As Martin Tolchin concluded from interviews with state and local government officials:

> Although the "New Federalism" approach was intended to give states and municipalities more flexibility and authority, it was undercut by an avalanche of mandates imposed in Washington, from monitoring pollution to removing asbestos from schools to supervising nursing homes. . . .
>
> One paradox of the Reagan years is that while Mr. Reagan cultivated the image of being a "deregulator," his Administration forced state and local governments to assume new regulatory duties—in terms both of new rules to enforce and of responsibility for enforcing old ones.[18]

Tolchin quoted Governor Carroll A. Campbell, Jr., a Republican from South Carolina, as saying, "Instead of giving the power to the states, and giving us the flexibility of addressing the problems of the states, Congress keeps giving us new mandates."[19] And Republican Mayor Robert M. Isaac of Colorado Springs, who was president-elect of the United States Conference of Mayors at the time of the interview, stated, "I don't think there was any New Federalism. I don't think there's been any transfer of power. I think it's gone the other way."[20]

Conclusion

The Reagan administration failed to make a lasting imprint on the three branches of the federal government or on federalism. The developments in many parts of the government were just the opposite of what should have occurred in a conservative Reagan revolution.

Future presidents will probably follow President Bush's course and shun Reagan's decision-making style. All the Republican and Democratic candidates for president in 1988 vowed to adopt a much different administrative style from Reagan's. The Iran-Contra scandal and the kiss-and-tell books of several high officials in the Reagan administration created the image of Reagan as an inept and uninformed administrator.

The federal bureaucracy should have declined substantially if a fundamental conservative change in government happened in the 1980s, but instead the bureaucracy grew. The number of federal employees increased considerably and the cabinet departments increased from thirteen to fourteen rather than dropping down to eleven as Reagan had proposed.

In Congress the major change in the rules and decision-making patterns of the past several decades occurred in the late 1960s and in the 1970s. The 1980s were a continuation of the "postreform" period in Congress.

Rather than the 1980s ending with conservatives and Republicans in control of Congress, Democrats had majorities in both chambers, and moderates and liberals dominated the most powerful positions. In fact, the moderate and liberal Democrats, who held the party leadership positions, the committee chair positions, and the key subcommittee chair positions, were as liberal, if not more so, than any other similar group in several decades.

Probably the most important development in congressional politics during the 1980s was the decline and almost disappearance of the conservative coalition. In past decades, the conservative coalition formed on over 20 or 30 percent of the roll-call votes. During some years of the 1980s, the conservative coalition formed on less than 10 percent of the votes. This developed primarily from a substantial liberal shift in the voting patterns of southern Democrats.

The Supreme Court maintained the basic decision patterns of the 1970s with the continuation of the Burger Court for the first half of the 1980s and the shift to the Rehnquist Court in the last half. The important change in Supreme Court eras did not occur in the 1980s, but with the shift from the Warren Court to the Burger Court.

Finally, no historic shift of power occurred from the federal government to the state and local governments. The federal government's share of total government spending even increased. The

Reagan administration contradicted its federalism policy on many important issues by favoring federal power over state and local power.

Notes

1. Richard P. Nathan, "Institutional Change Under Reagan," in *Perspectives on the Reagan Years,* ed. John L. Palmer (Washington, D.C.: Urban Institute Press, 1986), 122–23.
2. On the Republican candidates, see Bernard Weinraub, "G.O.P. Hopefuls Backing Away from Reagan," *New York Times,* 13 July 1987, pp. 1 and 11.
3. David S. Broder, "Reagan reduced to a joke," *Plain Dealer,* 15 May, 1988, p. E–1.
4. Nathan, "Institutional Change Under Reagan," 122–23.
5. Based on data in U.S. Bureau of the Census, *Statistical Abstract of the United States: 1989* (Washington, D.C.: U.S. Government Printing Office, 1989), 318 and 335.
6. Ibid., 318.
7. For a discussion of some of the changes, see Larry M. Schwab, *Changing Patterns of Congressional Politics* (New York: D. Van Nostrand, 1980).
8. Lawrence C. Dodd and Bruce I. Oppenheimer, "Consolidating Power in the House: The Rise of a New Oligarchy," in *Congress Reconsidered,* 4th ed., ed. Lawrence C. Dodd and Bruce I. Oppenheimer (Washington, D.C.: CQ Press, 1989), 39–64.
9. Richard E. Cohen and Christopher Madison, "A Piece of the Action," *National Journal* 21 (28 January 1989): 174–92.
10. The ADA and ACU ratings are listed in Michael Barone and Grant Ujifusa, *The Almanac of American Politics 1990* (Washington, D.C.: National Journal, 1990).
11. The operational definitions for the ideological categories are as follows: liberals, ADA rating − ACU rating = 50 to 100; moderates, ADA − ACU = 49 to −49; conservatives, ADA − ACU = −50 to −100.
12. Stuart Taylor, Jr., "Rehnquist's Court: Turning Out The White House," *New York Times Magazine,* 11 September 1988, 38–41, 94–5, 98.
13. Ibid., 41.
14. U.S. Bureau of the Census, *Statistical Abstract of the United States: 1989* (Washington, D.C.: U.S. Government Printing Office, 1989), 267.
15. W. John Moore, "Just a Principle," *National Journal* 19 (17 January 1987): 161.
16. Neal R. Peirce, "Reaganites are uncorking a super federalism campaign," *Plain Dealer,* 1 December, 1986, pp. 9–13.

17. Martin Tolchin, "States Take Up New Burdens to Pay For 'New Federalism,' " *New York Times,* 21 May 1990, pp. 1 and 11.
18. Ibid., p. 1.
19. Ibid., p. 11.
20. Ibid.

9

Conclusion

The first part of the chapter summarizes the main points of the book. The second section presents several reasons why no fundamental conservative and Republican change occurred in the 1980s.

Summary

Through the 1980s, the United States remained in the same political era that started in the 1930s. No fundamental changes occurred in public opinion, politics, and public policies to shift the political system into a new conservative and Republican era. The so-called Reagan revolution is an illusion. In fact, many of the major developments in the 1980s, such as the decline in public support for defense spending, the enormous budget deficits, and Democratic victories in the 1980–88 House elections, were just the opposite of what should have happened in a conservative Reagan revolution.

In the 1980s, U.S. public opinion moved a little to the left overall rather than significantly to the right. National polls showed that the position of the majority or plurality of Americans remained the same on most issues. The majority continued to hold the liberal position on some issues and the conservative position on others. Most of the few changes which did occur were in the liberal direction.

Rather than a historic shift against government programs, strong support for most programs continued in the 1980s. A high propor-

225

tion of U.S. citizens maintained their support for programs such as Social Security and federal aid to education.

The major change in U.S. public opinion during the 1980s was a dramatic decline in support for defense spending. By the middle of the 1980s, public opinion studies indicated that less than 10 percent of the population favored increases in the military budget. This shift against defense spending, of course, meant a significant change in public opinion toward the liberal position.

When asked in national polls about priorities in government spending, military funding always lost to social spending. Several survey research studies showed that Americans favored cuts in defense spending over cuts in social spending by a two-to-one margin.

Support remained high among the public for strong environmental protection laws. The polls showed such high support for environmental laws that George Bush distanced himself from the Reagan administration's policies and tried to run for president as an environmentalist candidate.

No opinion shift occurred toward the New Right's position on social policy in the 1980s. The majority of Americans remained conservative on some social issues and liberal on others. For example, polls indicated that majority support continued for organized prayers in public schools as well as for the Equal Rights Amendment.

New Right conservatives failed to gain public support for their position on two of their main concerns—abortion and women's rights. According to national studies, the majority of Americans continued to oppose most aspects of the conservative position on abortion. Public opinion in the 1980s continued to move toward the acceptance of greater equality for women in many aspects of society.

Furthermore, the elections during the decade did not indicate that a conservative change occurred in public opinion. According to election studies, Reagan and Bush won because of factors such as economic conditions, not because of overwhelming public support for conservative policies. In fact, survey research studies showed strong opposition by the majority of Americans to many of Ronald Reagan's key conservative policies.

In the Senate elections, liberals gained almost an equal amount of voter support as the conservatives. In the House elections, liberals had an amazing record. Not only did they receive more voter support than conservatives, but almost all the liberal incumbents won reelection in the 1980s by landslide proportions.

In another aspect of public opinion, most reporters, columnists, and other political analysts greatly exaggerated Ronald Reagan's popularity as president. Reagan was not one of the most popular presidents of the past sixty years. The Gallup poll's measure of presidential popularity, which is the most often used index of presidents' public approval, shows that Reagan's popularity ratings were well below those of Roosevelt, Eisenhower, and Kennedy, the three most popular presidents of the last several decades. While the approval ratings of the popular presidents were usually above 60 percent, only a small portion of Reagan's ratings were above this mark. President Reagan's overall average in the Gallup poll rating was only a few points above the presidents with the lowest overall averages. Reagan had the lowest popularity scores for any of the recent presidents during the early part of the first term. His overall average for the first term was about the same as the average for the supposedly unpopular Jimmy Carter. Reagan's ratings were low during part of the second term from the effects of the Iran-Contra scandal.

In party politics, the predicted party realignment never occurred in the 1980s. The Democrats clearly remained the number one party overall in the political system. In 1988 the Democrats held the majority of House seats, Senate seats, governorships, and state legislatures. For a realignment to have taken place, the Republicans would have had to control the majority of positions in most of the different parts of the system.

Republicans did win the presidency during the 1980s. These victories, however, did not mean the U.S. party system entered into a new era, because the Republicans had won the presidency several times during the previous thirty years. The same party era continued through the 1980s with Republicans being highly competitive in presidential elections, but relatively weak in the elections for other offices.

The Republican victories in the 1980–84 Senate elections were not based on a significant shift in voting patterns toward the Republicans. In the 1982 election, for example, the Democrats won the majority of the national vote. The Republicans won the Senate majority by winning most of the seats in the small states and winning an amazing proportion of the close races in 1980.

In the early 1980s, many political commentators predicted that the Republicans would maintain their control of the Senate for a long time and win the majority in the House before the end of the decade. Their predictions were off by a wide margin. The Democrats won back the Senate majority in the 1986 and 1988 elections and continued to win landslide victories in the House.

While the Republicans did come closer to the Democrats in party identification in the 1980s, this did not constitute a new era because the Republicans had narrowed the gap before. The Republicans, for example, were close to the Democrats in party identification during the period from the mid-1940s through the early 1950s. Moreover, in the late 1980s the Democrats increased their lead to fourteen points in the Gallup poll, which was just one point below their average lead in the poll for the previous fifty years.

No fundamental conservative shift in public policies occurred in the 1980s. Instead of the $100 billion budget surpluses President Reagan promised, the deficit soared to record levels of over $200 billion for several years. Instead of cutbacks in spending, the federal budget skyrocketed to record highs. From 1979 to 1987, the federal spending increased from $504 billion to over $1 trillion. Federal spending had hit a plateau in the 1970s of a little over 20 percent of GNP. But in the early and mid-1980s, federal outlays jumped to nearly 25 percent of GNP.

Rather than the moving toward laissez-faire capitalism, the federal government's role in the economy expanded. By far the largest expansion of the government's agriculture program developed in the 1980s. This occurred after the shift toward a more free-market approach in agriculture during the 1970s. The incredible increase in the national debt and the savings and loan bailout significantly expanded the federal government's impact on the financial sector of the economy. The amount of business deregulation was small in the 1980s compared to the substantial deregulation activity of the 1970s.

Instead of federal taxes declining from the 1979 level of 18.9 percent of GNP to 16 or 15 percent, federal revenues remained above 18 percent of GNP during the 1980s and even climbed above

19 percent for several years. President Reagan signed several tax increases including some of the largest increases in history.

Rather than a historic military buildup, the mid-1980s began the greatest military cutback in the post–World War II period. By the late 1980s, military spending was growing at a very slow rate and declining as a percent of GNP. The military budget was not even growing enough to match the inflation rate. Congress ended up spending many hundred billion dollars less on the military in the 1980s than would have been spent if defense spending had grown at the rate Reagan proposed in his first five-year budget projections. Moreover, the defense budget would have been larger at the end of the 1980s than it actually was if the budget had increased at the rate proposed by Jimmy Carter and Walter Mondale.

Instead of a decade of disaster for the environmental movement, the 1980s turned out to be an excellent period overall for liberal environmental policy. Environmental groups gained new support and enthusiasm in their fight against the Reagan administration. The scandals and controversies surrounding the administration's environmental program discredited the conservative position on environmental policy. Reagan was unable to persuade Congress to significantly cut back any major environmental law. Several environmental programs were expanded with greater funding and stronger regulations.

Instead of enormous cutbacks in social programs, federal social spending hit record high levels in the early 1980s. Human resources spending, which includes the major social programs, was higher in the 1980s than in the 1970s as measured by the yearly average of percent GNP. While some social programs were cut, many others such as Medicare grew enormously during the decade. In addition, the legitimacy and long-term prospects of the federal social programs were enhanced because these programs so successfully survived the attack of the Reagan administration and congressional conservatives.

Instead of winning many victories in the 1980s, the New Right lost on almost all of their legislative proposals and failed to reverse the major social trends they opposed. For instance, the New Right failed to pass any of their proposed constitutional amendments, Congress passed child care legislation, legal abortions continued in the 1980s, and many more married women held jobs outside the home.

Rather than significant gains for conservatives in foreign policy, the late 1980s began a historic change that severely damaged the conservative position. Strong anticommunism had been the core of the conservatives' foreign policy beliefs. They effectively attacked liberals for being soft on communism. In the late 1980s, however, President Reagan abandoned his previous position and adopted policies advocated by liberals. Several leaders of conservative groups vehemently criticized Reagan, particularly for accepting the INF treaty with the Soviet Union. In addition, the decline of the Communist party in the Soviet Union and the communist regimes in Eastern Europe pulled the rug out from under conservatives' policies and left conservative foreign policy groups in shambles with decreasing financial support and membership.

Furthermore, no historic changes occurred in government institutions during the 1980s. The Reagan administration probably will not have a long-term impact on how the government functions.

If the 1988 presidential campaign and the Bush administration are reliable indicators, future presidential candidates and future presidents will not follow President Reagan's approach to the presidency. The 1988 presidential candidates and President Bush went out of their way to stress that they would use a much different administrative style than President Reagan utilized in the White House.

Also, President Reagan did not significantly change the relationship between the president and Congress. His success with Congress was exaggerated by most commentators. Rather than having the best record in congressional relations since FDR, President Reagan, after his successes of 1981, had one of the worst records of any president in office during the past several decades.

Rather than declining substantially, the federal bureaucracy grew during the 1980s. Congress kept the bureaucracy from growing by an even greater amount by cutting several hundred billion dollars from Reagan's defense proposals.

The House of Representatives continued to be dominated by moderate and liberal Democrats during the decade. Democrats won all the House elections in the 1980s. The Republicans have not won a House election since 1952. After the Democratic victories in the

1986 and 1988 elections, moderate and liberal Democrats returned to the lead in the Senate.

Probably the most important change in congressional politics in the 1980s was the substantial decline in the conservative coalition's influence. This developed primarily from more liberal voting by southern Democrats.

The Supreme Court did not experience a fundamental shift to a new era. The post-Warren Court era established in the 1970s continued through the 1980s.

The predicted shift of power from the federal government to the state and local governments never happened in the 1980s. The federal government even increased its share of total government spending. The major part of Reagan's New Federalism programs died in Congress, and federal mandates to state and local governments increased. In addition, the Reagan administration contradicted its federalism policy by promoting federal power over state and local power on many important policy issues.

In conclusion, it is amazing to consider all the records and near records which occurred in the 1980s and early 1990s that were just the opposite of what should have happened in a conservative Reagan revolution. For example, the federal budget deficits, the national debt, and U.S. foreign debts hit record levels. The first trillion dollar budget was passed. Federal spending was at record high levels for the post–World War II period in current dollars and percent of GNP. Of the past five decades, the 1980s had the most years in which federal revenues amounted to 19 percent or more of GNP. President Reagan supported some of the highest tax increases in history. If present budget trends continue for a few more years in the 1990s, the defense budget, as a percent of GNP, will be at the lowest level in the post–World War II period. Social spending hit record high levels in current dollars and as a percent of GNP. Many records were set in spending on agriculture programs. Also, the Reagan administration initiated the greatest acreage-diversion program in the history of U.S. agriculture policy. Different parts of the federal government expanded to record size. The number of cabinet departments increased to a new high of fourteen.

According to national polls, support for defense spending was at record or near-record low levels. On the other hand, support for several of the liberals' programs and policies were at record or near-record high levels.

Of the presidents in office during the 1952–88 period, Reagan had the lowest approval score in the first Gallup poll rating taken at the beginning of the first term. He also set several Gallup poll records for low popularity for presidents during the early years of their first term. For the 1952–88 period, President Reagan received the two lowest presidential support scores in congressional voting.

Democrats set records or extended records for the most years controlling the major parts of the political system. Except for a few years since 1932, the Democrats have led the Republicans in congressional seats and state and local offices. No other U.S. political party or party era even comes close to this record.

Also, record low levels were set for the formation of the conservative coalition in congressional roll-call votes. Party cohesion among congressional Democrats, especially southern Democrats, was at some of the highest levels for the past several decades. During the late 1980s in Congress, the liberal ADA ratings for southern Democrats, committee chairmen, and the Democratic leadership were at record or near-record levels.

Why No Conservative Reagan Revolution Occurred

Several factors could be mentioned to explain why no conservative Reagan revolution occurred in the 1980s. Six of the most important are examined in this section.

First, as emphasized before, no fundamental conservative shift could develop in public policies because of contradictions in conservatives' ideology. The conflict between conservatives' belief in less government and their belief in an enormous expansion of military spending, the biggest part of the federal budget, creates particularly difficult problems. The federal government influences the economy the most through defense spending. Military spending has been the major factor in making the national government the largest level of government in the federal system. Therefore, the attainment of all the major goals of conservatives would be impossible because the goals conflict so much. If President Reagan had persuaded Congress to increase the defense budget at the rate outlined in his first five-year projection, the impact of the federal government on the economy would have expanded considerably, and the power of the federal government would have increased substantially compared to state and local governments.

The conflict between conservatives' belief in less government and their support for government actions to promote their social policy also makes it impossible to achieve several major goals at the same time. If, for example, conservatives were able to make abortion illegal in all situations, the government's involvement in society would increase enormously. Similarly, a large increase in the government's role in Americans' lives would develop if conservatives were able to pass much stronger laws on pornography and to convince the federal courts to accept these laws as constitutional. In these examples on abortion and pornography, the conservatives would have achieved some of their goals on social policy, but they would have violated their belief in less government.

Second, a fundamental conservative shift in politics and policy would have been very difficult to achieve because U.S. public opinion never moved significantly to the right. President Reagan and congressional conservatives faced the nearly impossible task of producing fundamental conservative changes in the political process and in policies without a strong shift in the public's attitude to support these changes. In the 1980s, polls indicated that the majority of Americans continued to support the conservative side on some important national issues. However, conservatives were unable to gain strong support on a wide range of issues that previously had majority support for the moderate or liberal side.

Furthermore, a historic conservative shift in policies was almost impossible because polls showed that the majority of the public opposed many of the key policies of the Reagan administration. In many of these unpopular policies, majorities formed in Congress to reverse, stop, or at least restrict the initiatives of the administration. For example, strong congressional opposition developed on unpopular Reagan policies such as cutbacks in social spending, large increases in defense spending, cuts in environmental programs, and on the administration's Nicaraguan policy.

Third, the recession of the early 1980s hurt the Republicans' efforts to significantly alter public policies and the political system. In 1981 President Reagan and the Republicans were on a roll. Reagan had recently won a landslide victory, the Republicans had won the Senate majority for the first time since the early 1950s, and House Republicans had gained over thirty seats in the 1980 election. In addition, President Reagan had led the Republicans to several important victories in Congress. Many Republicans and political commentators predicted that the Republicans would win the House within a few years, maintain their Senate majority for many years, and continue to significantly change public policy.

Then the recession hit. The economic downturn had a devastating impact on the Republicans' program and future prospects. The popularity of President Reagan and the Republicans dropped. While the Republicans lost some of their enthusiasm, confidence, and unity, the Democrats' morale and cohesion improved considerably. The recession was an important factor in helping the Democrats post a big victory in the 1982 House election. It also aided the Democrats in gaining a big triumph in the national vote in the Senate election, although they could not regain the Senate majority. In 1983 the House Democrats were much more effective against President Reagan and the Republicans because of their increased numbers and greater unity.

The recession significantly harmed the Reagan administration's efforts to cut social programs. The costs of the social-welfare programs always soar in recessions because many more people need benefits and are able to qualify for them during periods of economic problems. Also, the recession made cuts in social spending less politically feasible. Many Americans began to question the morality of a policy that reduced benefits to recipients of social programs at a time when so many people faced severe economic difficulties.

The recession was a major cause of the increase in the deficit, which produced many problems for the Republicans. The GOP and Reagan lost a great deal of public support when the president's promised $100 billion budget surplus ended up being a $200 billion deficit. The deficit also put pressure on the president and congressional Republicans to support tax increases. It increased government spending enormously through the increase in the cost of financing the debt. The deficit was one of the major reasons why the growth rate of the defense budget dropped so much after the early 1980s.

The recession and the deficits also caused much dissension

among conservatives and within the Republican party. Ideological warfare broke out between moderate and conservative Republicans, and among supply-side conservatives, monetarists, and traditional conservaties over issues such as budget priorities, proposals for tax increases, and the impact of deficits.

Fourth, no monumental event such as the Depression occurred in the late 1970s to fundamentally change the social and economic structure of the nation. An event or events of far-reaching proportions seems to be needed for a historic restructuring of politics and policies in the United States. The problems of the late 1970s were large enough to reduce Jimmy Carter's popularity and to pave the way for Ronald Reagan's victory in 1980. But these problems of the 1970s were of a very small magnitude compared to the Depression of the 1930s. It was too much to expect of President Reagan and the Republicans to produce a fundamental change similar to the New Deal without an event at least close to the magnitude of the 1930s' Depression.

Fifth, no fundamental changes developed because Ronald Reagan's budget plan, the centerpiece of the Republican program, was severely flawed. Historic changes in a proposed direction will not come about from a plan out of fantasyland. A plan of this sort may help gain votes in an election, but it will face great difficulties in the real world. Anyone who had a basic knowledge of American politics and the federal budget, and who knew how to add and subtract, would have been skeptical of Reagan's budget claims. Among those who did question Reagan's plan were most of his Republican opponents in the 1980 election, including George Bush of "voodoo economics" fame. It did not take a political and economic genius to question the feasibility of a plan that claimed even though the budget had a $74 billion deficit in 1980, a $100 billion surplus could be produced within three years by doubling the biggest part of the budget (i.e., defense) in five years, cutting the major source of revenue (i.e., income tax) by 30 percent, and keeping the main social programs. The $200 billion deficits, instead of $100 billion surpluses, were absolute proof of how unrealistic the plan was as originally proposed.

Finally, the rise of Mikhail Gorbachev and the decline of the Communist parties in Eastern Europe undermined U.S. conservatives' military and foreign policy positions. The decline of the communist threat was one of the main reasons why in early 1990 Congress was considering huge cuts in military spending rather than large increases. For this reason, strong anticommunism was no longer the central focus of U.S. foreign policy.

Index